N

WITHDRAWN
WORDPRESS® 24-HOUR TRAINER

W9-BPP-301

WordPress®
24-Hour Trainer

WordPress®
24-Hour Trainer

Third Edition

George Plumley

wrox™

A Wiley Brand

WordPress® 24-Hour Trainer, Third Edition

Published by
John Wiley & Sons, Inc.
10475 Crosspoint Boulevard
Indianapolis, IN 46256
www.wiley.com

Copyright © 2015 by John Wiley & Sons, Inc., Indianapolis, Indiana

Published simultaneously in Canada

ISBN: 978-1-118-99560-0

ISBN: 978-1-118-99581-5 (ebk)

ISBN: 978-1-118-99639-3 (ebk)

Manufactured in the United States of America

10 9 8 7 6 5 4 3 2 1

For general information on our other products and services please contact our Customer Care Department within the United States at (877) 762-2974, outside the United States at (317) 572-3993 or fax (317) 572-4002.

Wiley publishes in a variety of print and electronic formats and by print-on-demand. Some material included with standard print versions of this book may not be included in e-books or in print-on-demand. If this book refers to media such as a CD or DVD that is not included in the version you purchased, you may download this material at http://booksupport.wiley.com. For more information about Wiley products, visit www.wiley.com.

Library of Congress Control Number: 2015930537

This book is dedicated to the memory of my mother, Adelaide, who passed away during its writing, and to the memory of my father, Stan. It is also dedicated to my wife, Kim, and daughters, Grace and Ella, my sister, Patricia, and my in-laws, Gord and Carole— your support and encouragement always mean the world to me.

ABOUT THE AUTHOR

 **GEORGE PLUMLEY** has been developing small business websites since 1993 and has worked almost exclusively with WordPress since 2007. In addition to writing about WordPress, he does live online coaching and produces video training series for VTC.com and Infinite Skills. He lives on Vancouver Island where he tries to go offline at least a couple of hours each day.

ABOUT THE TECHNICAL EDITOR

JOHN PELOQUIN is a software engineer with over 10 years of web development experience. John earned his B.A. in Mathematics from U.C. Berkeley and is currently a lead engineer for a healthcare technology startup where he makes heavy use of MySQL, PHP, and JavaScript (the technologies upon which WordPress is built). John has used WordPress to build custom content management solutions for a variety of professional and personal projects. Prior to editing this volume, John edited *Professional Website Performance* by Peter Smith (Wiley 2012) and *Professional JavaScript for Web Developers, 3rd ed.* by Nicholas Zakas (Wiley 2012). When he is not coding or collecting errata, John can sometimes be found doing stand-up comedy at open mics in NYC.

CREDITS

EXECUTIVE EDITOR
Carol Long

PROJECT EDITOR
Chris Haviland

TECHNICAL EDITOR
John Peloquin

PRODUCTION EDITOR
Rebecca Anderson

COPY EDITOR
San Dee Phillips

**MANAGER OF CONTENT DEVELOPMENT
& ASSEMBLY**
Mary Beth Wakefield

MARKETING DIRECTOR
David Mayhew

MARKETING MANAGER
Carrie Sherrill

**PROFESSIONAL TECHNOLOGY & STRATEGY
DIRECTOR**
Barry Pruett

BUSINESS MANAGER
Amy Knies

ASSOCIATE PUBLISHER
Jim Minatel

PROJECT COORDINATOR, COVER
Brent Savage

PROOFREADER
Jen Larsen, Word One New York

INDEXER
Johnna VanHoose

COVER DESIGNER
Wiley

COVER IMAGE
©Getty Images/Westend61

ACKNOWLEDGMENTS

I WANT TO THANK Carol Long for her guidance and patience over the years, the whole Wiley team, in particular the editors headed by Chris Haviland, who had to deal with more than just a third edition, San Dee Phillips, who kept my voice consistent and my syntax clear, and John Peloquin for many helpful technical suggestions. Thanks also to my wonderful agent, Carole Jelen, for her keen insights into publishing and for being my cheering section, the programmers who make WordPress possible, and the WordPress community from whom I've learned and continue to learn so much. Finally, I want to thank all my clients and students over the years who, by asking great questions, have helped me learn to explain things more clearly.

CONTENTS

INTRODUCTION

IN THE FEW SHORT YEARS since the first edition of this book, WordPress has grown to power about 20% of all the websites in the world. This success is not due to some massive marketing campaign; it was mostly viral, as web site owners, designers, developers, and marketers spread the word. And I think they told others because WordPress is:

➤ Easy to set up

➤ Easy to maintain

➤ Easy to grow and adapt

It's this last quality—ease of growing and adapting—which I think is particularly important. **WordPress helps make your website future-proof,** meaning no matter what happens on the web—new social media platforms, new technologies, new requirements—it allows you to respond pretty easily to those changes.

Since I began building websites exclusively with WordPress, I've noticed an important change in my clients: they look forward to updating and expanding their sites. When changing some text, let alone adding a new page, is like pulling teeth, you're less likely to do it. With WordPress, not only are my clients making their own changes, but they're excited about it and that's also made them more involved in their sites. Instead of having a site built and then sitting back, my clients are actively thinking about what they can change or add to make their sites better, because they can go in and do it themselves when the thought strikes.

That's the real power of WordPress: putting more control in the hands of the website owner.

But WordPress won't magically build a great site for you. It's only a tool that makes it easier for you to build a great site. You need to know how to use WordPress, as well as understand its potential, so you can use the tool most effectively. This book will help you with both.

WHO THIS BOOK IS FOR

This book is for beginners at two levels: those who've never built a website and those who've never built or used a WordPress website. You should be aware that there are two versions of WordPress:

➤ The free hosted version at `WordPress.com`

➤ The open-source downloadable version from WordPress.org, which you then install on your own server (commonly referred to as the self-hosted version)

The important difference between the two is that with the hosted version you don't control which plugins or themes are available to use. For personal blogging or, with some paid features, even some small businesses, the hosted version can be a good choice. But for complete control or customization of your site, the self-hosted version is the better choice.

Though this book deals with the self-hosted version of WordPress, much of it—how to enter content, how to upload photos and documents, how to lay out content, and so on—still applies to the hosted version.

WHAT THIS BOOK COVERS

Since the second edition of this book, WordPress has undergone significant changes, all of which make it even easier to use and even more flexible for managing any type of website. This new edition includes features up to and including Version 4.0, with indications of some changes expected in 4.1.

You'll learn how to set up a WordPress website from scratch, using the default features of the software. Each lesson covers a related set of tasks, so you can follow the lessons in order or easily dip into any one of them to quickly learn one thing. Because we're in an increasingly mobile world, the book also covers important differences when using WordPress on a mobile device. And at the end of most lessons there will be a list of free plugins that extend the functions discussed in that lesson.

Keep in mind, this book is not what I call an extended manual. It does not aim to cover every feature of WordPress. Instead, it focuses on the key tasks you need in the day-to-day running of a website, and covers them in great detail. I do that by showing you not just the basics, but the tips and tricks that make things as simple as possible. The addition of videos for key points helps make things clearer and reinforce the concepts.

HOW THIS BOOK IS STRUCTURED

The 36 lessons are grouped into themed sections:

➤ **Section I: Before You Start**—Get to know how WordPress thinks about content and what planning you need to do before starting your site.

➤ **Section II: Firing Up WordPress**—Instructions for installing the software, an overview of the administration interface, and the basic settings you'll need to get going.

➤ **Section III: Working with Written Content**—Entering your content and publishing it.

➤ **Section IV: Working with Media Content**—The ins and outs of uploading images, video, documents, and more, as well as how to use them on your site.

➤ **Section V: Managing Your Content**—Navigating through various types of content, editing it, and moving it around.

➤ **Section VI: Making Your Site Social**—Dealing with social media, comments, links, RSS feeds, and multiple users.

➤ **Section VII: Choosing and Customizing Themes**—How to choose from the astonishing array of themes, and some basics for making the site look exactly the way you want.

➤ **Section VIII: Becoming Search Engine–Friendly**— Keeping an eye on your site statistics, and basic techniques for optimizing your site so that you get indexed in the best possible way.

➤ **Section IX: Maintenance and Security**—Making sure your software is up to date, and getting into good backup habits.

➤ **Section X: Added Functionality Using Plugins**—Using plugins that give WordPress new features, such as e-commerce, events calendars, and much, much more.

When you're finished reading the book and watching the videos online, you'll find lots of support in the p2p forums, as you'll see in a moment, but there's also the WordPress community on the Web. Hundreds of thousands of people around the world are using this software, and a lot of them give back in so many ways. It's a spirit that's reflected in the quality of WordPress and its continued improvement.

From the people who created and maintain WordPress, to the people who make plugins and themes, to the people who write about WordPress on their blogs or contribute to the official and unofficial forums, there are thousands of bright minds giving back to the community with code, ideas, fixes, and more. You never have to feel you're alone when you're using WordPress. I like to think of it as a worldwide 24-hour help line. Whether you need help or can offer help, you're welcome any time.

INSTRUCTIONAL VIDEOS

Nothing beats watching how something is done, and that's why I've provided several hours' worth of video about how you can use WordPress. Most lessons in the book have an accompanying video which not only illustrates several of the examples in the lesson, but goes well beyond what can be covered in print. You'll also gain more insight into the creation of the sample website discussed in the book: Island Travel.

If you have an existing WordPress site—a self-hosted version or a blog on WordPress.com—I encourage you to work along in the admin screen. If you don't have a site, you could install WordPress if you have a web hosting account (see Lesson 3) or you could open an account with WordPress.com. The main thing is that you be able to practice what's covered in the book and on these videos, which can be viewed at `www.wrox.com/go/sp2010-24`.

Also online you'll find a PDF with links to each of the more than 400 plugins mentioned in the book. You can find the plugins under the lesson where they were mentioned. Click on a link and you'll be taken to the listing in the WordPress.org Plugin Directory.

CONVENTIONS

To help you get the most from the text and keep track of what's happening, we've used a number of conventions throughout the book.

> **WARNING** *Boxes like this one hold important, not-to-be-forgotten information that is directly relevant to the surrounding text.*

> **NOTE** *Notes, tips, hints, tricks, and asides to the current discussion are presented in boxes like this.*

> **PLUGINS**
>
> At the end of virtually all the lessons, you'll find a box like this with a list of plugins from the WordPress Plugin Directory related to the topics of that lesson. Commercial plugins are not covered here, with the occasional exception.

> **REFERENCE** *References like this one point you to the website at* `www.wrox.com/go/wp24vids` *to watch the instructional video that accompanies a given lesson.*

As for styles in the text:

➤ We *highlight* new terms and important words when we introduce them.

➤ We show URLs and code within the text like so: `persistence.properties`.

ERRATA

We make every effort to ensure that there are no errors in the text or in the code. However, no one is perfect, and mistakes do occur. If you find an error in one of our books, like a spelling mistake or faulty piece of code, we would be very grateful for your feedback. By sending in errata, you may save another reader hours of frustration and, at the same time, you will be helping us provide even higher quality information.

To find the errata page for this book, go to www.wrox.com and locate the title using the Search box or one of the title lists. Then, on the Book Search Results page, click the Errata link. On this page, you can view all errata that has been submitted for this book and posted by Wrox editors.

> **NOTE** *A complete book list, including links to errata, is also available at* www.wrox.com/misc-pages/booklist.shtml.

If you don't spot "your" error on the Errata page, click the Errata Form link and complete the form to send us the error you have found. We'll check the information and, if appropriate, post a message to the book's errata page and fix the problem in subsequent editions of the book.

P2P.WROX.COM

For author and peer discussion, join the P2P forums at p2p.wrox.com. The forums are a web-based system for you to post messages relating to Wrox books and related technologies and interact with other readers and technology users. The forums offer a subscription feature to e-mail you topics of interest of your choosing when new posts are made to the forums. Wrox authors, editors, other industry experts, and your fellow readers are present on these forums.

At p2p.wrox.com, you will find a number of different forums that will help you not only as you read this book, but also as you develop your own applications. To join the forums, just follow these steps:

1. Go to p2p.wrox.com and click the Register link.

2. Read the terms of use and click Agree.

3. Complete the required information to join, as well as any optional information you wish to provide, and click Submit.

4. You will receive an e-mail with information describing how to verify your account and complete the joining process.

> **NOTE** *You can read messages in the forums without joining P2P, but in order to post your own messages, you must join.*

Once you join, you can post new messages and respond to messages other users post. You can read messages at any time on the Web. If you would like to have new messages from a particular forum e-mailed to you, click the Subscribe To This Forum icon by the forum name in the forum listing.

For more information about how to use the Wrox P2P, be sure to read the P2P FAQs for answers to questions about how the forum software works as well as many common questions specific to P2P and Wrox books. To read the FAQs, click the FAQ link on any P2P page.

SECTION I
Before You Start

Thinking Like WordPress

WordPress provides you with the tools to create, organize, and update your website content. Those tools function in specific ways, just as one type of word processing software has its specific buttons for creating, say, lists. But there's a difference between knowing which button to press to create a list and thinking about ways to use lists in your documents. That's what this lesson is about: learning to think like WordPress so that you can build or rebuild your website in an efficient and flexible manner from the start, and to use it in new and useful ways.

The driving principle behind this way of thinking is: *Store everything in the smallest possible piece; then assemble as needed*. It's the way of the digital world—photographs assembled out of pixels, data stored in database fields, or video recorded in bytes. WordPress operates with this kind of thinking, and you can make better use of its power if you think of your website and its content in this way.

STATIC VERSUS DYNAMIC WEB PAGES

If you right-click while viewing a page in your web browser, you'll see a tool called View Source, which displays the HTML of the page you're currently viewing. If you try this tool, it appears as though you're viewing a single file, but for most websites today, that's an illusion. In most cases there is no corresponding file sitting on a web server. Instead, the server has combined dozens and dozens of files in a split second to create what you're seeing with View Source.

That was not the case in the early days of the Internet, when most web pages were stored as single HTML files. The fact that no assembly was required to produce the code you see in your browser is why they are called *static files*. They're easy to create and they load quickly (an important factor at a time when computers and Internet speeds were slow), but they aren't flexible. Suppose you decided to change the logo at the top of each of your website's pages, and it had a new file name. With static files, you would need to manually go in and replace the HTML in every file. Not so bad on a 5-page site, but what if you had 5,000 pages? Yes, there's such a thing as search-and-replace functions in HTML editors, but aside from the fact that methods like that are not user-friendly, they solve only one limitation of static files. Suppose you wanted an entirely different header area depending on what part of your site the visitor is on?

The answer is to break up the structure of web pages in such a way that different files control different parts of the final page. So instead of storing web pages as single files, the server would store a series of files that are then assembled into a single file at the moment the page is requested by someone's browser. It is this assembly process that leads us to refer to these types of web pages as *dynamic*. Figure 1-1 shows one way to split up a static HTML file.

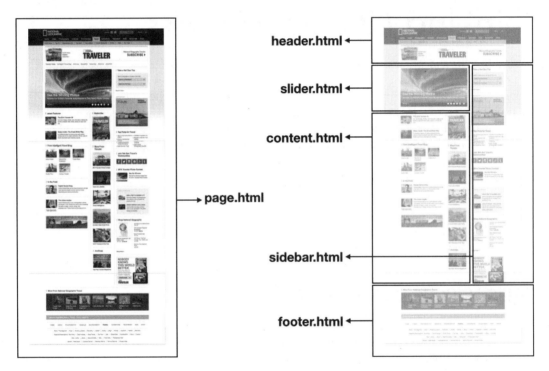

FIGURE 1-1

Notice in Figure 1-1 that the only file that would be unique to this particular web page is content .html. The rest of the files—header, footer, and so on—would be shared by the other pages on the site. So changing that logo for 5,000 pages would simply be a matter of changing the header .html file. If you can start thinking of your web pages in this way—as a set of parts that can be assembled on-the-fly in different ways—you're more likely to think of ways to use this ability to your advantage.

For example, it could be that the actual content of a web page (the material in content.html in Figure 1-1) might be broken down further to allow for greater flexibility. News stories, press releases, or testimonials are good instances of this kind of content. Using testimonials as an example, you can see in Figure 1-2 how dynamic web page thinking could be applied:

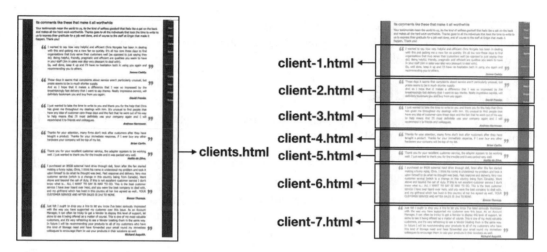

FIGURE 1-2

Although the value of dynamic web pages is obvious, the concept is not of much use to website owners unless the files required to run them are easy to manage. You could build a dynamic website—even a sophisticated one—with just a set of simple text files. But that would require the website manager to know HTML and other assorted languages, and to be comfortable working with tools such as file transfer programs. Moving those simple text files into a database to increase their flexibility only further complicates the work of the website manager. Enter the *content management system*, or *CMS*.

CONTENT MANAGEMENT SYSTEMS

Most of us tend to think of a CMS merely as a way to avoid having to learn HTML, but editing the text and media on a web page is just a part of what a CMS does. A content management system is a user interface for dynamic web pages.

Imagine for a moment you had a CMS that provided only a WYSIWYG interface for the full HTML of each individual web page. If you had a 5-page website that rarely changed, that might be enough. But suppose, even on a 5-page website, that you decided you didn't like the top section or header that appears on all the pages of your site. Yes, the CMS makes it easy to drag and drop a new graphic into the header area of the pages, but you'd still need to change the graphic on all 5 pages separately. Now imagine that task on a site with 500 pages or 5,000! Even with search-and-replace capabilities, you would need to upload all 5,000 pages back onto the server to replace the old version, and then do it all again for the next change. Ouch!

A CMS, however, is much more than a WYSIWYG editor. You want the CMS to keep separate all those elements of a dynamic web page that you saw earlier: the header, footer, sidebar, and so on, and to manage not only their contents, but also how they interact with each other. A CMS instructs the server how to assemble any particular web page based in part on elements you control using its interface.

From the look of the page to which sidebar elements to include, a CMS provides ways for nontechnical users to control their web pages. The question then becomes: Does your CMS offer a lot of control and an easy-to-use interface?

Why Choose WordPress?

There's no shortage of content management systems these days—good ones—but the reason for choosing WordPress as your CMS is twofold:

➤ The simplicity and flexibility of WordPress's design make it easy to learn, easy to expand, and easy to customize.

➤ The WordPress community is so large and so vibrant that you have a huge number of add-on functions and designs to choose from, as well as excellent support, and will have for years to come.

It's important to keep in mind that no CMS can fulfill everyone's needs right out-of-the-box. The more a CMS tries to be all things to all people, the more bloated it becomes, and that means a steeper learning curve and a greater chance it will break down. A good CMS follows the principles of digital thinking and keeps as many elements separate as possible, meaning each one is fairly simple but when assembled offers great power.

WordPress is built on this principle. The core software does only basic functionality, to which you then easily add other functions as you need them or remove them when you don't. The look of WordPress is entirely separate from the core software, so it, too, is easily changed. And all these elements outside the core can be modified or new ones can be created to match your exact needs.

But even the best CMS is only as useful as the community that supports it, and WordPress has community. Whether there is someone building new add-on functionality, offering advice in forums and blog posts, or selling development services, WordPress is the most-supported CMS on the planet.

How WordPress Assembles Pages

Part of thinking like WordPress is having a general grasp of how it works. There are four elements of WordPress that interact to create HTML pages: the *core files*, the *theme files*, *plugin files*, and the *database*.

The core is the set of files that you download from WordPress.org that provide not only the basic functionality, but also the coordination between all the other elements.

The theme files have two key functions: Provide the set of HTML files that assemble the final web pages, and control the design of those pages.

Plugins are groups of files that add more functionality to WordPress. Some plugins consist of a single file, whereas others can have dozens or even hundreds.

The database has several functions. It keeps track of all the parameters of your WordPress installation, from which themes and plugins you have to the preferences of each individual user. It also stores the text portion of your content. When you write a blog post, for example, it is stored in the database, along with any references to media files, which are stored in folders on the server.

Figure 1-3 shows a simple diagram of how these four elements interact.

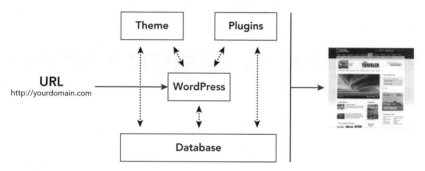

FIGURE 1-3

The arrows going back and forth between the elements begin to demonstrate the incredible amount of interaction required to generate a web page in a matter of seconds. The number of requests or queries made to the database averages approximately 40 or 50 for a typical WordPress page. Dynamic web pages are not cheap. They can place a heavy load on server resources if a lot of people try to access the site at one time. That's why many sites use a caching system with their CMS, which means that snapshots are taken of each page and stored as single, static HTML pages, avoiding all the back and forth between files and the database. The caching system keeps track if any changes are made to a page and takes a new snapshot as needed. That way you have the advantages of both dynamic page generation and static page serving.

The advantages of keeping these four elements of WordPress separate are many. Changing the look of your site is as simple as changing the theme. If a plugin starts causing problems for your site, you simply remove it and plug in a new one. If a new social media platform becomes the next big thing, someone will come up with a plugin to interact with it—or you can have your own made. When WordPress needs updating, your site's options and preferences remain untouched in the database. And if your host gives you poor service, you just copy all the files and the database, and move them to a new server.

But, although WordPress by its nature as a CMS and through its particular design produces dynamic web pages, its built-in tools can go only so far. Sites using WordPress can be more or less dynamic in nature depending on how the user works with WordPress's tools. Some of the power and flexibility in your site comes down to you.

YOUR ROLE IN MAKING YOUR SITE FLEXIBLE

As mentioned earlier, a good CMS needs to have a simple user interface, and WordPress lives up to this requirement. Actually, it was that ease of use that first led me to use WordPress on my clients' sites. Even as it has grown more complex, the developers of WordPress have continually worked to keep the interface user-friendly.

The menu system, for example, enables an unlimited number of menus; each can handle dozens and dozens of menu items with multiple levels of drop-downs, and those menu items can be virtually any type of content within WordPress: pages, posts, categories, tags, and more. Yet, as you can see in Figure 1-4, all this complexity is handled with simple check boxes, drag-and-drop interfaces, and drop-down selections.

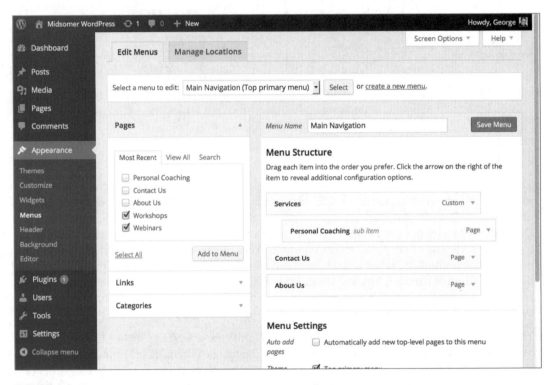

FIGURE 1-4

But with great power comes great responsibility. You're the one who has to create a useful and easy-to-follow navigation system for your users; WordPress cannot do that for you. It just makes it easy for you to do the creating. The more you can understand what's possible with WordPress, the better you'll become at making use of its powerful tools to create the best website for your visitors.

Understanding the difference between two ways of handling content in WordPress is particularly important to making your site easier for you to use and more useful to your visitors, and that is the difference between posts and pages.

Posts and pages share a lot of similarities, in particular the way their user interfaces or, in WordPress terminology, their admin screens work (which means there are many functions you'll have to learn only once). Where they differ brings you to the heart of the principle in this lesson: Store everything in the smallest possible pieces.

Take testimonials. For many websites it is absolutely crucial to have testimonials from satisfied customers or clients. So you grab those e-mails and letters people have written praising your services and you open up WordPress. You want a web page of all those testimonials, so under Pages in the WordPress menu, you select New Page. The WYSIWYG editor makes it easy to copy the text over from your e-mail or Word document, add any extra formatting, and get the page looking nice indeed.

Fast forward 6 months, and you decide that you would like to group some of the testimonials onto another web page because they all relate to a particular service. Not so bad; you just copy the text of the page, create a new WordPress page, paste it in, and then delete the testimonials you don't need. Then a month later you get a new testimonial that belongs on both pages. You copy and paste into both. But suppose you have several categories of testimonials; you can see how this could get both tedious and complex to manage.

Remember earlier in this lesson the diagram of the testimonials page (refer to Figure 1-2) and how you might break it up instead into individual testimonials? Well that's what posts in WordPress are for: groups of related content that you can categorize. That's all we mean when we talk about a blog: groups of similar content. So now, instead of putting all the testimonials in a WordPress page, you can create a category of posts called Testimonials and enter individual testimonials as posts, assigning them to that category. Then put the category on your site menu, and when visitors click that link, WordPress gathers all the relevant posts and outputs them as a single web page.

Fast forward 6 months again and you decide you need a category of testimonials for a particular service. Just create a subcategory of Testimonials called, say, Workshop Testimonials. Through an easy WordPress interface, you can assign 2, 20, or 200 testimonials to that new category with a single click. Then you just put the Workshop Testimonials on your menu or create a link to the category wherever you want. When visitors click, they see only testimonials about your workshop.

By keeping those testimonials individual, the possibilities are endless. Need rotating testimonials on the front page? Want to feature a particular testimonial on the sidebar of a specific page? It's only possible by keeping them as separate posts. That's the power of thinking like WordPress. In the next lesson you start applying that thinking to a sample site, and throughout this book you see ways to use WordPress's tools to increase the power and flexibility of your site.

> **NOTE** *Okay, having just told you how posts and pages differ in WordPress, I use the term* posts *throughout this book to mean both posts and pages. Partly, it's to avoid potential confusion with the term* page, *but mainly, it's for the sake of simplicity. The way you enter and edit content for posts and pages is basically identical because they both share the majority of content management features. Where necessary, I'll distinguish between them, but unless I do you can assume that when I say* posts, *I mean both posts and pages.*

TRY IT

There isn't anything specific to try based on the material in this lesson, but one thing you can do is examine your favorite news website, and in the content area of the site, try to image how those pieces of content might be separated in the site's CMS. Then go to another page, compare what's common with the previous page, and try to imagine how the builders have divided up the structure of the page—map it out on paper.

> **REFERENCE** *There is no video to accompany this lesson.*

Planning Your Site for WordPress

It's beyond the scope of this lesson to go into the entire planning process for a website. Rather, the goal is to map out a website and plan generally how to implement it in WordPress.

If you're setting up a personal blog, WordPress has done much of the structuring for you, and you could skip to the next lesson, but there's still plenty here that can be of use. For everyone else, this is an important step because with the right kind of planning upfront, not only can you save a lot of time and energy in the future, but it also can help you think about ways to make your website even more useful and easier to navigate.

To build a site in WordPress, you have three key things to consider during the planning process:

➤ What content will you have? (Including areas such as the header and footer)

➤ What special functionality will your site need? (E-commerce, events calendar, and so on)

➤ What do you want the site to look like? (Layout, colors, and so on)

The main focus in this lesson is on the first item—the content—because people have the hardest time with it.

The site used as an example throughout the book is for a company called Island Travel, a small travel agency with two locations, specializing in vacations to the Caribbean. Its primary goal is to have a website that provides a personal touch, with information largely written by its staff, and of course, the company wants it to be as easy as possible to update and expand.

MAPPING OUT YOUR SITE CONTENT

There are two kinds of maps you'll create for the travel site: a site map and a page map. The first will show every page on the website, and you want them organized. The second is an outline of elements that you want to appear on every page of the site: header, footer, and sidebar, at the end of every article/blog post, or wherever. In either case, "map" can be a bit intimidating, so you'll begin each one with a list.

The Site Map

For your site map, start writing a list of pages you think you might need, or more to the point, pages you think your visitors will want. Don't worry whether you've thought of everything—that will never happen—just write things down as you think of them. Don't do it in one sitting; come back the next day, and the next, and so on.

Here's a list for Island Travel:

- ➤ Vacation packages—One page per destination, listing all packages for that destination.

- ➤ Destination guides—One page per island destination, talking about what to see, tips for traveling, and so on.

- ➤ Supplier pages—One for each supplier of vacation packages, maybe with a list of their packages, if possible?

- ➤ About Us—A bit of history, our travel philosophy.

- ➤ Our Team—Short introductions to each of our staff members.

- ➤ Contact Us—Phone numbers, e-mail addresses, and showing our two locations with maps.

- ➤ Testimonials—clients happy with our service or their vacation.

- ➤ Current Specials—temporary travel deals.

- ➤ A page for our customers—Maybe specials just for them?

- ➤ A travel blog—Our own travel experiences, travel industry news, and so on.

Notice how every destination or every supplier isn't listed here and some notes to myself are added about what the pages might consist of, even if I'm not sure at this point if I can have what I want.

When you can't think of any other pages for your site, stop and make the first draft of your site map. The best way to think of this map is to picture something we're all familiar with on websites: the navigation menu. A site map, in the end, is the plan for the main menu of your website. It can also get more involved by showing links you want to make directly between pages, but for your purposes here keep things simple.

Speaking of simple, your site map does not need to be anything elaborate. You can hand draw it on a piece of paper or your tablet. Since I'm not much at drawing and you'd never be able to read my writing, I use a presentation program to create my site map such as PowerPoint (Windows) or Keynote (Mac). It can be easier to use than a graphics program or a word processor, but if you're a whiz with Word or some other program, by all means use them.

In Figure 2-1 you can see the site map I created. The top row of boxes shows the visible menu items, and the boxes below them would drop down as visitors mouseover the respective top-level menu item. There's no need to show every possible box, so the arrows indicate more menu items below.

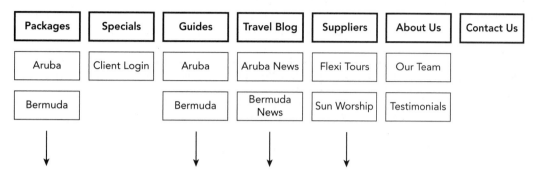

FIGURE 2-1

Now, keep in mind that this is a plan for the web pages that visitors will see, but as you learned in the previous lesson, what they see is not the same as how it might be organized in a content management system (CMS) such as WordPress.

Of course, you could build the exact structure shown in my site plan using WordPress pages. But remember that example about testimonials? If you just create a single WordPress page and keep adding testimonials to it, you can't do anything more with the individual testimonials. You can't reuse them in any way. But if you enter each one as a post in WordPress, the sky's the limit. Now go back and review the site map from the standpoint of what should be a WordPress page and what should be a post.

Clearly, testimonials need to be entered as individual posts and categorized as testimonials. So what you would have on your site map or menu is a WordPress category and not a page.

It's actually the same thinking that led to the first draft of the site map showing suppliers and destinations as subpages. You could put all the suppliers on a single page, but not only might that make for a large page (not friendly for visitors), it also wouldn't be as flexible, such as having a link to a specific supplier. So, suppliers were broken down into their smallest possible chunks—same as with the vacation destinations. Now that you know a bit about how WordPress works, you can specify how the content should be entered using WordPress structures that make your organizing even more efficient.

Another way to think of this process is to look at content and ask if it can be used in multiple ways throughout the site. If it can be or even if you think it might be in the future, it's better to enter the content as a post.

If the content is one of a kind (there won't be different versions of it) as in the case of About Us, that content should be entered as a WordPress page.

And finally there's another important consideration: Don't be stingy with page or post creation. You can have an unlimited number of WordPress pages or posts. In fact, the more you can break down your content into individual web pages, the better. For the contact page, for example, you can mention your two locations, but then link to a separate page with details about each (photos, staff greetings, map, and so on).

Based on these parameters, now go back and redo the site map. The top row of thick-bordered boxes is what would be visible on the navigation bar of the site; the boxes underneath would drop down from their respective top-level items. Items with gray backgrounds will be categories that display a list of posts, whereas the items with a white background are WordPress Pages. A dashed border indicates a child or sub-page in WordPress. Figure 2-2 shows the finished product.

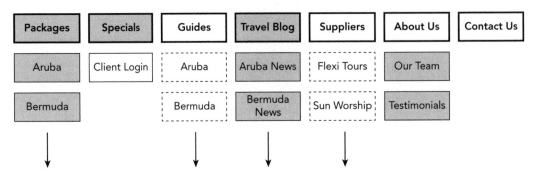

FIGURE 2-2

I say finished product, but this site map isn't written in stone. First, you're likely going to think of new content as the site progresses, such as a category for staff picks or a resource page for links to useful websites. Second, you may decide to rearrange the order of items on the map.

As you'll see throughout the book, changing how content is organized is easy with WordPress, but the more you can develop a good, clear plan early, the less likely or the smaller the changes will be in the future.

How to Organize Posts

While creating the site map, you saw how much of the content for the travel site is better as posts rather than WordPress pages. And because posts are organized by categories, the way those categories are set up is another important aspect of planning your WordPress site.

The site map contained numerous category menu items, but exactly how those categories are set up in WordPress remains to be decided. Take the Vacation Packages posts, for example. They could be set up as a main or parent category, as they're called in WordPress, with a set of child categories, one for each destination (Aruba Packages, Bermuda Packages, and so on). Or each destination could be a parent category, with children such as Aruba Packages, Aruba Testimonials, Aruba News, and so on.

A third approach involves the use of *tags*, another tool in WordPress for grouping posts (such as the index of a book, while categories are the table of contents). By creating a tag for each of your destinations, you can filter categories by that tag. For example, if you have a category called Vacation Packages, you can get a menu item of Aruba Packages by creating a link to Packages and filtering with the Aruba tag. (Don't worry about the details of this; it is covered in detail in Lesson 20, "Managing Post Categories and Tags.")

Table 2-1 shows how these three approaches play out (parent categories in bold, child categories in regular text, tags in italics).

TABLE 2-1: Three Approaches to Categorizing

SUBJECT-BASED	TYPE-BASED	TAG FILTERING
Aruba	**Testimonials**	*Individual Destinations*
Aruba Packages	Aruba Testimonials	*Individual Suppliers*
Aruba Testimonials	Sun Worship Testimonials	*Packages*
Aruba Travel News		*Specials*
Sun Worship Holidays	**Travel News**	*Testimonials*
Sun Worship Packages	Aruba Travel News	*Travel News*
Sun Worship Testimonials	Sun Worship Travel News	
Sun Worship Travel News		

At first glance, it might look as if the Subject approach is nicely geared toward what your visitors are most interested in: destinations and their favorite vacation suppliers. But what about flexibility of grouping posts?

Now go back to the example of testimonials for a moment. If you choose the Subject approach, it wouldn't be easy to have a single testimonials page displaying all testimonials at one time. You'd need to figure out some way to gather together the various testimonials categories rather than lettingWordPress's parent-child category structure do the work for you. You would have the same problem if you want to have a random testimonial from the list of all testimonials appear on the site's sidebar; unless they're all under one parent category, there'd be some customization work needed.

With the Type approach, however, not only can you easily have an "all testimonials" page by simply displaying the Testimonials category, you also can link the Sun Worship Holidays testimonials category to the Sun Worship Holidays page. Like the Subject approach, though, it does mean creating a lot of child categories. However, the way categories appear on the posts admin screen makes it much easier for you or your staff to be sure you're accurately placing a post in all the right spots.

The Tag Filtering approach is even more flexible, but it does take a bit more work when entering a new post or creating a menu item. You'll need to remember to use the WordPress tag system, not just categories, and how to create special URLs that filter a category using tags. And don't let Table 2-1 leave you thinking that with Tag Filtering you can't have child categories.

In any of these approaches, remember there's the ability to create child categories of child categories for even greater flexibility. Under the Packages category you could have child categories by price level or type of package (resort versus tour and so on).

So you can see there's a lot to think about for organizing your post content; all of it is influenced by knowing how WordPress works. As you move through the book, the process should become clearer, and you'll start to develop your own ideas. Every site will have different needs, of course, but hopefully this lesson gives you some broad guidelines to create your content organization.

The Page Map

Having mapped out individual web pages for your site, it's time to create a map of common elements you want on all those pages (or sometimes on just a few of them).

Figure 2-3 shows a visual page map, but yours can simply be a list with headings indicating the portion of the page you're talking about.

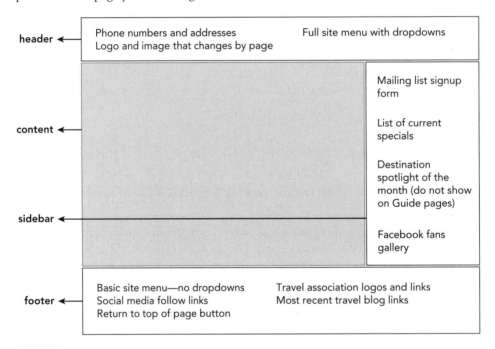

header ←

Phone numbers and addresses
Logo and image that changes by page

Full site menu with dropdowns

content ←

Mailing list signup form

List of current specials

Destination spotlight of the month (do not show on Guide pages)

sidebar ←

Facebook fans gallery

footer ←

Basic site menu—no dropdowns
Social media follow links
Return to top of page button

Travel association logos and links
Most recent travel blog links

FIGURE 2-3

Notice in the sidebar the qualification put on "Destination spotlight of the month." You don't want to distract visitors with another destination while talking about one destination. Content in any area of the website, not just the sidebar, can be hidden from some pages or only shown on others, so be sure to make notes about that on your page map.

Remember, this map does not need to represent your final site layout; it's about site content outside the main content area. For example, the layout that you choose for Island Travel might have two menus in the header area, which split up the "full site menu," or you might decide later to move those travel association links into the sidebar. And maybe some of your pages won't have a sidebar.

The key here is to have something in mind as you progress through learning WordPress and creating your site. It will make learning easier and make a better site.

SPECIAL SITE FUNCTIONALITY

It's now time for another list. You won't need it right away, but it's good to have it as you work your way through this book and through WordPress. It will begin as a list of every function you want your site to perform. As you learn more, you can cross some items off the list until it becomes a list of the things your site needs that WordPress doesn't do. Eventually it will become a list of plugins, the add-on programs that provide WordPress with additional functionality.

For the moment, you just need to write down all the things you think your site needs to do. Following are some examples:

➤ Run a slider on the homepage.

➤ Allow visitors to sign up to your mailing list.

➤ Accept online payments.

➤ Automatically post to Facebook, Twitter, or other social media.

➤ Allow visitors to easily pin your pictures to Pinterest.

➤ Create a pricing table of your services.

➤ Display an events calendar.

➤ Track how many visitors download certain files.

➤ Play video on the site (from YouTube or other sharing sites).

➤ Display galleries of photos.

➤ Track the number of visitors and other statistics.

➤ Create forms.

➤ Have rotating testimonials on the homepage or in the sidebar.

Try to be as comprehensive and as specific as you can with your list. Some of the items in the example here were items from the page map, and that will often be the case. The page map was about where you want things; this is a list about what you need WordPress to do, so you can figure how it's going to get done. Don't worry if it's a long list or whether you're actually going to have all this functionality on your site (at least right away). This is a wish list to help guide you.

Some of these functions, you'll discover, are built in to WordPress, whereas others will require a plugin. And the more you know exactly what you need from each of these functions, the better you're going to judge which plugin is right for a particular function. In any case, having the list can make you a better WordPress user; **learning any software is about knowing what you need it to do, not knowing everything it does.**

> **WARNING** *You're going to discover that WordPress themes may offer to do some of the functions on your list. In some cases that will be a good thing, whereas in others I'm going to warn you not to accept the offer. That's because the function the theme wants to perform is a function you'd want even if you switched themes. In that case the function should be performed by a plugin. This happens a lot these days as themes become more sophisticated; often that sophistication becomes misplaced in an attempt to be all things to all people. I'll be sure to warn you about this throughout the book.*

HOW YOU WANT THE SITE TO LOOK

The final list you should make in planning your website is the visual elements of the site. When choosing a theme for WordPress, this list can help focus the process.

Site Design

The first part of this list should be a series of URLs for websites you like the look of. Along with the web address of the site, be sure to write a short note about which elements you liked in particular, such as "open, airy feeling with lots of white space" or "dark, textured background in the footer." Not all the elements may fit together well, but with modifications or eliminations, the result should be a good picture of what you're looking for.

The best place to begin your search is with competing websites. It can help you to spot trends within your field, either to incorporate them or to deliberately break away from them. After that you can expand your search to sites of any kind. If you make this a habit during your normal web surfing, you can build up a good collection of sites with not much additional effort.

Hopefully, there will be a few sites whose overall look would be good candidates for yours. This can make the process much easier than trying to piece together a site design only from elements on numerous sites.

Two elements are particularly important to pay attention to when looking through all these sites: color schemes and typography. They have become increasingly important as web design has become more minimalistic. If you have a logo or company colors, watch for color schemes that match or complement them. Don't worry about finding color codes at this point. Lesson 27, "Overview of WordPress Themes," discusses tools for grabbing those. If you don't have a company color to work with, focus on the effect of the color scheme on the mood of your site: professional versus light-hearted versus folksy, and so on.

When looking for great typography on sites, don't simply pay attention to the font. It's only one element of typography. Watch for easy-to-read font sizing, comfortable spacing between letters, lines, and paragraphs, and the overall look of the type on the screen. Font color and the color of links is another part of readability on the web. Again, just make notes along with the URL of the site—the tools for finding technical details, such as the name of a font or the font sizing, spacing, and so on will be discussed later.

What's been said so far concerns the common design governing all the pages on your site, but there's one page that needs its own examples and notes: the homepage. This is your business's introduction to the world and it needs to stand out. That doesn't mean a lot of fancy graphics (though if that would benefit your business, by all means), but it does mean more color, more images, wider variations in typography, and more elements that require design.

One word of warning as you make your way through all these sites: Don't get caught up in the *magpie effect*: being dazzled by bright, shiny objects. From time to time you'll see, for example, a cool animation and think, *I need that*. Sometimes, though, these effects that impress us on first glance become annoyances when you see it on every page of the site or every time you return to the homepage. Be dazzled, by all means, but don't rush it to the top of your design list.

Site Layout

In the broadest sense, there isn't much to think about for site layout: header, content, footer, and probably a sidebar. Perhaps the sidebar is on the right instead of on the left, but what more is there to say about site layout? Of course, there's a lot more to say when you start filling in the details of these broad areas of the site. And if it sounds like you already went through this with the page map earlier in this lesson, that was simply about what common content is planned for all web pages. Now you're concerned with positioning that content.

A drawing is going to be the most effective way to visualize the layout and again, while a hand-drawn outline is fine, Figure 2-4 has been done with presentation software:

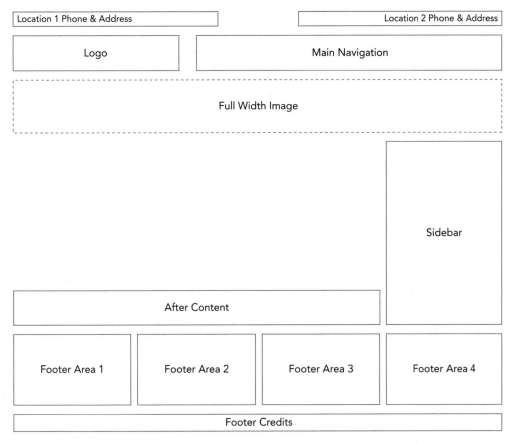

FIGURE 2-4

Armed with an outline like this you'll have another set of criteria when eventually looking for a WordPress theme. Either the theme will have a layout close to this or the capability for you to easily customize areas of the site to match your vision. Not that you can't change your mind as you go along, but you'll have something to change.

Now there's one other important element of site layout you'll want to plan for: the homepage. Because it's meant to be an introduction to your business, it needs a different layout. In some cases the layout may not be all that different, but typically it takes on a different form, as illustrated in Figure 2-5.

FIGURE 2-5

The goal here is to quickly convey the key benefits of what you're offering and guide the visitor to the areas of the site with more details. The flow of the layout and where it draws your eye becomes important. You don't want to overwhelm the visitor.

TRY IT

This lesson does not have a step-by-step instruction other than to encourage you to make the lists and drawings outlined here. They will not only help make your site better, they can also help you learn to use WordPress by giving you specific goals—a context for why you want to use a particular WordPress function.

> **REFERENCE** *There is no video to accompany this lesson.*

SECTION II
Firing Up WordPress

- ▶ **LESSON 3:** Installing WordPress

- ▶ **LESSON 4:** Admin Area Overview

- ▶ **LESSON 5:** Basic Admin Settings

3

Installing WordPress

Because this book covers the self-hosted version of WordPress, you need to have a hosting account on a web server. This is different from having a domain name. A domain name points to a hosting account on a server where the files and a database for a WordPress website are stored. If you don't have a hosting account, following are some things to keep in mind when looking for one.

HOSTING WORDPRESS

At www.WordPress.org, you can find a list of currently recommend hosting companies, but there are many others that are just as good. There are a few software requirements for hosting WordPress, but most hosting packages these days—even the most basic—should meet them. Still, it's best to double-check, so here's what to look for as of Version 4.0:

➤ PHP Version 5.2.4 or greater

➤ MySQL database Version 5.0 or greater

➤ The recommended server software is Apache or Nginx, but as long as the minimums for PHP and MySQL are met, everything should be fine.

> **NOTE** *If you're not sure how to word your question to your hosting company, the WordPress site provides you with the text for an e-mail you can send at* http://wordpress.org/about/requirements/. *The letter adds a third item to the list: the* mod_rewrite *Apache module. This module is needed for the custom permalinks feature in WordPress; although there is a way to use custom permalinks without it, it just makes life a bit easier. Most Linux servers have the module installed.*

Of course there's more to choosing a host than meeting these requirements. In particular, you want to look for:

➤ **Reliability**—How often are they down? How good are their security measures? What is their backup policy?

➤ **Support**—Do you have 24-hour access? How quickly do they respond? Do they have a useful knowledge base?

➤ **Speed**—How quickly will your site load?

Don't rely on advertising or most of the so-called hosting review sites you'll find. Look for individual bloggers who have performed actual tests or provided reviews with pros and cons based on real-world experience. You can also search through the forums of hosting companies or webmaster forums to see what people complain about. And put the question to social media for direct feedback.

As Figure 3-1 shows, many hosting companies these days promote that they do WordPress hosting. Often this simply means that they offer automated installing of WordPress. That's a valuable feature, but be aware that it isn't anything special or unique.

FIGURE 3-1

In other cases, WordPress hosting means it offers services such as:

➤ **Managed hosting**—The host provides regular backups and performs all WordPress updating (even plugins). This can extend to offering a separate version of WordPress where you can test your site or allow only certain plugins to be used.

➤ **WordPress support**—This could include support specialists who know WordPress or detailed WordPress documentation using videos or screen shot tutorials.

➤ **Optimized servers**—This can range from ensuring that server software is configured to help WordPress and its database perform well all the way to using Virtual Private Servers (VPS) and fewer sites on a machine than the shared hosting packages most people use.

➤ **Caching**—This is like taking a snapshot of each of your pages and serving those snapshots instead of having to go back and forth to the database, and that helps speed up site loading for visitors. There are plugins for this, but they can be tricky to set up. Here the host takes care of all that for you.

Naturally, with these special hosting features typically comes a higher monthly cost. Although regular shared hosting accounts (without multiyear plans or introductory pricing) are in the $6 to $9 range, specialized WordPress hosting starts at approximately $16 per month and goes up from there.

This book shows you how to do such tasks as backups and updates, and ways to keep your WordPress site loading quickly. However, you may prefer to pay someone else to do them. Managed hosting is a cost-effective way of off-loading these important ongoing tasks.

After you decide on a hosting company and have your account, it's time to install and activate WordPress. As previously mentioned, most hosts these days have programs that enable you to do a one-click installation of WordPress, but now look at an old-fashioned manual install.

MANUALLY INSTALLING WORDPRESS

If you want complete control over how WordPress is installed on your hosting account and you're comfortable working with file transfer programs (FTP) and hosting control panels (such as cPanel or Parallels/Plesk), this method is for you. Or if you're hiring someone, this can help you understand why he should not be charging for more than 15 minutes worth of work.

The steps are outlined here, but on the DVD you can watch the process in detail using cPanel, the most popular hosting control panel available. There's also a working file on the DVD with instructions for the downloading and uploading of WordPress files.

Because there are two main elements to WordPress—the files and the database—the outline follows that structure.

Uploading the WordPress Files

Self-hosting WordPress means you need to put the files onto your server using the following steps:

1. Download and save the latest version from WordPress.org.
2. Unzip WordPress.
3. Using an FTP program (such as Filezilla), upload the unzipped WordPress files (the ones inside the folder wordpress and not the folder itself) to the location you want on your server.

Creating the Database

WordPress requires a database in order to function, so you need to set one up through your hosting control panel:

1. Locate the MySQL database section of your hosting Control Panel.
2. Click the button for creating a new database.
3. Enter a name for the database. If you have several databases, be sure to name it so that you know it's WordPress for this site.
4. Click the button for creating a new user. (Not all control panels have this step.)

5. Enter a username.

6. Enter a password for the user, and make sure it is strong.

7. Be sure to have the database name, username, and password handy for use later in the process.

8. If you are asked to assign permissions or privileges for this user, make sure you select ALL.

9. In some cases you may be asked to assign the new user to a database; make sure it's the right database.

10. Check where your database is located and make a note of the server name for use later. If no server name is specified, it's likely the default *localhost*.

Connecting the Files to the Database

This is what WordPress actually means by "our famous 5-minute install." There are two ways to do this install: manually creating the configuration file or having WordPress lead you through a semi-automated process.

You can see the manual configuration process in one of the videos accompanying this lesson; however, here is the semi-automated process, which you begin by entering your site's domain name in your browser (or if you put the WordPress files in a subdirectory, enter the full path).

1. The first screen asks you to choose an installation language; then click Continue.

2. Next, you are asked to gather some information about your database (what you were told to make note of in the previous section). When you're ready, click Let's Go!

3. Here you enter all that database information. The final field asks if you want to change the default WordPress database prefix. The prefix will be placed in front of all the tables in the database to help distinguish them from any other tables. You can put whatever you want here, but I recommend keeping the default wp- at the beginning so that you can quickly see that it's a WordPress table. When you finish, click Submit.

4. Now confirm that you can talk to your database and can do the actual install, then click Run the Install.

5. You need to provide a title for your WordPress installation, along with an administrator username and password. Do NOT use "admin" or "administrator" because hackers automatically try these. And make sure your password is a strong one; weak passwords are the number-one way hackers get into WordPress. When you're ready, click Install WordPress.

6. Screen #6 tells you you've successfully installed WordPress and offers to take you to the login screen.

> **NOTE** *If you plan to use the multisite feature of WordPress—the capability to run multiple sites from a single installation—you can find the additional installation instructions here:* http://codex.wordpress.org/Create_A_Network.

AUTO-INSTALLING WORDPRESS

Most hosting companies offer some form of automatic WordPress installation. In a few cases, this means that they'll actually do the installation for you, but mostly it means that they have a program that you use to do the auto-install.

The two most common auto-installer programs are Softaculous and Quick Install, but there are others, and some hosts have their own proprietary installers. They all work in mostly the same way: You enter a bit of information and press a button.

> **NOTE** *For many years Fantastico was the auto-installer used by most hosting companies, but it has since been discontinued.*

The first step is to tell the auto-installer where you want it to put the WordPress files. Referring to Figure 3-2, Quick Install offers a choice of existing domains or subdomains that are on your hosting account with the opportunity to enter a subdirectory. (If that subdirectory doesn't exist, the installer creates it.)

FIGURE 3-2

After the location is chosen, you need to enter information such as your e-mail address and username—information varies by programs. Referring to Figure 3-3, you can see that Quick Install also needs the title of your site (ignore that it says Blog Title), your first name, and last name.

FIGURE 3-3

Although Quick Install creates a password for you (you can change it later in WordPress), other installers ask you for a password. Some also allow you to choose the database prefix for WordPress.

> **NOTE** *Auto-installers should install the latest version of WordPress, but if yours doesn't, don't worry. WordPress will tell you if it needs updating, and that process is easy—especially after installation when you have no content or plugins. The steps for updating are outlined in Lesson 32, "Keeping Up to Date."*

WHEN THE INSTALLATION IS FINISHED

Whether you do an auto-install or a manual install, your WordPress site is now up and running. You can check by going to your domain name (or subdirectory, depending on where you did the install) and looking at your new site (see Figure 3-4).

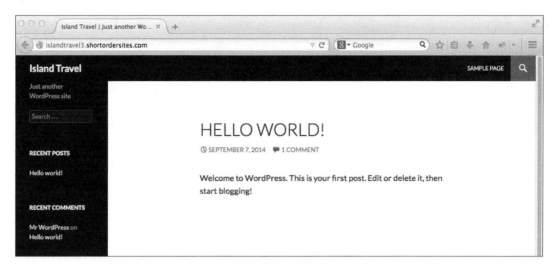

FIGURE 3-4

It may not have much —a sample post and a sample page—but this is a fully operational website waiting for you to add content and customize the look and the functionality. But before getting to that, become familiar with the way WordPress works in the back end. That's the subject of the next two lessons.

> ## PLUGINS
>
> There are no plugins to help install a new WordPress site because WordPress isn't running yet. However, there may be times when you need to move an existing WordPress site within your hosting account (perhaps to a new directory) or to a new server. In that case, here are some plugins that can help:
>
> ➤ *Duplicator*—takes care of the entire process of copying your site and restoring it in a new location.
>
> ➤ *WP Clone by WP Academy*—utility for copying and moving your WordPress site to a subdomain, a new server, or a new domain.

TRY IT

There's nothing additional to try in this lesson—hopefully, you completed the installation using these instructions. If you don't plan on doing the installation right now, you could always set up an FTP program if you don't have one or download WordPress for use later.

> **REFERENCE** *Please select the video for Lesson 3 online at* www.wrox.com /go/wp24vids. *You will also be able to download resources for this lesson from the website.*

Admin Area Overview

One of WordPress's greatest strengths is the user-friendliness of its administration interface. From both an organizational and a design standpoint, it's laid out in a way that's intuitive. As with any system, of course, you need to take some time and learn how it works, where things are, and so on, and that's what this lesson is about: helping you become familiar with the WordPress administration area.

LOGGING IN

At the end of the installation process, you're either sent automatically to the default login page, as shown in Figure 4-1 A, or there will be a link to take you there.

FIGURE 4-1

It's a good idea to bookmark this page in your browser. Some themes include a login link—often in the footer area—but even without a bookmark or a link, you always have this fallback: add `/wp-admin` to the end of your site URL, like this:

```
http://yourdomainname.com/wp-admin
```

This takes you to your login screen. Of course if you installed WordPress in a subdirectory, you'll add **/wp-admin** at the end of that subdirectory URL.

> **WARNING** *If you can't login, double-check that you're not at* `WordPress.com`. *A common mistake—and not just for newbies—is to think that because you have a WordPress site, you have to log in at* `WordPress.com`. *If you installed WordPress on a hosting account, the login will be through the domain name for that account.*

Logging in is a matter of entering the username and password you chose during the installation process. If you forget or can't find your password, there's a link on the login page for setting a new password, as shown in Figure 4-1 B. You can use either your e-mail address (the one given during installation) or your username to set a new password. In either case, the instructions for setting the new password are sent to that e-mail address, so always make sure it's a functioning address. In Lesson 5, "Basic Admin Settings," you learn how to keep your e-mail address up to date through your Profile.

As mentioned, during installation the importance of having a strong password is the best way of protecting yourself from hackers. If you do reset your password, WordPress has a strength meter: Pay attention to it. There are other ways to make your login process more secure, which are discussed in Lesson 34, "Keeping Your Site Secure."

One option you have during login is a check box that says Remember Me. By selecting that option, the cookie that WordPress always creates when you log in will last for 14 days instead of the default 2 days. This is particularly handy when you're first setting up your site and likely to be coming back to it over the course of many days.

Logging into WordPress means you're going into the administrative area of your website: the back end. This is where you create content, update content, control the look of your site, add or remove functionality, and much more. The admin area of WordPress is well laid out and easy to use, but you need to become familiar with it, and that's what this next section is all about.

> **WARNING** *Even if you close your browser or your tab, you're still logged into WordPress for 2 or 14 days; that's the value of the cookie. But it's also the danger. If you're at a public terminal or in an environment in which someone could access your device, be sure to log out.*

NAVIGATING THE ADMIN AREA

The first time you log in to WordPress, you get a welcome message at the top of the Dashboard screen, as shown in Figure 4-2.

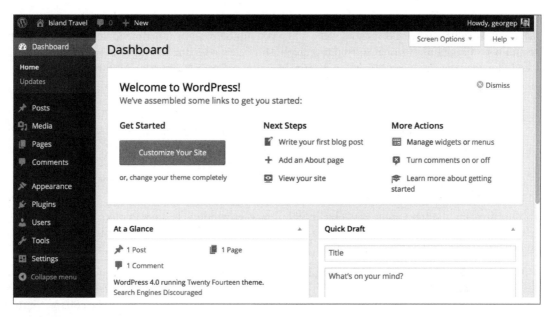

FIGURE 4-2

The *Welcome to WordPress!* area provides beginners with helpful links to key areas of WordPress for starting the site. You can dismiss the welcome area, but it is well worth leaving in place until you become more familiar with the software.

The Main Admin Menu

The most important tool for getting around WordPress is the main admin menu (Figure 4-3 A), which is on the left side of all admin screens. *Get to know this menu.* One of the most common problems is users simply being unsure of where to find what they need.

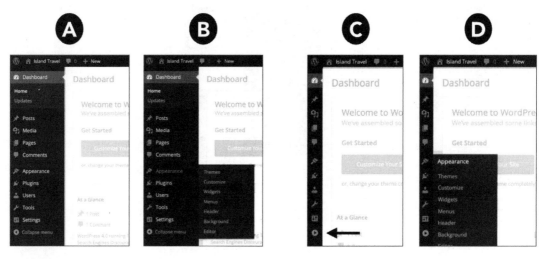

FIGURE 4-3

The first level of the main admin menu shows all the admin sections. When you're in one of the sections, its submenu items display as well. When you mouseover any other menu item, you see a fly-out menu with all the links for that section (Figure 4-3 B). When referring to one of these submenu items, the following convention is used: Main Admin Menu Item ⇨ Sub-Menu Item. So for example, to edit post categories, you see, Click Posts ⇨ Categories.

> **NOTE** *The main admin menu referred to in Figure 4-3 is the default menu. Depending on the theme you use and the plugins you activate, the main admin menu items and the submenu items could look different.*

If the entire main admin menu is visible in your browser window, it stays in place as you scroll through other content on the screen. If part of the main admin menu is not visible, it automatically scrolls as you use the browser's scrollbar.

After you're familiar with the main admin menu, you might find it unnecessary to see the names of each of the main admin menu items, or you simply might want the screen to be less cluttered. In that case you can collapse the main admin menu so that it looks like Figure 4-3 C. (The collapse button is highlighted.) If you mouseover any of the icons, the submenu items appear as usual, complete with full names (refer to Figure 4-3 D). If your browser window becomes narrow enough, WordPress automatically collapses the main admin menu.

On mobile devices, WordPress's admin area shifts to a single column with a menu icon at the top left, as shown in Figure 4-4. When you tap the icon, the full menu appears. Just tap the icon to collapse the menu again. When you tap a top-level menu item, the submenu slides down rather than becoming a fly-out to the right. The submenu remains open until you tap the parent again, and you can have as many submenus stay open as you want.

FIGURE 4-4

The Toolbar

The toolbar is at the top of WordPress admin screen (Figure 4-5).

FIGURE 4-5

The Toolbar provides additional navigation for the admin area, including (from left to right) the following:

1. Links to WordPress.org, the Codex (documentation), the support forums, and a feedback page
2. A link to the front end of your site
3. An icon indicating how many comments await moderation
4. A quick link menu for creating a new Post, adding Media, creating a new Page, or adding a new User
5. Your user display name (here it's the username), your profile photo, and links to your Profile and to Log Out

As with so many elements of WordPress, this toolbar will vary according to what theme you have and which plugins. You can turn off the toolbar for the front end of your site (see Lesson 5, "Basic Admin Settings") but not for the back end or admin area. And, as mentioned at the end of this lesson, there are plugins to give you control over what's on the toolbar.

> **NOTE** *At one time there was an admin header area with an Admin Bar above that. They were both combined into what is now called the Tool Bar, but you'll often hear people still using the term Admin Bar.*

THE DASHBOARD

Whenever you log in to WordPress, the first screen you see is the Dashboard, which is the homepage for the administration area. In default mode it consists of five modules, or widgets (as they're sometimes called). Here they are referred to as boxes.

You saw something of the Dashboard earlier when you saw the Welcome to WordPress box. It's meant for beginning users, although many people leave it in place permanently as a reminder of functions they can perform. The other four boxes on the page basically summarize what's going on with your site and in the world of WordPress.

I don't use the Dashboard much. I do pay attention to the At a Glance box because it tells you the version of WordPress and whether you're blocking search engines from indexing your site. (Lesson 5 explains when you might want that turned on.) I also keep an eye on WordPress News because it talks about new versions, security issues, and so on. Other than that, I don't spend much time with the Dashboard.

For others with busy blogs, the Dashboard has a handy summary of your recent activity, the latest Comments and whether some need approval, and a running total of your Posts, Pages, and Comments. And if you need to jot down some notes for a possible Post, there's a box for writing a Quick Draft.

However, the Dashboard may do a lot more, depending on your theme and the plugins you have. An e-commerce plugin, for example, may show your recent orders, whereas an SEO plugin may show you some statistics.

For all these reasons, the Dashboard is a personal admin screen that can vary greatly from one WordPress installation to the next. There's another way the Dashboard can be personalized: by physically changing the screen. Actually, most admin screens have this capability, but the next section illustrates the tremendous flexibility you have with WordPress.

CUSTOMIZING ADMIN SCREENS

Here are some common ways you can structure admin screens to suit your needs, using methods built in to WordPress. At the end of the lesson I mention some plugins that provide additional customization options.

WordPress screens are divided into boxes; each one performs a function or set of functions. Most boxes enable you to customize them in one of four ways:

➤ Minimize a box.

➤ Show or hide available boxes using Screen Options.

➤ Reposition a box.

➤ Change the number of columns of boxes.

Minimizing Boxes

To minimize or collapse a box, click anywhere on its header area, as shown in Figure 4-6.

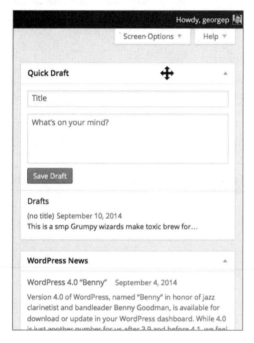

FIGURE 4-6

To restore the box, click again in the header area. This is handy when you need the box out of the way temporarily. After you minimize the box, it stays that way even if you leave the screen and come back. It won't restore until you click the header.

Hiding or Showing Entire Boxes Using Screen Options

You can completely hide (or show) a box from the Screen Options button at the top right of the screen, as shown in Figure 4-7. Dropping down this area allows you to pick and choose from the boxes available for that screen.

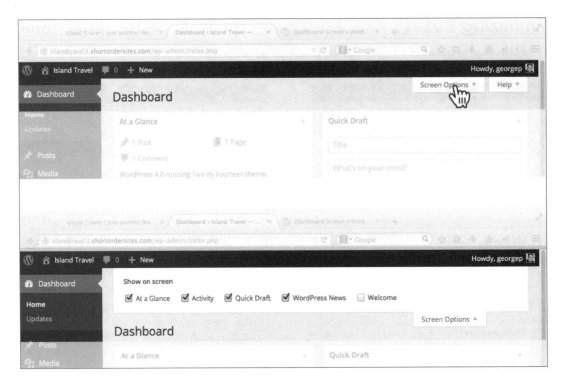

FIGURE 4-7

Checking a box makes the element appear, and unchecking it makes it disappear. What's nice is that this happens in real time, so you can see what the change looks like before closing Screen Options.

Again, the boxes available for a screen vary tremendously depending on your theme and plugins. The key is to remember that Screen Options exists. If you're not seeing something on a screen that's mentioned in instructions or shown on a video, remember to check Screen Options. If a box that you remember from a few months ago is not showing on the screen, remember to check Screen Options.

Screen Options can also control more than just box visibility. You learn about these additional functions throughout the book, but here's one good example: On screens that list items such as Posts or Pages, you can customize how many display on one screen by going to Screen Options.

Repositioning Boxes

The third way to customize the display of boxes is to physically move them around the page. For example, if you don't use the QuickPress feature much, but often read the WordPress News, you can switch places by moving them around. On Post screens you can move the Featured Image box up to the top to remind you whether you assigned a featured image yet.

All you do is mouseover the header of the box and you'll see the cursor change to the hand icon or crossed arrows icon, depending on your operating system. At that point, you can click and drag. (For mobile, hold your finger down on the header and drag.) As the box moves from its original location, a rectangle with dashed borders appears when your cursor approaches a point where the box can be dropped, as shown in Figure 4-8.

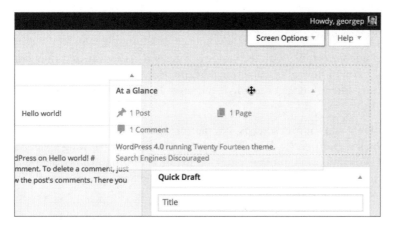

FIGURE 4-8

When you see that dashed outline in the spot you want, release the mouse button, and the original box now appears there. It will remain there until you move it again.

> **NOTE** *With larger boxes, it can be easier to collapse them first and then move them around.*

Changing the Number of Columns

The fourth way to customize the admin screen is to change the number of columns available to display boxes. By default, WordPress displays admin screen boxes in two columns on a desktop, laptop, or large tablet, whereas smaller tablets and smartphones default to one.

On most screens, the only choice is between one or two columns, but some offer up to four columns. You can find this under Screen Options. Because WordPress now adjusts to one column automatically if your browser is below a certain width, the column feature is less important, but there may be situations in which you want this kind of manual control.

> **NOTE** *Previously when you switched from one column to two, you had to manually move boxes back to the second column, but in recent versions of WordPress, the boxes realign themselves into columns when you make the change in Screen Options.*

GETTING COMFORTABLE

The point of this lesson has been for you to become comfortable with the WordPress admin screens. In addition to slowing you down, being uncomfortable with any software has an even worse effect: You stop using it. A website is a living, growing, adaptable tool for your business (or your personal life) and unless you keep working on it, it will die. And the more you work on it, the better it becomes. Don't let your website suffer because you don't "get" WordPress.

Part of what makes people feel uncomfortable with technology in general is the fear that they don't know everything about it—they don't know all its functions. Many people using WordPress only know how to write some content, add an image or a video, and press Publish. They learned only what they needed.

There's a sense in which WordPress is its admin screens. No matter what you need to do with WordPress, you need to find your way around, adapt the admin screens to your working style, and understand the "language" of WordPress. It's another part of learning to think like WordPress, the concept introduced in Lesson 1, "Thinking Like WordPress." And the more you can think like WordPress, the more comfortable you'll be using it.

The next lesson starts to shape WordPress into the tool you need by adjusting some administrative settings—or you at least learn where to go if you need to change those settings later.

> **NOTE** *If you need help on any WordPress admin screen, remember to use the Help drop-down at the top right of the screen.*

PLUGINS

From this brief overview of the WordPress admin area, you might have had some thoughts about how you want things to be different. Thankfully, so have a lot of other people, and they've created plugins to make the customizations easy. Following are a few to help you start:

THE LOGIN SCREEN

➤ **Custom Login**—Customize the look of your login screen, such as adding your own logo. Also includes add-ons such as hiding the URL of your login page. In Lesson 34, "Keeping Your Site Secure," you learn more about security for the login page, along with lots of plugins to help with that.

➤ **Login Logo**—Simply replaces the login screen's WordPress logo with your own.

➤ **Erident Custom Login and Dashboard**—Control the look of the login screen and the Dashboard screen.

THE MAIN ADMIN MENU

➤ **Admin Menu Editor**—Reorder, hide, or add menu items.

➤ **Adminimize**—Reorganize menu items, but also change many aspects of admin screens in general.

THE TOOLBAR

➤ **Custom Admin Bar**—Add your own menu to the toolbar.

➤ **Admin Menu**—Enables you to put any items from the main admin menu on the toolbar.

➤ **Auto Hide Admin Bar**—When you mouseover the top of the screen, the toolbar displays.

Note that when you are searching for Toolbar plugins, be sure to search for **Admin Bar** as well.

THE DASHBOARD

➤ **Dashboard Commander**—Control the display of default dashboard boxes (or widgets, as the plugin calls them) as well as any that are installed by plugins; you can control based on a user's role.

➤ **Dashboard Widget Sidebar**—Creates a widget area under Appearance ➪ Widgets, which displays on the Dashboard.

➤ **Announce from the Dashboard**—Enables you to add your own box to the Dashboard and decide which users are able to see it.

PLUGINS FOR SPECIFIC FUNCTIONS

A lot of plugins add a specific function to the Dashboard. Following are a couple examples:

➤ **Google Analytics Dashboard for WP**—Displays reports and real-time stats from Google Analytics on your Dashboard.

➤ **WordPress Dashboard Twitter**—Enables you to control your Twitter account directly from the Dashboard.

With the AG Custom Admin, you can customize the main admin menu, Dashboard, login page, and toolbar—just about anything in the admin area.

Plugins such as Selfish Fresh Start make a lot of changes on the back end of WordPress, removing admin elements, such as the ability to edit Plugin files (which the author thinks should not be there). You need to check precisely what the plugin can do in case you don't agree with all the options, or better still, look for a plugin that gives you the option of turning things off.

TRY IT

In this lesson, you reorganized the boxes on the Dashboard using a variety of techniques and you're tested on knowing the main admin menu.

Lesson Requirements

WordPress installed.

Step-by-Step

➤ Main Admin Menu Quiz (answers at the end of the lesson): What is the parent menu item of these submenu items?

1. Discussion

2. Categories

3. Menus

4. Permalinks

5. Updates

➤ Reorganize the Dashboard using a mouse:

1. Move the Quick Draft box. Click the header of the box and while pressing the mouse button, drag the box downward.

2. When you get below WordPress News, stop and let go.

3. Collapse the At a Glance box (which should be at the top of your left-hand column) by clicking the box's header area.

4. Collapse Other WordPress News the same way. You should now see Quick Draft without having to scroll.

5. Go to Screen Options at the top right of the screen, and click it.

6. Uncheck Activity, and you should see it disappear.

7. Close Screen Options by clicking the button again.

8. Return the Dashboard to the way you want it.

➤ Answers to the quiz:

1. Settings

2. Posts

3. Appearance

4. Settings

5. Dashboard

> **REFERENCE** *Please select the video for Lesson 4 online at* www.wrox.com/go /wp24vids. *You will also be able to download resources for this lesson from the website.*

Basic Admin Settings

WordPress has dozens of administrative settings at your disposal, but you'll probably use most of the default settings for as long as you run your site. So, the good news is you don't need to mess with more than a few settings as you begin to build your site.

This lesson familiarizes you with the pages on the default Settings menu and shows you how to change those truly important few settings. Later lessons deal with other admin settings as they're needed.

THE SETTINGS MENU

The Settings heading on the main admin menu is where you control various site-wide parameters for WordPress, and its submenus are divided by functions. Figure 5-1 shows the menu and a list of key functions for each of the submenu items:

General	site title, tagline, location, admin email, date/time formats
Writing	default Post category/format, Press This bookmarklet, posting via email
Reading	control front page display, how many posts to show, search engine visibility
Discussion	detailed settings for comments, avatar control
Media	control the sizes of the images created from originals that you upload
Permalinks	control the way URLs are created for your site's pages

FIGURE 5-1

This is the Settings menu when you first install WordPress. Depending on your theme or installed plugins, this Settings menu may show more choices. Now walk through each of these settings pages and focus on the key settings you may want to change at this point.

> **NOTE** *On most Settings screens, the Save Changes button is at the bottom of the page, so you need to remember to scroll down to save any new administrative settings.*

Settings ⇨ General

There are only a few settings here that you should need to touch after installing WordPress, and a few you shouldn't touch unless you know what you're doing.

Site Title

This was set during the installation of WordPress, but, of course, you can change it any time using the setting shown in Figure 5-2. Before you launch your site, make sure you've decided on the title. It's an important part of your identity, and search engines use this as well—if you change in midstream, it can make things difficult.

FIGURE 5-2

Tagline

Change this right now! As you can see in Figure 5-3, the default wording is "Just another WordPress site" and if you Google that phrase, you'll see how many millions of people have not made this important change.

FIGURE 5-3

The Tagline is meant to be a more descriptive phrase about your site and is often displayed by themes somewhere near the Site Title. It will also get used by SEO plugins, so you want to make sure that it provides useful information about what you do or what your site is about.

WordPress Address/Site Address

Do not touch these settings! Putting the wrong information into the fields shown in Figure 5-4 will break your site. These are created during installation, so you have no need to touch them.

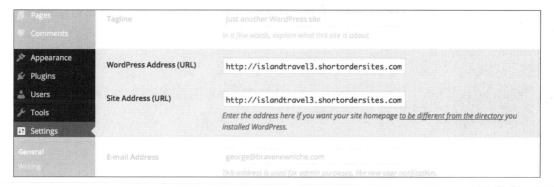

FIGURE 5-4

Although these are often the same URL, they have different functions. The WordPress address tells WordPress where to look for files, whereas the Site Address tells it what to use when constructing URLs.

If you decide to change the domain name of your site down the road, do not simply change the domain name here. There's more to it than that. Look up "move wordpress site" in Google to find instructions.

E-mail Address

This is the e-mail you entered as the administrator's personal e-mail during the installation process. WordPress used it as a default for all site functions, but you can change it here in the field shown in Figure 5-5.

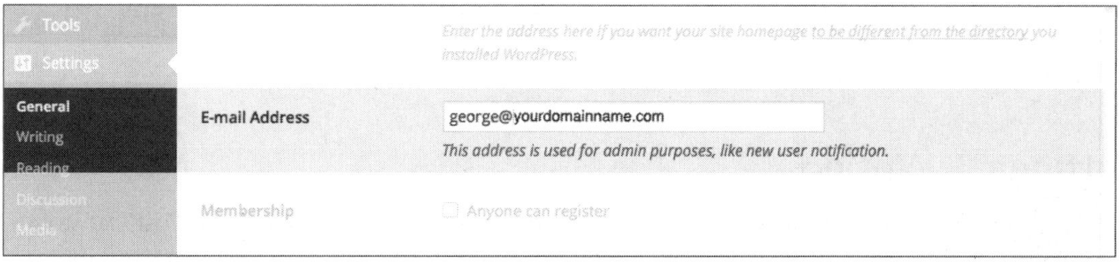

FIGURE 5-5

This e-mail is used by WordPress to send out notifications, such as automated WordPress updates, new users being added, or new comments being posted on the site. Many plugins also use this address for their settings, such as sending out a form or accessing PayPal. Plugins enable you to change the address in their settings.

Membership

Leave the box in Figure 5-6 unchecked. If you want visitors to become users or members of your site, you should use a membership plugin rather than simply checking this box and trying to manage user registrations. Without a plugin to help manage things, you're likely to get spam subscribers.

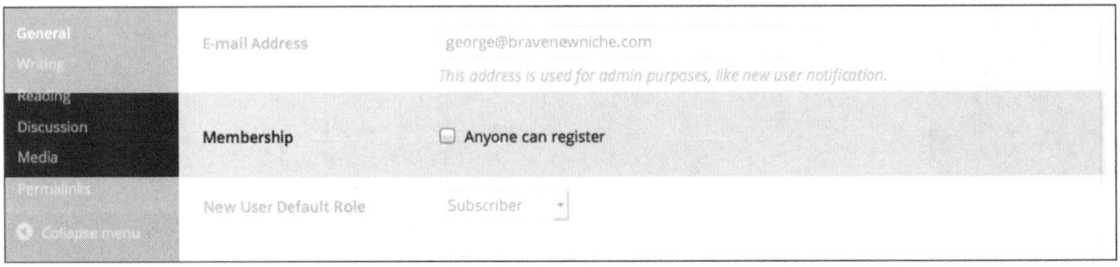

FIGURE 5-6

Timezone

Change the time zone to match your region so that dates and times are accurate when you publish or schedule content on your site. WordPress makes this easy by providing a drop-down menu of major cities around the world, as shown in Figure 5-7. Just find a city in your time zone, click Save Changes, and the correct date and time should show up in the Timezone setting area.

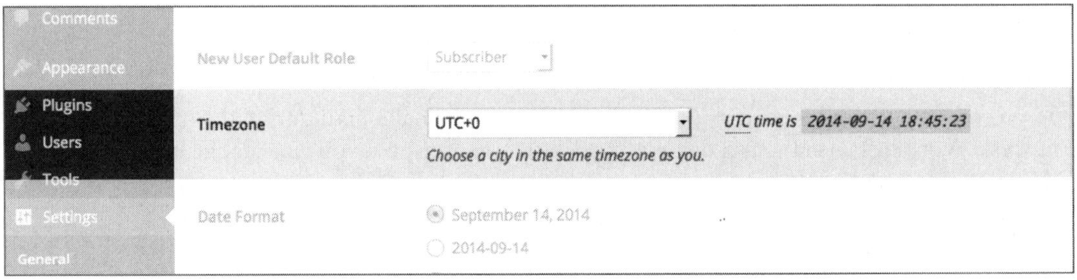

FIGURE 5-7

Settings ⇨ Writing

There's nothing to deal with on this screen when you start your site. The Default Post Category is important, but you have no categories to choose from yet, so Lesson 20, "Managing Post Categories and Tags," covers this setting.

Settings ⇨ Reading

One of the key settings on this screen is for your homepage or front page; it controls what displays when people enter your domain name in their browser. However, what setting to choose depends on what your theme needs, as well as having any pages to choose from, so this setting is discussed later at different places in the book.

Search Engine Visibility

Checking the box shown in Figure 5-8 tells search engines not to index your entire site. Depending on what you chose during installation, this box could be unchecked or checked when you first visit this screen. The default in WordPress is to have it unchecked.

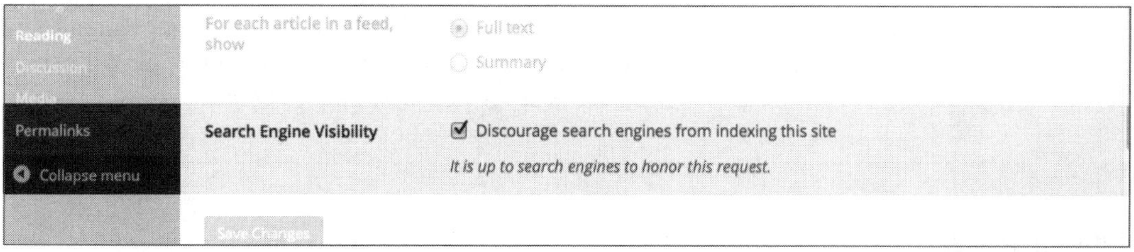

FIGURE 5-8

Blocking search engines can be valuable while you build your site, especially if you build on a test site with a different domain name. **But if you do check the box, be sure to uncheck it before your site goes live.**

You must keep two things in mind about this setting:

➤ Visibility refers to search engines, not to whether anyone can see your site.

➤ Search engines do not have to obey this setting; it's up to each search engine whether they honor the request.

> **NOTE** *Some plugins, such as SEO plugins, provide a warning message telling you if the Search Engine Visibility box is checked.*

Settings ⇨ Discussion

Discussion is just another word for Comments, and the settings on this screen default to the most common way of handling comments:

➤ Comment authors must submit both a name and e-mail address.

➤ All comments are held for moderation, unless the visitor has already had one comment approved.

➤ Comments are displayed in threaded fashion; that is, if someone directly replies to a particular comment, then that reply is shown below the original comment.

➤ You will be e-mailed whenever a comment is posted and whenever one is held for moderation.

➤ A comment is held for moderation if it has two or more links in it (a sign of spam).

This is the standard for comments on a website, so unless you have good reasons, just leave these settings on default.

Default Article Settings

Even though the term "article" is used in Figure 5-9, these settings refer to both Posts and Pages. You must understand that particularly for the third check box, *Allow people to post comments on new articles*. The default setting is checked, which means that all Posts and Pages will have a comments area. Typically, you don't want a comments box on pages, so it might be tempting to uncheck this setting, but then any Posts you create after that won't have comments.

FIGURE 5-9

My recommendation is to leave this box checked. It's simple to remove comments from individual Pages (or Posts), even large numbers of them. You learn how to do this in Lesson 10, "Adding a New Page," and Lesson 18, "Managing Posts and Pages."

Settings ⇨ Media

These settings affect the media files you upload to WordPress.

Image Sizes

When you upload an image to WordPress, a set of smaller versions is created based on the sizes you see in Figure 5-10. You can change these dimensions, but a lot depends on the particular theme you use. For example, if the theme has a wide area for actual content, you might want to increase the Medium setting to 400 px or more, or a theme may create its own versions of images to fit particular layouts for that theme.

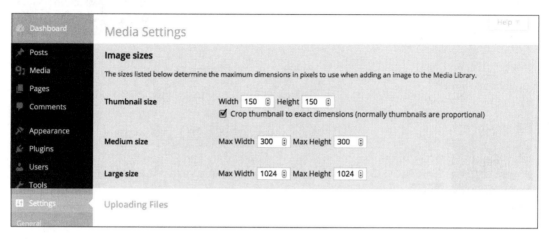

FIGURE 5-10

It makes sense not to touch these dimensions until you know whether they need changing and, most important, what to change them to.

Settings ⇨ Permalinks

A default link to a WordPress web page looks like this: `http://yourdomainname.com/?p=8723`. It's nicer for visitors and better for search engines if these links have words relating to the topic of the particular page. That's what the Permalinks settings enable you to do.

Working with Permalinks, however, is no quick or easy decision and can have negative consequences if you do it incorrectly. So ignore this for the moment; you return to the topic in some depth when you get to Search Engine Optimization in Lesson 31, "Optimizing Behind the Scenes."

PROFILE SETTINGS

The Profile page is where users control personal preferences for the admin area and information for the site in general. For example, if your posts display the author's name, this is where you set what name displays. You can access the Profile page from the top-right area of the Toolbar and from the Users submenu on the main menu, as shown in Figure 5-11.

FIGURE 5-11

> **NOTE** *There is no default option in Profile to allow users to upload their photo. WordPress automatically finds your profile photo from Gravatar.com based on your profile e-mail address, but there are plugins that add this functionality. See the list at the end of this lesson for details.*

There are three key items in Profile settings that you need to pay attention to at this point.

Toolbar

This setting determines whether the Toolbar displays on the front end of the website while logged in. As shown in Figure 5-12, the option is turned on by default. Although you can turn off the Toolbar on the front end, there is no option to turn it off on the back end, that is, on admin screens.

All Users		
Add New		
Your Profile		
Tools	Keyboard Shortcuts	☐ Enable keyboard shortcuts for comment moderation. More information
Settings	Toolbar	☑ Show Toolbar when viewing site
Collapse menu	Name	
	Username	georgep Usernames cannot be changed.

FIGURE 5-12

> **NOTE** *Some of the Toolbar plugins listed in Lesson 4, "Admin Area Overview," give you the option of turning off the Toolbar on the back end or making the Toolbar hide and show automatically on the back end.*

Display Name Publicly As

Although the username you entered during installation can never be changed, your Profile has fields for a First Name, Last Name, and Nickname. The Nickname is required and by default WordPress adds in your username, but you can change that on this screen. After you have at least one name other than the username, you can change the setting *Display name publicly as*, as shown in Figure 5-13.

FIGURE 5-13

This setting controls how WordPress lists you in various places around the website; the most obvious is on Posts and Pages for which you're the author.

> **NOTE** *Aside from the embarrassment of having your author name show up as your username, such as "georgep," not changing how your name is displayed allows hackers to easily see one-half of your login information.*

Password Strength Indicator

The Profile page enables users to change their passwords. To try and ensure they don't choose bad passwords, WordPress provides a strength indicator that tracks the quality as the new passwords are entered. Figure 5-14 shows the four levels of strength and an example of a password that would trigger each level.

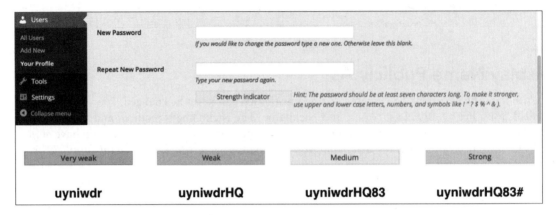

FIGURE 5-14

Referring to Figure 5-14, WordPress also provides instructions on how to make passwords strong. One thing you should add to those instructions is to not make the password a natural language word—a word you would find in a dictionary or use in speaking to someone. The more random a password, the better.

> **WARNING** *Remember to scroll to the bottom of the screen to update your profile. There is no warning if you navigate away without saving changes.*

PLUGINS

There aren't many plugins that directly target admin settings, but if you search for plugins by admin setting functions, such as Permalinks, Comments, or Media, you can find plugins that override or expand on admin settings. For example:

➤ **Disable Comments**—You can globally disable comments for Posts, Pages, or Custom Post Types. The plugin removes all comment-related fields from the edit screens of the post type chosen, so users cannot turn on comments for individual items.

➤ **Simple Image Sizes**—Enables you to add new image size options to the Media settings page and then have those new sizes available when inserting images into Posts or Pages, for example.

PROFILE PLUGINS

➤ **Cimy User Extra Fields**—Adds new fields to user profiles, including the capability to upload user images.

➤ **User Meta Manager**—Enables you to create new fields for user profiles (but the free version is limited to 100 users, which would not work for situations in which you have customers or members as users).

➤ **Profile Builder**—Enables you to create a page on the front end of the website where users can edit their profile (assuming they're logged in).

➤ **WP User Avatar**—Enables you to use any image uploaded to the WordPress Media Library as a user's profile image.

➤ **Simple Local Avatars**—Creates a section on the Profile screen where users can upload their own images.

There are also plugins that put specific social media fields on the user profile, such as Facebook or Twitter.

TRY IT

In this lesson, you're tested on where to find admin settings, and you practice changing the most essential data under General Settings.

Lesson Requirements

WordPress installed.

Step-by-Step

➤ Admin Settings Quiz (answers at the bottom): On which settings pages would you perform these functions?

1. Change the number of links allowed in comments.

2. Change how WordPress creates your website page links.

3. Change which page is displayed as your homepage.

4. Change whether WordPress organizes uploads by month and year.

5. Change the date and time formats used by WordPress.

➤ The following is the process for entering important general settings.

1. Mouseover the Settings link on the main menu.

2. Click General.

3. Find the Tagline box and change it to your new tagline.

4. Find the E-mail Address box and make sure it's correct.

5. Find the drop-down menu for Timezone, and choose a city in your time zone, or if you know your time zone, choose that.

6. If the changes look good, click Save Changes at the bottom of the page.

➤ Answers to the quiz:

1. Discussion

2. Permalinks

3. Reading

4. Media

5. General

REFERENCE *Please select the video for Lesson 5 online at* www.wrox.com/go /wp24vids. *You will also be able to download resources for this lesson from the website.*

SECTION III
Working with Written Content

Adding a New Post:
An Overview

You've seen how quickly you can get WordPress installed; now learn how fast you can create a web page on your new site. This lesson covers the basics of adding a new post: entering the text, categorizing it, adding a featured image, and then publishing it. Virtually everything here applies to writing pages. The term *post* also refers to pages. You see important differences as they come up and Lesson 10, "Adding a New Page," covers the elements unique to pages.

NAVIGATING TO ADD A NEW POST

You can add a new Post from two locations on any admin screen:

➤   The Add New link on the main admin menu under Posts (Figure 6-1, item 1)

➤   The drop-down menu near the top left of the Toolbar (Figure 6-1, item 2)

And from two additional locations on the Dashboard screen:

➤   The Welcome to WordPress box (Figure 6-1, item 3)

➤   The Quick Draft box (Figure 6-1, item 4)

Any of these links take you to the Add New Post screen, the default version, as shown in Figure 6-2, along with a sample web page to show the relationship between the front end and back end.

There are a number of other meta boxes for this screen, but to help keep things uncrowded, WordPress hides them by default. You can display them using Screen Options, which is covered in Lesson 9, "Advanced Post Functions."

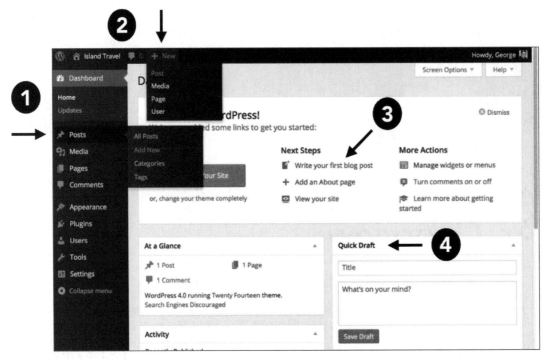

FIGURE 6-1

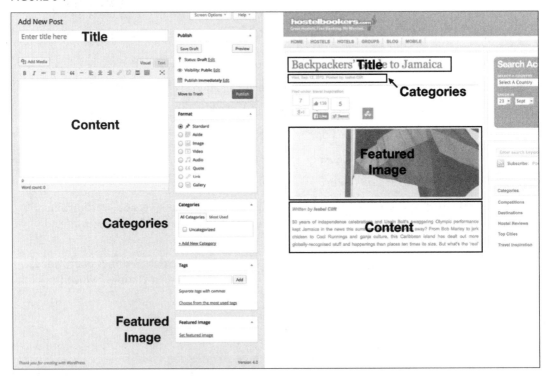

FIGURE 6-2

The default version of the Add New Post screen in mobile browsers is simply the same meta boxes in a single column of various widths, depending on the device. Figure 6-3 shows the full column as it displays on a smartphone.

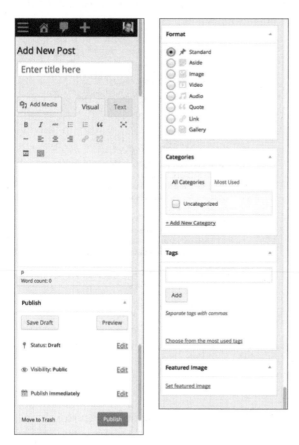

FIGURE 6-3

> **NOTE** *Posting from a mobile device, such as a smartphone, is best suited to short posts with one or two images or links.*
>
> *Automattic, the company that runs WordPress, has IOS and Android apps for posting to your site. These have a different interface than the browser, but again, it is difficult to do anything more than a quick post.*

ADDING A NEW POST

The following four steps are the only ones required to publish a post and have it show on your website.

Title

Just below the Add New Post screen title, there's a box that asks you to *Enter title here* (Figure 6-4). In this example I'm writing about a vacation package to Kingston, Jamaica, so I entered the title **7-Day Capital City Package.**

FIGURE 6-4

Content

The actual content of your web page is entered in the large box below the title in Figure 6-4, referred to in this book as the Content Editor.

There are two modes for the Content Editor: Visual Mode and Text Mode. The easiest way to think of them is WYSIWYG or "What You See Is What You Get" Mode (how it will look to visitors on the site) and HTML Mode (the coding behind the scene). By default, WordPress shows Visual Mode, but if you switch to Text Mode, it will stay that way until you change it back.

> **NOTE** *This box is referred to in the WordPress documentation as Post Box or Post Editing Area. The term Post can be misleading because this editing area is used for Pages and other types of content in WordPress.*
>
> *In previous editions I used the term Text Editor, but now that WordPress uses the term "Text Mode," rather than "HTML Mode," that name would be confusing. Also, some people thought I meant the box was only for text, so I now use the term Content Editor, because what you enter here appears on the front end web pages in what's usually referred to as the content area (as opposed to header, footer, and so on).*

You can do your writing in the Content Editor or you can paste in text you've written elsewhere, such as a Word document. WordPress will try to maintain any basic formatting that's in the document you're pasting from (bold, italic, lists, and so on), but in this case (Figure 6-4, right side) I'm pasting text that has no formatting so I can show you in Lesson 7, "Working with Text in the Content Editor," how to use the editor to style your text.

> **NOTE** *In the past, writing in Word and then pasting into the Content Editor often caused problems with styling because hidden coding would interfere with a theme's styling in WordPress. In fact, there was a special button in the Content Editor to help strip that coding. As of WordPress 3.9, that button has been dropped because the Content Editor now automatically removes that coding.*

Categories

Because you're creating a Post, WordPress requires you to place it in at least one Category, using the meta box, as shown in Figure 6-5. You won't need this step when creating a Page in WordPress because there are no categories for Pages.

Referring Figure 6-5, you can see that there's already a Category in WordPress called Uncategorized, which is the default category. That means, if you don't choose at least one Category for your post, WordPress automatically places it in the default. This is why it's important to either change the name or create new categories and remember to place Posts in them. (Enter **"uncategorized wordpress"** in Google to see how many people failed to do either.) In Lesson 21, "Managing Widgets and Menus," you can see how to choose a different default category.

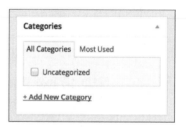

FIGURE 6-5

For the Island Travel site in Lesson 2, "Planning Your Site for WordPress," one of the main categories is Packages. If a Category does not already exist, you can add one from the Categories meta box. Simply click the Add New Category link, and it drops down the area shown at the bottom of Figure 6-6 A.

You enter the name, click Add New Category, and it immediately appears at the top of the categories list, with the box beside it checked, as shown in Figure 6-6 B.

Now you could simply leave this post under Packages, but as discussed in Lesson 2, it's better to separate out packages by their destination. This means you need a subcategory or child category of Packages called Jamaica Packages.

First, uncheck Packages. (If your Post is in a child category, it's automatically included in the parent.) Next, enter your new category title in the field, and then drop down the menu called Parent Category, as shown in Figure 6-6 C. Choose Packages and click Add New Category.

You can see Jamaica Packages with the checked box beside it in Figure 6-6 D. The Categories meta box displays categories in alphabetical order, with child categories grouped below their parent and indented, but the categories chosen for a Post displays out of sequence at the top of the list.

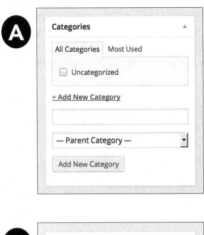

FIGURE 6-6

Featured Image

Technically, this step isn't necessary for publishing a Post, but so many themes use the Featured Image for displaying posts in various ways that it's good to get in the habit of setting one. In the case of the default Twenty Fourteen theme, the Featured Image appears full-sized at the top of individual Posts and as a thumbnail in lists of Posts.

You can find the meta box, as shown in Figure 6-7, at the bottom-right area of the default screen. Drag it up somewhere near the top, because it's helpful to quickly see if you've put one in before publishing, which is covered in the next lesson.

Featured Image ▲
Set featured image

FIGURE 6-7

When you click Set Featured Image, the pop-up window displays, as shown in Figure 6-8.

By default, this window shows all the images in your Media Library, but because you haven't uploaded anything yet, it's showing the Select Files option to browse your computer or mobile device. When there's something in the Media Library, you need to click the Upload Files tab at the top left. You can also drag and drop to the upload area.

After an image uploads, it displays both in the media library listing and on the right, as shown in Figure 6-9.

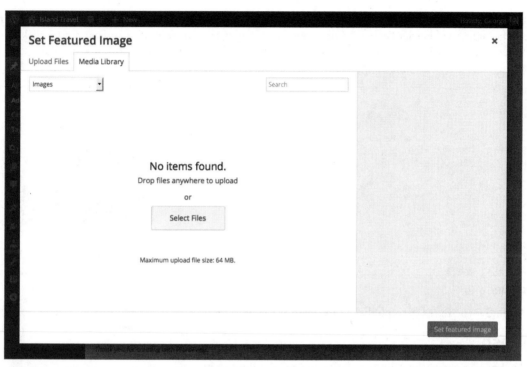

FIGURE 6-8

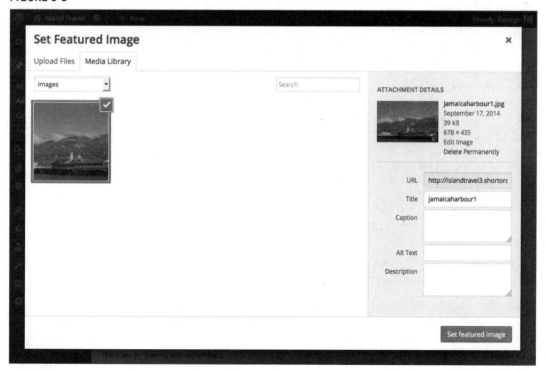

FIGURE 6-9

Until an image has been chosen, which is indicated by the blue check mark and shown in the gray area on the right, the blue Set Featured Image button at the lower right stays dim and cannot be clicked. When you have selected an image, click that button and the pop-up window disappears. You see a thumbnail version of your image in the Featured Image box, as shown in Figure 6-10.

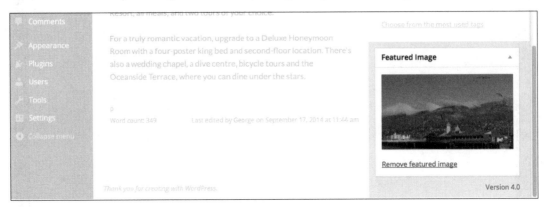

FIGURE 6-10

And now you're ready to publish your Post for the world to see.

Publish

At the top right of the Add New Post screen is the Publish box, as shown in Figure 6-11.

Lesson 9 covers all the options available under Publish. For now, all you need to know is that if you click the Publish button, your Post will be live on your website for the world to see. So do that now.

There are several ways you'll know your item has been published. Most important, WordPress creates a success message at the top of the screen, as shown in Figure 6-12.

FIGURE 6-11

FIGURE 6-12

> **NOTE** *Always pay attention to this message area. No matter what you think has happened, if you're not getting a success message, it means that WordPress has not published, saved, updated, or whatever it is you meant to do. The color of the bar at the left side of the message area indicates success (green) or an error (red).*

You'll also see that the blue button in the Publish box now says Update, and the title of the admin screen is now Edit Post instead of Add New Post. In the success message area, there's a View Post link. Click it to view your handiwork.

Figure 6-13 shows how the default Twenty Fourteen theme displays my first Post on the front end of the website:

FIGURE 6-13

That's all there is to it.

Now, there's clearly an issue with the sizing of the Featured Image and the way this theme uses it, and my text could use some formatting to make it more readable. I'll get to those and other details in the next few lessons, and you'll see how easy it is to make changes and additions.

The point of this lesson was to give you a sense of how easy the basics are for adding new content to your site. It demonstrated how WordPress frees you from the technical issues of creating web pages so that you can concentrate on what's important: coming up with useful content for your visitors.

A Rant Before Moving On

After you've been working on content and publishing to your site, I urge you to get in the habit of doing the following:

➤ Always click Update (or Save Draft) before leaving a screen.

➤ Don't try to remember if you did. Even a successful update message at the top of a screen may have happened before you made additional changes. Don't think, just click Update.

I've had people tell me that the You Have Unsaved Changes warning or the Auto-Save feature make my ranting unnecessary. To which I reply, I've seen people ignore the warning or leave before Auto-Save has had a chance to work.

It costs you nothing to click Update before leaving a screen, and it costs you time, embarrassment, or worse to miss saving a change, so why wouldn't you always click Update?

PLUGINS

There are hundreds of plugins dealing with Posts and Pages, but I don't want to distract from learning the basics of adding content to WordPress. There's plenty of time to talk about these plugins in future lessons.

I will, however, mention one plugin (and there are others like it) because it provides another way of adding new Posts or Pages or other content types: *Duplicate Post.* If you want to create a new Post or Page which has all the same parameters as another (categories, author, custom fields, and so on), this plugin will do it. Of course, you'd be changing the actual title and content of the new item. The goal here is to avoid having to repeat adding parameters or re-creating a complex layout like a table; you just change the content of the layout in the new Post or Page (or Custom Post Type).

Some plugins, like ones for e-commerce, often have their own copy function so that if you have a lot of products with similar settings, you just click a button and then change the details of the new item.

TRY IT

In this lesson, you practice creating a new Post.

Lesson Requirements

WordPress installed, a document or web page with some text you can use, and a large image (approximately 800 pixels wide).

Step-by-Step

Following are steps for creating a post:

1. Click Add New under the Post section of the main admin menu.

2. Enter a title.

3. Check that the Content Editor is in Visual mode.

4. Copy some text from a document or from a page in your browser, and paste it into the Content Editor. Watch for the formatting. Is it all being retained?

5. In the Categories meta box, click Uncategorized.

6. In the Featured Image meta box, click Set Featured Image.

7. In the media upload window, if you do not see a Select Files button, click the Upload Files tab near the top of the window. Click Select Files.

8. Find your image on your hard drive, and click Open to begin the upload process.

9. When the image uploads, click the Set Featured Image button. Check that the image thumbnail now appears in the Featured Image meta box.

10. Click the Publish button and look for the success message at the top of the screen.

11. Click View Post to see what your Post looks like on the site.

> **REFERENCE** *Please select the video for Lesson 6 online at* www.wrox.com/go /wp24vids. *You will also be able to download resources for this lesson from the website.*

7

Working with Text in the Content Editor

In Lesson 6, "Adding a New Post: An Overview," you had a brief introduction to the WordPress Content Editor; now, it's time to examine its capabilities in more detail. You'll learn the functions of each of the buttons on the button bar, including a few tricks to help make it easier to use this powerful tool.

ANATOMY OF THE CONTENT EDITOR

While the Content Editor is built to look and act like word processing software programs, it also has its own unique features. Here are the key parts of the editor.

Visual vs. Text Mode

The Content Editor runs in two different modes: Visual and Text. Visual Mode shows you what your content looks like to visitors, whereas Text Mode displays the raw HTML. Figure 7-1 shows the same content viewed in Visual Mode (left) and Text Mode (right).

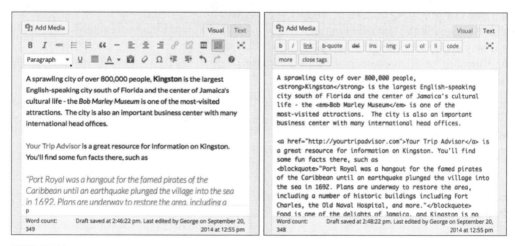

FIGURE 7-1

Visual Mode is the default setting for the Content Editor, but you can switch back and forth using the tabs at the top right, as shown in Figure 7-2.

WordPress remembers what you choose and keeps showing the Content Editor in that mode until you switch back.

Visual Mode does not always show you exactly how your content will look to visitors. It all depends on whether the theme you use has styled the Content Editor. WordPress has a default styling, so you

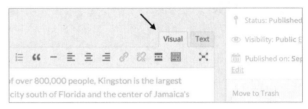

FIGURE 7-2

can always see a kind of WYSIWYG in Visual Mode, but to exactly match what visitors will see, it depends on your theme.

One sign of a well-written theme is that it matches the styling of the Content Editor with the styling on the front end of the site. Keep this in mind when learning about choosing a theme in Lesson 27, "Overview of WordPress Themes."

> **NOTE** *If you prefer working only in Text Mode, you can completely turn off Visual Mode from your Profile page. If you have other users on the system, they will not be affected by your setting.*

Add Media

The Add Media button enables you to add images, documents, video, and audio to your content. The button is located at the top left of the Content Editor, as shown in Figure 7-3.

Just as you saw with Featured Images in Lesson 6, this button pops up a Media Upload Window, as shown in Figure 7-4.

Referring to Figure 7-4, you can see the window opened at the Upload Files tab, but it may open at the Media Library tab, depending on what you did last with uploading media.

FIGURE 7-3

The lessons in Section IV, "Working with Media Content," go into detail about the Media Upload Window and about adding various types of media to your content, as well as how to lay out images and other media within text.

The Status Bar

After you begin entering content, the bottom area of the Content Editor displays some useful information, as shown in Figure 7-5.

FIGURE 7-4

"Port Royal was a hangout for the famed pirates of the
Caribbean until an earthquake plunged the village into the sea
in 1692. Plans are underway to restore the area, including a
number of historic buildings including Fort Charles. the Old

blockquote » p

Word count: 349   Last edited by George on September 21, 2014 at 2:55 pm

FIGURE 7-5

On the bottom left is the word count, and on the right is the last date and time the content was edited, with the name of the user who made the edits.

The area above the word count tells you what HTML tags are governing the text your cursor is pointing to. Referring to Figure 7-5, for example, it says *blockquote >> p*, which means this text has a paragraph tag within a blockquote tag. If you click a tag, the content editor highlights the relevant text. Be aware that the HTML tag status line only displays in Visual Mode.

The Button Bar

The Button Bar is the heart of the Content Editor, providing all the tools for styling and formatting your content. You'll sometimes see it referred to as the toolbar, but because the area at the top of admin screens has that name, and the icons all act like little buttons, I prefer to say Button Bar.

In Visual Mode it resembles a word processor, and in Figure 7-6 you see the default Button Bar, with each button labeled for reference.

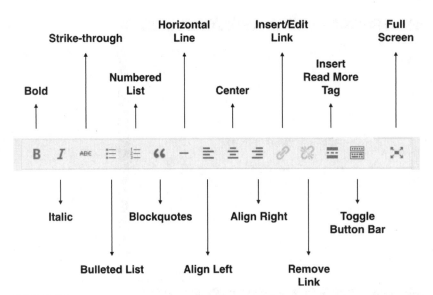

FIGURE 7-6

Now consider the second row of key buttons. On the right side of the first row there's the Toolbar Toggle button (for a long time this was called Kitchen Sink), as shown in Figure 7-7.

Clicking this button reveals the second row of buttons, and they'll stay visible until you click the Toolbar Toggle again. Figure 7-8 shows this second row of buttons with their functions.

FIGURE 7-7

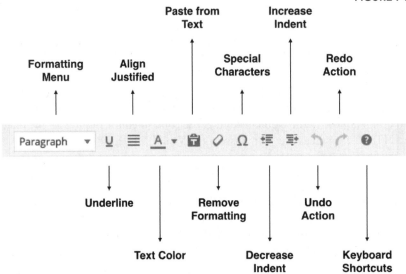

FIGURE 7-8

> **NOTE** *The two rows of buttons in Visual Mode may not look exactly like this, depending on your theme and plugins. Adding buttons is fairly common, and there are even plugins that replace the entire Content Editor. See the end of this lesson for more details.*

On mobile browsers, the Button Bar looks and operates exactly the same way, except, of course, the width of it causes some narrower screens to take two lines per row. Having both rows open at the same time makes for a cumbersome Button Bar on smartphones, as shown in Figure 7-9.

This is a good reason for mobile users to toggle the second row off most of the time, and display it only as needed.

FIGURE 7-9

WORKING WITH THE CONTENT EDITOR

Although you'll hear some people say that aspects of working with the Content Editor in Visual Mode can be frustrating, it's still the easiest way for the average user to work with content. That's why this lesson is conducted in Visual Mode. Included are some tips that can help smooth over those minor quirks, but they're few and far between, and the advantages of Visual Mode far outweigh such issues.

Sizing the Content Editor

Up until WordPress 4.0, working with large amounts of content meant resizing the height of the Content Editor or making sure your cursor was inside the Content Editor before scrolling (or else you'd end up scrolling the entire browser window).

Now the Content Editor automatically scrolls no matter where you have your cursor and no matter how long the content. This is why you won't find any resizing option—you don't need it.

Distraction Free Writing Button

You can resize the Content Editor by clicking the Distraction Free Writing button on the far right of the Button Bar (in Visual or Text Mode). (This button used to be called Full Screen and I still think of it in those terms.)

The idea is to get rid of any other boxes on the screen and let you focus on writing. Figure 7-10 compares the same Post in regular screen mode on the left and Distraction Free Writing on the right.

Referring to the right side of Figure 7-10, you may ask, "Where's the Button Bar?" To keep you focused on writing, WordPress hides any options until you mouseover the top portion of the screen.

At that point you can access all key functions, including Update and Exit full screen mode, as shown in Figure 7-11.

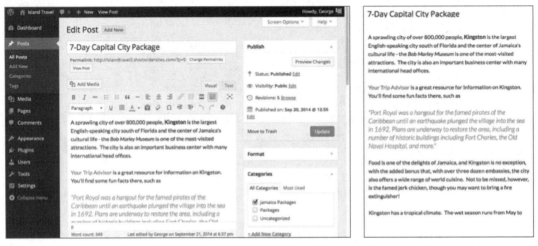

FIGURE 7-10

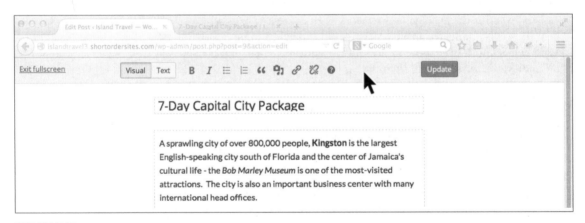

FIGURE 7-11

You might also ask where the Add Media button has gone in Distraction Free Writing mode. It's now an icon—the one near the middle that looks like a camera and music notes. Clicking that button produces the usual Media Upload Window.

> **NOTE** *If Distraction Free Writing feels too Spartan, remember you can collapse or hide as many meta boxes on a screen as you want and still keep your writing largely distraction free.*

> **NOTE** *In WordPress 4.1 there is a major change to Distraction Free Writing. When it's turned on, as soon as you begin typing in the Content Editor, all other boxes move off the screen, but the Content Editor and the Button Bar remain in place.*
>
> *If you move your mouse outside the Content Editor, the other boxes move back into place. When you move your mouse back inside the Content Editor, the boxes disappear again.*
>
> *If you click outside the Content Editor, the boxes reappear and will remain there until you click inside the Content Editor again (simply mousing over will not make the boxes disappear).*

Styling Text

Styling buttons on the Button Bar, such as Bold or Italic work as follows:

➤ They're toggle switches. That means if some text is in italics, clicking the Italic button removes the italics, and vice versa.

➤ Highlight the text you want to work with and then click the button to apply the change.

I'll demonstrate by working with some of the text in the first Post for my website. I want to emphasize the name Kingston in the opening sentence and to italicize the name Bob Marley Museum. As shown in Figure 7-12, I simply highlight the text first and click the corresponding button, just like any word processor.

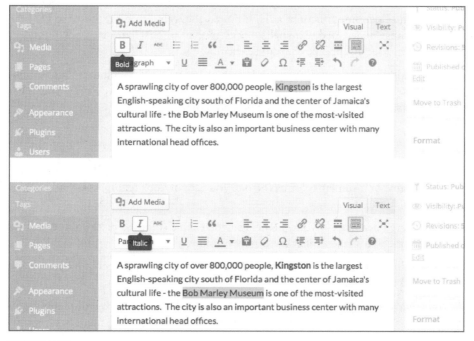

FIGURE 7-12

If you prefer working with keyboard shortcuts, those all work in the Content Editor, too. (For a complete list of shortcuts, click the question mark icon on the Button Bar.)

Lesson 6 mentions that WordPress usually retains most types of basic styling when you copy and paste text from a program such as Word. But it's always important to check for any that might have been missed.

> **WARNING** *If you copy from a web document, it's better to use the Paste from Text button on the Button Bar. It will strip out HTML that could interfere with how your theme styles the text.*

Although WordPress provides you with powerful tools for styling your text, with any power comes responsibility. The following suggestions aren't about WordPress, but they're important for your visitors.

Bold

Please **use this button wisely**. If you use **too much bold text** on a page, **the purpose begins to get lost**. Everything **becomes important** so nothing **stands out**. Like **that**.

In addition, bolding is next to all caps, and no one likes writing that "shouts." Search engines, too, take a dim view of excessive bolding. They can see it as a sign that the author is trying to manipulate the way the page will be interpreted and ranked.

Underlining

I'm not a fan of using the Underline function, at least not on the web. I think it's just too confusing to your visitors, because underlined text spells "link" in their minds. They try clicking the underlined text and you either disappoint or confuse them.

I know some uses of underline are actually required, such as in scholarly documents, but for cases like that, the visitor has some context and is familiar with the underlining. If you need to emphasize text, it's usually best to stick to bold and italics, or perhaps color.

Coloring Text

Having mentioned coloring text, remember a few things before you start using it:

➤ Don't use the same or a similar color as the one you use for your text links—that's going to confuse visitors.

➤ If you have colored headings in your theme, using the same color for pieces of text can also be confusing, though a shade of that color may be okay.

➤ Always think about the background color behind the text. You want enough contrast with the background to keep the text readable.

How, then, do you color text? It's the button with the letter A, on the second row of the Button Bar. If you highlight some text and click that button, the text turns the color of the small bar displayed at the base of the button. If you want to change that color, click the down arrow and you see some preset choices. Click More Colors and you see a pop-up window where you can choose from any color, as shown in Figure 7-13 A.

FIGURE 7-13

> **WARNING** *Changing color this way bypasses your theme's style sheet by inserting what's called inline styling (refer to the HTML in Figure 7-13 B). If you change your theme, this kind of coloring remains, so if it clashes with the new look, you have to manually go in and change it.*

> **NOTE** *Whenever you think about styling text in any way, keep these two points in mind:*
>
> ➤ *Does the styling help visitors understand what you're saying in the post or is it simply adding clutter to what they see? Too much styling is distracting.*
>
> ➤ *Is the styling needed for this content alone, or is it something that might better be handled by your theme's style sheet because you want to develop a standard style across the site?*

I often see people create special styles for a section heading. Those headings are already controlled by your theme. Creating a style for a particular heading overrides what's in the style sheet, and that's okay, but maybe what you actually want to do is change the style sheet so that all headings of that type look the same. Lesson 29, "Advanced Design Customization," mentions how a change like that could be made.

Linking Text

You may know that the HT in HTML stands for Hyper Text and what makes text hyper is linking. Indeed, one of the primary goals in developing HTML was to make it possible to jump to other locations. Whether you want to link to another site or to a page on your own site, WordPress makes it easy.

As with styling text, linking is a matter of highlighting the text where the link will show and then clicking the Insert/Edit Link button.

In my "7 Day Capital City Package" article, I want to link to a website, Your Trip Advisor, where I found a quote. In Figure 7-14 I've highlighted the text and, as soon as I did that, the grayed out link buttons became live, and I could click on them. Because I'm starting a new link, I click Insert/Edit Link:

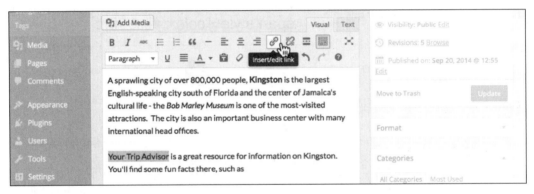

FIGURE 7-14

Clicking Insert/Edit Link produces a pop-up window where you enter the URL. The easiest way with an external website is to copy the address from your browser's address bar or right-click a link, copy the address, and then paste into the URL field, as shown in Figure 7-15.

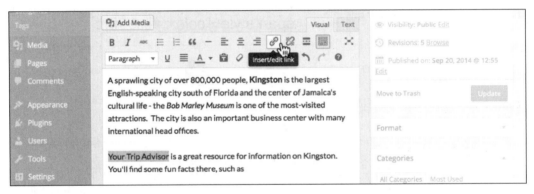

FIGURE 7-15

Below the URL there's a Title field; use this to say a few words about where the link is going.

Below Title is a check box. If you check it, the link opens in a new tab or new window. By default the link opens in the current tab or window. Some people like to have external sites open in a new tab so that visitors still have the current site open, and that's the approach I take. Others feel it's a better user experience if links open only in the current tab or window.

When you're finished, click the Add Link button. The window disappears and the text you highlighted now displays as a link.

Exactly how the link displays in the Content Editor depends, as I've said before, on your theme. By default, WordPress shows the link in traditional HTML purple with an underline, so no matter what, you should see the link displayed differently than the other text. (If your theme styles links exactly like other text, I'd look into getting a different theme.)

> **NOTE** *What text your link displays on is important. Say you had the text "Click the link to Your Trip Advisor." Do not simply highlight the word "Click" and make that your link.*
>
> *Good user experience and search engine optimization demand that link words, or anchor text, as they're called, should indicate what visitors will get when they click the link. That's why I highlighted the words "Your Trip Advisor."*

Internal Linking

It's valuable to visitors if you can help them find material on your site by creating links to other pages. But it can be time-consuming to open a separate tab, go find that other page, and then copy the URL from the address bar. That's why there's Link to Existing Content.

As Figure 7-16 shows, clicking that link drops down a new area where you can search for any content on your site.

Start entering a phrase in the search box, and you see a list of possible content. If you have a lot, you can just scroll until you find what you want. (It's an infinite scroll; that is, it keeps scrolling as long as there's content to choose from.)

Found what you need? Then just click it, and the URL for that content is automatically placed in the URL field, and the title of the content is placed in the Title field. Clicking the Add Link button wraps your link around the text you originally selected.

Of course, I have virtually no content on my site right now, but imagine the time saving when you have hundreds of Posts and dozens of Pages (and other types of content).

Editing Links

After you create a link, it's easy to go back and make changes to it. Simply place your cursor anywhere in the text that's linked. You do not need to highlight all the link text. The link buttons become live. You want to click the left one: the Insert/Edit Link button.

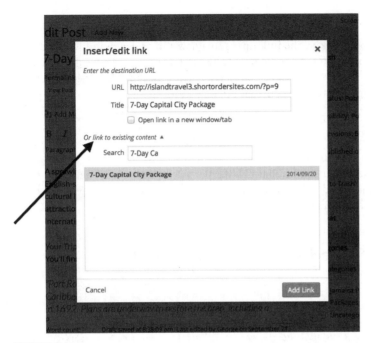

FIGURE 7-16

The usual window pops up with all the settings for the link. Just change anything, including linking to a completely new location. When you're ready, click the Update button.

> **WARNING** *This is just one example of the many times you'll see something changed on your screen and assume it's been saved. You'll leave the screen and discover later that you don't see the change on the front end of the site. You forgot to click Update in the Publish meta box.*

Removing Links

As with editing links, to remove one, you don't need to highlight all the link text. Place your cursor somewhere in the link text, and then click the Remove Link button (the one that looks like a broken chain link, to the right of the Insert/Create button). The text, of course, will still be there, but the link will be gone.

Formatting Text

Formatting text is another way to help visitors read your content easily, and the Button Bar offers many formatting options. By formatting, I mean how text is structured: paragraphs, lists, groups of paragraphs separated by headings, alignment (left, center, or right), and indenting.

Following are some examples of each of these so that you can more easily associate that look with each button. The exact nature of the look will vary by theme, of course, but the general concept always holds.

Aligning Text

There are four alignment buttons: left, center, and right alignment are on the first row of the Button Bar, and justified alignment is on the second row. To use any one of them, simply place your cursor in the paragraph you want to align, and click the appropriate button. You cannot align a single sentence within a paragraph.

You may think that to return alignment to the normal position of left-aligned, you must click the Left Align button. This works, but it's better if you simply click the button of your current alignment and thereby toggle it off. HTML defaults to left alignment, so if you just remove the current alignment, the text will be left-aligned.

Blockquotes

Blockquotes are meant to distinguish blocks of text from regular paragraphs, often with some nice styling. As the name suggests, the most common way to use blockquotes is when quoting someone else. Figure 7-17 shows you how it works in our sample package.

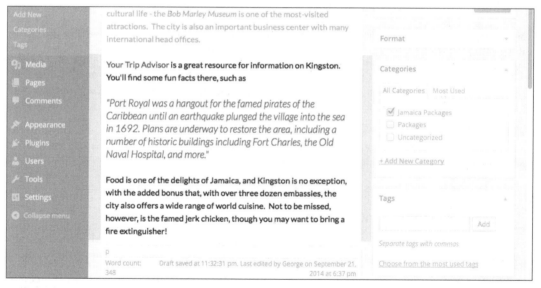

FIGURE 7-17

Keep in mind that the font styling you see here is based on the default Twenty Fourteen theme. What you'd see would depend on your theme. One common styling is to indent the left side or even the right side as well.

Applying blockquotes works only on entire paragraphs. If you try to highlight just one sentence of a paragraph, clicking Blockquotes would format the entire paragraph. It follows from that, you need to place your cursor only somewhere in a paragraph to make it all a blockquote.

If you want to make more than one paragraph into a blockquote (assuming they're all in a row), you need to highlight the entire group.

> **WARNING** *Whatever way you use blockquotes, be sure to use them only that way on your site. If, like most people, you use it for quotes, do not use it to simply emphasize a point. Formatting helps provide context and even meaning, so changing uses randomly is confusing to visitors.*

Lists

One of the most effective ways to present information on the Internet is with the use of lists, because they:

➤ Emphasize points by separating them visually

➤ Allow the eye to scan through material quickly

➤ Provide a roadmap when giving instructions or long explanations

➤ Help readers remember points

WordPress makes it easy to create lists with bullets or with numbers; there's a button for each on the Button Bar. The basics for each type are the same, so following are a couple specific items.

The key to making lists in the Content Editor is to remember that each list item needs to be separated by a return before using the Button Bar. Another way to think of it: Each item needs to be a paragraph.

Assuming, of course, that each of these separated lines follow one after another, creating a list is just a matter of selecting the entire group and clicking one of the list buttons. You can see the before and after in Figure 7-18.

The result is a bulleted list. As always, the exact way it looks depends on your theme.

Writing a List in the Content Editor

If you create your list in the Content Editor, begin by pressing Return/Enter after the paragraph and before the point where you want to put in the list. Then click the button of the list type you want.

A bullet or number appears, and you can begin writing the first list item. Press Return/Enter at the end of the item, and another bullet or number appears. Repeat until you complete the list.

When you finish, press Return/Enter once. You see a bullet or a number; then press a second time. The bullet or number disappears, meaning the list is complete, and you're on a new line ready to start writing a new paragraph.

Pasting List Items into the Content Editor

If you paste a list of items into the Content Editor, WordPress may display it as a list immediately. It all depends on the source. Lists from Word, for example, should carry over just fine.

However, if your list is not formatted after pasting (Figure 7-19 A), you need to manually do it. The problem is, highlighting your list items and clicking a list button is likely to produce something odd: a single bullet or number, with all the original items as one list item, as shown in Figure 7-19 B.

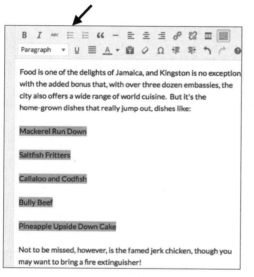
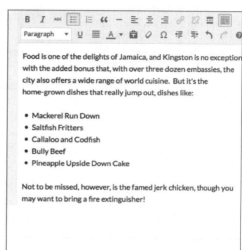

FIGURE 7-18

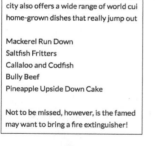

FIGURE 7-19

No worries; just put your cursor at the beginning of each original item and press Return/Enter. Figure 7-19 C shows you the result part way through the process: A bullet or number appears each time you do this, until your list is fully formatted.

Multilevel Lists

If you have complex lists with sublevels, WordPress can handle that using the Indent buttons in combination with the List function.

To create a subitem, press Return/Enter to start a new list item, and then press the Increase Indent button. The list item moves to the right, and for numbered lists, you see numbering begin again for the new level. For bulleted lists, the bullet for the new level may be the same or different, depending on your theme.

The Decrease Indent button moves a list item to the left and returns the bullet or number to the type for that level of the list.

You can see a new multilevel version of my food list in Figure 7-20 in bulleted form on the left and using a numbered list on the right:

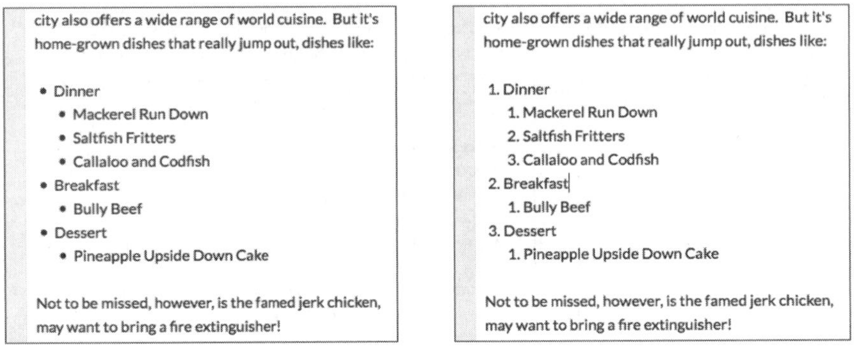

FIGURE 7-20

The number of levels you can have is limited only by the width of your content area.

The Formatting Drop-down

The drop-down menu on the second row of the Button Bar is one of the most misunderstood and misused elements of the Content Editor. Following is a description of each of the formats in the order on the drop-down.

Paragraph

The default formatting when you enter text in the Content Editor is a paragraph. Even a single line of text followed by a return creates a paragraph in the technical sense of having HTML paragraph tags.

About the only time you need to use the Formatting drop-down for paragraphs is when you want to change some text back from some other format.

Paragraphs by default are left-aligned and their styling is controlled by the theme's style sheets.

> **NOTE** *Paragraph tags are automatically added by WordPress when a page is viewed on the front end. You don't see the tags in Text Mode unless there's a specific formatting added to the paragraph (like centering or other alignment).*

Address

Despite the name, do not use this to format a mailing address. The address tag is actually intended to designate the contact information for the author of a web page or a portion of a page designated in HTML as an article. Typically, that contact information would be an e-mail address, a web link, a Skype handle, and so on.

Even though your theme gives this a particular styling, do not simply use it for styling. Search engines and other web reader functions look within this tag for specific kinds of contact information.

Pre

The "pre" is short for preformatted content, and the idea here is that the text in question has a particular spacing, and the job of this tag is to preserve it. By default, HTML ignores white space and puts a single space between elements. The pre tag, however, maintains the original white space, as shown in Figure 7-21.

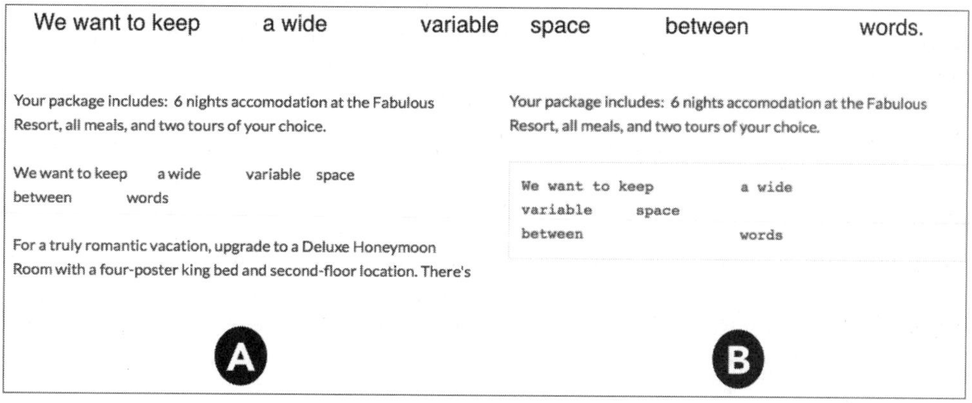

FIGURE 7-21

You can see in Figure 7-21 A how the Content Editor tried to keep some of the spacing, but when the preformat was applied in Figure 7-21 B, all the spacing displayed exactly as in the original.

Usually the pretag displays using a fixed width font, such as Courier (the typewriter font), and sometimes without any word-wrap function. Coupled with the ability to maintain the original white space, the tag is often used for displaying computer code; though there is a specific HTML tag called "code" for that purpose.

Headings 1 Through 6

Many people try out the formatting menu and discover that if they use one of the Heading settings, they can make their text look different (larger, bolder, and so on). But this is a misuse of headings.

The reason your theme styles each heading differently is to help visitors see the relationships between headings. The numbers 1 through 6 are derived from the HTML tags h1, h2, and so on. Heading 1 is meant to be the most important on a page, or as of HTML5, the most important within an HTML Section. Heading 2 is less important, and so on down the line.

And the term Heading is also important here. It means a word or short phrase. A series of two sentences is not a heading. Headings introduce and mark out groups of paragraphs and other content.

Consider this outline:

Heading 1

    Heading 2A

        Heading 3A

        Heading 3B

    Heading 2B

        Heading 3C

        Heading 3D

The H1 tells you the overall topic, the two H2s divide that topic in some related way, and the H3s divide their respective areas in some further way.

The value to visitors is tremendous. By glancing at the wording of the headings, they should get a good sense of what the page covers, while the styling of each heading conveys the importance of relationships between the segments.

If your goal is simply to style text, do not use Headings. If you don't know how to use CSS to achieve specialized styling, plugins can help go beyond the default Content Editor. See the end of this lesson for some suggestions.

If you use Headings to divide up your content and make its structure clearer to visitors (and search engines), make sure you are clear and consistent with the different levels of headings. Unless you know what you're doing, for example, there should be only one H1 on the page, and that should be the Title of the Post or Page. Your theme should take care of that automatically, so do not to use H1 in the Content Editor.

> **NOTE** *If you have a long piece of content that warrants the use of headings, perhaps the sections might be better suited as separate Posts or Pages. There is no hard and fast rule about this, but often the thoughts in sections of a larger piece could stand on their own or as part of a series.*
>
> *A common example of this is the Service page you see on many websites. If you're going to put all the services and their descriptions on one page, be sure to use the same level of heading, probably an H2 for each of the services. However, it would be even better to make separate pages for each service so that visitors (and search engines) can easily find and focus on just the service they want.*

PLUGINS

Many themes and plugins, as part of their functionality, may add to what you have in your Content Editor. Also, plugins are specifically aimed at changing the way the Content Editor works or even replacing it in some form.

BUTTON BAR

➤ **Tiny MCE Advanced** enables you to add or remove the existing button bar functions as well as many others not natively offered by WordPress. You can even add a third row of buttons.

➤ **WP Edit** also enables you to add or remove buttons on the existing Button Bar. The free version limits changes to the first row, but for the average user, this should be plenty.

CONTENT LAYOUT

The WordPress Content Editor is designed to do basic content layouts of paragraphs and lists (with images and videos), but if you want to create columns, tables, tabs, and other complex layouts, without knowledge of HTML, shortcode plugins can be the answer.

Shortcodes are a WordPress feature that enables the user to insert simple instructions into the Content Editor to achieve complex effects. There are many of these plugins, but two of the most popular are:

➤ **Shortcodes Ultimate** is composed of more than 30 different shortcodes you can insert from a menu on the Button Bar, creating tabs, buttons, boxes, columns, and much more.

➤ **WordPress Shortcodes** includes more than 26 shortcodes, including the capability to trigger content based on certain conditions.

PAGE BUILDERS

Instead of shortcodes, there's a new breed of plugins, commonly called page builders, that work within the Content Editor and combine WYSIWYG editing with drag-and-drop functionality to make complex layouts simple. In their own ways they turn content items, such as text, images, tables, and so on, into modules that can be added, removed, and rearranged. Many of these page builders are paid plugins, but a few are free, including:

➤ Page Builder by SiteOrigin

➤ HTML Editor, Drag & Drop Visual Editor with Web Page Builder

➤ Aqua Page Builder

CONTENT EDITOR

The Content Editor used by WordPress is a version of an open source text editor program called TinyMCE, which you've probably used in dozens of different software programs and online tools. Some plugins actually replace the entire Content Editor:

continues

continued

➤ **CKEditor for WordPress,** although not under active development as of December 2014, has a large user base and uses an open source editor called CKEditor.

➤ **Foliopress WYSIWYG** uses a modified version of another open source text editor call FCKEditor.

➤ **WP Editor** replaces not only the Content Editor, but also the Theme and Plugin editors. This is more for those who work with HTML because it features line number and syntax highlighting.

TRY IT

In this lesson, you practice creating a new link.

Lesson Requirements

A post with text.

Step-by-Step

Practice creating a link using Visual mode.

1. Make sure you're in the Visual mode of the Content Editor.

2. Highlight the text you want to link to.

3. Click the link button (the unbroken chain icon on the top row) and the Insert/Edit Link window pops up.

4. Copy the URL from the address bar of your browser window or wherever you have the full URL you want to link to.

5. In the pop-up window, paste the URL into the URL box.

6. Enter a Title for the link.

7. Check the box if you want the link to open in a new window or tab.

8. Click Insert.

9. Verify that the text is linked the way you planned.

10. Click Update.

11. Click Preview to see how the link looks on the live site.

REFERENCE *Please select the video for Lesson 7 online at* www.wrox.com/go /wp24vids. *You will also be able to download resources for this lesson from the website.*

8

Basic Post Screen Functions

Lesson 6, "Adding a New Post: An Overview," shows some of the Post functions while quickly creating a new Post. Then, Lesson 7, "Working with Text in the Content Editor," went more in-depth on how to use the Content Editor. Now it's time to return to the meta boxes on an Edit Post screen and take a closer look at some of the key functions you need.

WordPress tries to keep the Edit Post or Add New Post screens as uncluttered as possible by showing only some meta boxes. Here you see more about the default screen items. Then Lesson 9, "Advanced Post Options," introduces you to the hidden functions. Much in this lesson applies to Page admin screens as well, and any differences are covered in Lesson 10, "Adding a New Page."

PUBLISH

There's a lot more to the Publish meta box than simply the Publish button. WordPress has a variety of tools to control the publishing process. Now consider all the options shown in Figure 8-1.

Status

This is the primary setting—essentially the on-off switch—which determines whether visitors can see your Post on the website. Clicking the Edit link reveals the possible states, as shown in Figure 8-2. Think of Draft as off and Published as on.

FIGURE 8-1

FIGURE 8-2

Normally, you won't actually use this drop-down setting. When you click Publish, that sets the status to Published, and clicking Save Draft sets it to Draft. A situation in which you might use this setting is if you published an item and later want to remove it from public view.

Draft status means that when you log in as an Administrator (or other Roles in WordPress), you can see what the Post will look like by clicking View Post or Preview Changes, but it won't show publicly anywhere.

> **NOTE** *Draft status is not the same as being in the Trash. At the lower-left corner of the Publish meta box is a Move to Trash link. Trashed items obviously aren't visible to the public, but neither are they destroyed. However, they never show up in lists of Posts the way Drafts do, and you can't edit or preview Trashed items. You would need to restore them to do that.*

The third state, Pending Review, is a kind of Draft mode but is used to signal Editors and Administrators that a Contributor's Draft is ready to be checked before publishing. (A Contributor can submit but not publish items.)

Visibility

The default visibility is Public, so you'll rarely need to touch the settings, as shown in Figure 8-3 A.

Sticky Posts

A setting that might come in handy is the check box that says Stick This Post to the Front Page.

When you have a default WordPress blog page—it does not have to be on your front page, as the wording suggests—the normal state is for a Post to gradually get pushed down the screen by newer Posts, until finally it disappears into archives when the screen quantity limit has been reached.

However, there may be an important Post that you'd like to have taken out of that normal flow and remain at the top of the list. Checking this box will do that, therefore the name Sticky Post.

Because Sticky Post is not visible without clicking the Edit link, it's easy to forget that it's here, under Visibility.

FIGURE 8-3

Password Protection

This means a visitor must enter a password to view the Post. As you saw in Figure 8-3 B, each Post can have its own password, so this is not like having a membership website, for example, where a user enters a single password to get into the whole site or portion of a site.

The classic example of passwording an individual Post is a photographer uploading photos to the Post and giving a client the password to view them.

Private

I've never fully understood the point of this setting. If chosen, it means that the Post technically is published, but only Administrators or Editors can see it. In other words, even if you have Subscribers (or Authors or Contributors) logging into your site, they cannot see Private Posts. To make it more confusing, Administrators and Editors can see Posts even if they're drafts, so I'm not sure what this setting is meant to do.

If you want to choose which Users can see a Post or if you want to hide your entire site from the public and allow only registered users to view content, there are plugins for that. (A few are mentioned at the end of the lesson.)

Revisions

WordPress keeps track of your content as you change it, enabling you to revert back to earlier edits. This is discussed shortly as an entire subject, and not directly related to the publishing status of the Post.

Publish

Think of this as the When setting. The default is to publish the Post immediately, and most of the time that's exactly what you want to do. But as you can see in Figure 8-4 A, there's the ability to set the date and time to anything you want, and that can be handy in certain situations.

FIGURE 8-4

The most common use of the Publish setting is to set a future date for publication; in other words, to schedule the Post. As you can see in Figure 8-4 B, the blue button changes to Schedule when you do that.

It's often easier to sit down and write two or three Posts at one time, but rarely would it make sense to publish all of them immediately. Better to spread them out over a few weeks and not have to think about posting to your website for a while. That's the power of scheduling.

Remember to use the time function when you schedule a Post. Everyone thinks about what day they want it to publish but often forget that timing can be important. From your website's statistics you can get a feel for when people tend to visit; try to schedule your Post for the time of day when they're most likely to return for new material.

There's another common way to make use of the publish date setting, and that's when you enter time-related material from the past. For example, when you start your site, you may have an archive of old press releases. If you enter each one as a Post (remember the rule from Lesson 1, "Thinking Like WordPress," keep content in the smallest possible units), you would want to set the publish date based on the release date. That means they'll show up in the correct order of when they were released.

Revisions

Although the Revisions link is in the Publish meta box, it's not a setting for the entire Post, only the Content Editor, because this is a way of reverting back to earlier versions of what you've written. In other words, a revision of a Post does not record things such as categories, tags, featured image, and so on—only what's in the Content Editor.

By default, WordPress keeps every revision you make, and that could be well into the double digits depending on your editing habits. (You can see the number in the Publish meta box.) However, there are plugins that enable you to control how many revisions are kept, which are mentioned at the end of the lesson.

> **NOTE** *The Revisions link and the Revisions meta box option in Screen Options will be visible only when there's at least one revision.*

When you click the Browse link for revisions, you're taken to a separate screen, as shown in Figure 8-5:

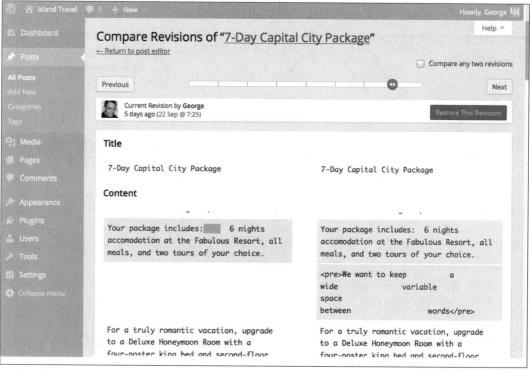

FIGURE 8-5

The default layout of this screen is to have the current content on the right and the most recent revision on the left. At the top of the screen is a timeline of all revisions, and as you drag the indicator along it, the content in the two boxes changes—always the more recent displays on the right and the older on the left.

In addition, differences between the two versions are highlighted: The right version displays in green and the left in red.

The blue button at the top right—Restore This Revision—refers to the version on the right. In other words, your decision will always be whether to restore the version that's shown on the right side.

The only exception to this—which can be a bit confusing at first—is when you first click through to this screen. In that case the current revision is on the right and the Restore This Revision button is not active. It's only when you start dragging the timeline indicator to the left that the button becomes active, because now there will be a revision that you can restore.

By default, the timeline indicator is a single blue circle with two arrows, and you're always comparing the two revisions next to each other. If you want to compare revisions far apart in time, you need to check the box that says Compare Any Two Revisions. As shown in Figure 8-6, you now have two separate timeline indicators, and you can select a From (left) and a To (right) revision.

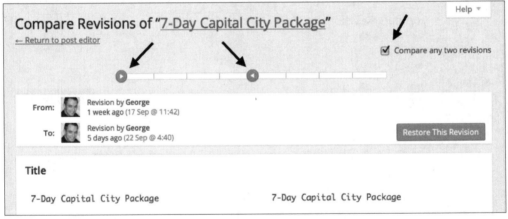

FIGURE 8-6

Again, the Restore This Revision button refers to the revision on the right. In other words, click the button, and WordPress makes the revision on the right the new current version.

In a mobile browser for smartphones, the Revisions screen is awkward to deal with because it requires a wide format. Landscape mode is a bit better, but this is a function best left to larger screen devices.

Format

The Format meta box (Figure 8-7) is visible when you first install WordPress because the default themes make use of it. However, it's entirely theme-dependent and may not always be visible.

WordPress has designated a set of names for Post formats: Standard, Aside, Image, Video, Audio, Quote, Link, and Gallery. You need to understand these are just names; how any particular theme lays them out or even uses one or more of them is completely open. In Figure 8-8, you see the same Post content with the different formats the Twenty Fourteen theme can assign:

FIGURE 8-7

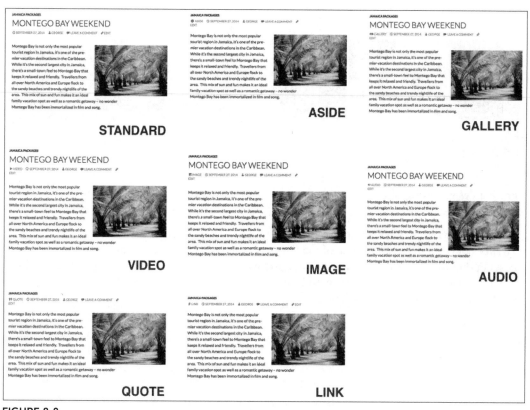

FIGURE 8-8

The only difference is that Asides, Quotes, and Links don't display the title, and the particular format is listed next to the date. It can be confusing for new users who may be expecting clear differences between the Formats.

Again for this particular theme, you can get nice formatting without the help of Formats. In Figure 8-9 there's no visual difference between using a WordPress Gallery in a Post (left) and designating the same Post with the Gallery Format (right).

FIGURE 8-9

From a design standpoint—with this theme at least—there doesn't seem to be any reason for using Format.

However, one reason might be as a way of categorizing Posts by the type of content. With the Twenty Fourteen theme, the name of the Format is linked, and clicking it produces a list of all other Posts in that format. If you want to see all Posts with a video in them, for example, this would be a way of doing it. You could do that with Post Categories, too, and because themes don't consistently use Formats, I prefer to go that route.

If your site is a personal blog, it could be useful to find a theme that displays different WordPress Formats in interesting layouts and styles, because that's a way of adding some nice visual appeal to your posts.

> **NOTE** *Remember, if your theme supports Formats and you're not using them, you can collapse the meta box or simply remove it by unchecking it under Screen Options (top right of your screen).*

Categories

Lesson 6 covers the basics of selecting Categories and adding a new one from this meta box, and Lesson 20, "Managing Post Categories and Tags," goes into more detail about Categories.

> **WARNING** *Remember: a Post must be in at least one category. And if you forget to choose at least one, WordPress puts the Post into the default category.*

Now briefly consider how Categories appear when there are child categories or subcategories. You can see the child category indented under its parent in Figure 8-10.

FIGURE 8-10

Tags

Tags are another way of organizing Posts and helping visitors find what they need. Lesson 6 compares Tags to the index of a book; they are meant to be specific, whereas Categories are general.

Don't ignore Tags. People tend to remember about categorizing because a Post must be in at least one category. Because tags are not mandatory, they often get left out, yet they can be as important for search engines and helpful to visitors.

Also, when creating a new Post, you see only a blank box for Tags, whereas Categories are displayed for you. It's just easier, for many people, to choose from a list that's offered to them than to try and think of their own. Yet that's part of the power of Tags: They're open-ended and you can make up as many of them as you need right on the spot.

There is, however, one sense in which a list of Tags is presented to you, and that is when you begin to enter a new Tag into the meta box, WordPress automatically matches any existing tags to what you start typing, as shown in Figure 8-11 A.

FIGURE 8-11

> **NOTE** *The list of possible tags has a bit of a time lag. If you type too fast, the list may not have time to appear. So go a bit slowly as you type the first few letters of the tag.*

The real importance of waiting to see if a Tag already exists is to avoid entering misspellings, or alternative spellings or phrasings; for example, entering **Fort Charles** and **Ft Charles**.

You can enter multiple tags at one time by separating each word or phrase with a comma. After you enter a tag, it displays below the box, as shown in Figure 8-11 B. Beside each tag is a circle with an X. Clicking the circle deletes the tag.

Unlike Categories that you add from inside a Post, which can exist even if no Posts are assigned to them yet, Tags entered from a Post exist only if there's at least one Post with that Tag. However, if you enter a Tag through Posts ➪ Tags, it continues to exist even if no Post uses it. (Lesson 20 covers more about Tags.)

Featured Image

When you last saw Featured Image in your sample post from Lesson 6, it wasn't looking so great in your theme, as shown in Figure 8-12.

It's both too narrow and too tall for the way the theme displays the Featured Image above the content and title.

Typically, the theme does not give you specifications for sizing a Featured Image, but here's how to rarely get caught with insufficient sizing: Always size any image to at least 800 pixels and no more than 1,900 pixels on the longest side before uploading to WordPress.

WordPress creates smaller versions for you to use inside Posts or as thumbnails, but if you have a good-quality, large original, you'll be fine. Just don't upload directly from your camera—a 100 K image will fill a computer screen. There's no need for 500 K images, let alone 2 MB or more. I'll remind you of this again in Part 4, but right now, let's fix the Featured Image.

After you upload a Featured Image, you see its thumbnail in the meta box, along with a link: Remove Featured Image (see Figure 8-13 A). Clicking that link simply removes the image, and you're left with a link to Set Featured Image (see Figure 8-13 B).

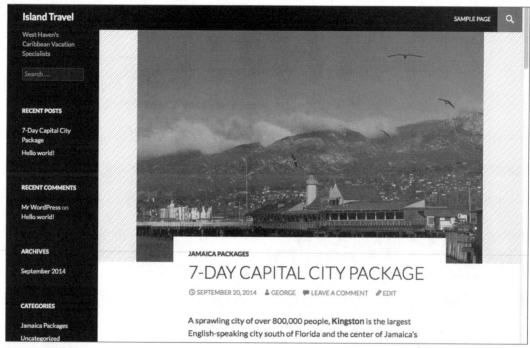

FIGURE 8-12

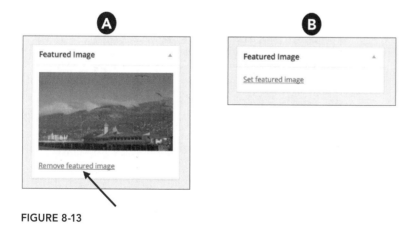

FIGURE 8-13

Using the method outlined in Lesson 6, the front end now looks like Figure 8-14.

This time I chose a wider and shorter image, which looks much better given this theme's layout.

Notice that the Featured Image does not appear in the body of the Post. It's used, depending on the theme, for places like listings of categories or at the top of the full Post. Sometimes, it will be a small thumbnail and other times a full-sized version.

> **NOTE** *In cases where a theme does not automatically display a Featured Image with the full version of a Post, you can still use that image to manually insert it into the content. In other words, being a Featured Image does not prevent use of that image in the usual ways.*

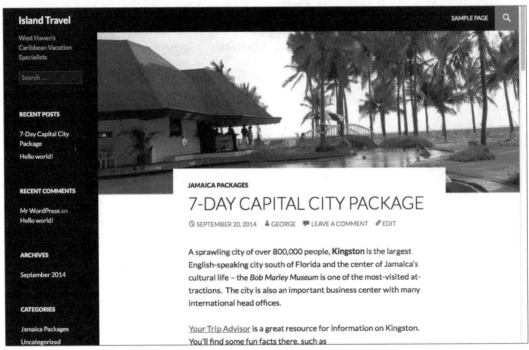

FIGURE 8-14

More Post Options

That's it, then, for the default meta boxes you'll see on a WordPress Post screen—the ones you'll use the most. There are more, hidden from view, that are covered in the next lesson.

And, as always, there may be more Post meta boxes, depending on what theme you choose and which plugins you add.

PLUGINS

Because Posts, Categories, Tags, and Images are covered in other lessons, I'm restricting these plugins to functions relating to the "Publish" and "Format" sections of this lesson.

PUBLISH

This is an example of a group of plugins that try to make the publishing process even easier. Others pop up an "Are You Sure?" message to make sure you don't accidentally publish something you shouldn't, and so on.

➤ **Post Expirator** can help if you need a Post or a Page to expire after a certain time (you can have it trashed or set to draft mode).

➤ **Toolbar Publish Button** duplicates the publish/update button on the admin Toolbar, so it's always visible no matter how far down the page you scroll.

PRIVACY

➤ **Members** is one of several plugins that enable you to make your entire website (or individual Posts or Pages) private; that is, visible only to logged-in users. Another in this group is User Access Manager.

➤ Membership plugins are another way of making entire sites or portions private, and usually this involves paid memberships. This group of plugins is covered in Lesson 36, "More Plugin Suggestions."

➤ **WP Hide Post** enables you to prevent a Post or Page from appearing in various areas of your site.

REVISIONS

➤ **Revision Control** controls the number of revisions globally or on an individual Post/Page basis. You can also delete specific revisions. There are many plugins like this, but this is the most popular.

➤ **Better Delete Revision**—If you've allowed unlimited or a lot of revisions, you might want to delete them later, and plugins like this enable you to do that. These kinds of plugins fall into the category of database optimization; they clean up your WordPress database to make it more efficient. Lesson 32, "Keeping Up to Date," covers more of those.

continues

continued

POST FORMATS

➤ **Disable Post Format UI**—I mentioned that you can hide the Post Format box if you don't use it, but if you have other users on your system and don't want them trying to use it, this plugin removes any trace of the Format box, even from Screen Options.

➤ **Bulk Convert Post Format**—Suppose you have a Category called Videos and you install a new theme that used the Video Post Format; this plugin enables you to give every Post in that Category a format of "video."

TRY IT

In this lesson, you make a couple changes to an existing Post, and then practice reverting to one of the earlier changes.

Lesson Requirements

A Post with some existing text.

Step-by-Step

1. Navigate to Posts ➪ All Posts, and click the title of the Post you want to use for this exercise.

2. Make enough alterations to the first paragraph that you'll easily recognize the changes later.

3. Click Update.

4. Now, make more major alterations to the first paragraph.

5. Click Update.

6. In the Publish meta box, you should see the Revisions link and the number 2 (or more if you'd made other changes to the Post earlier).

7. Click the Browse link. You should now be on the Revisions screen. Your most recent revision should be on the right side of the screen.

8. On the timeline at the top of the Revisions screen, move the indicator back two spaces. You should now see your original Post on the right side of the screen. If not, keep moving the indicator left or right until you do.

9. Click Restore This Revision. You should now see the Post as it originally was when you started this exercise.

REFERENCE *Please select the video for Lesson 8 online at* `www.wrox.com/go` `/wp24vids`*. You will also be able to download resources for this lesson from the website.*

Advanced Post Functions

In previous lessons, you have seen the most commonly used functions displayed by default on Add New Post or Edit Post screens. It's time now to look at the functions WordPress has been hiding to keep the screen less crowded. You unhide each function through the Screen Options tab at the top right of the admin screen, which reveals a series of check boxes, as shown in Figure 9-1.

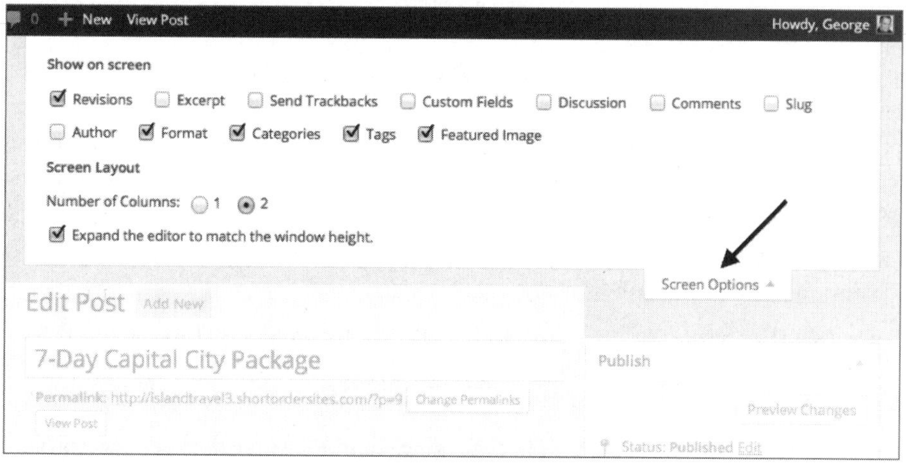

FIGURE 9-1

REVISIONS

Lesson 8, "Basic Post Screen Functions," shows how Revisions work, using the text link that appears in the Publish meta box as soon as there's at least one revision.

When there's at least one revision, Screen Options also displays a check box for Revisions. This displays a meta box, as shown in Figure 9-2.

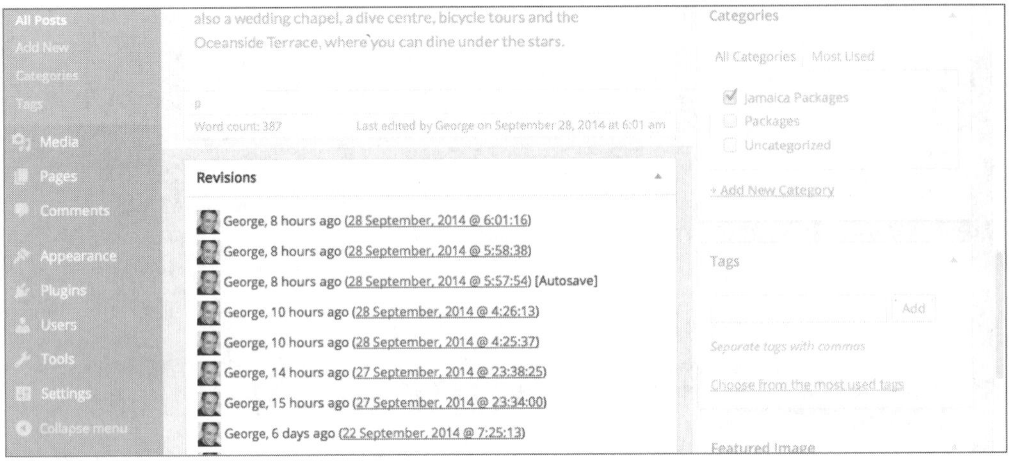

FIGURE 9-2

Clicking one of these links leads to the Revisions screen. The revision you click will appear on the right, and the revision dated immediately prior to it appears on the left.

EXCERPT

How excerpting works depends on which of two ways a theme can generate Post content for lists such as Categories, most recent Posts, and so on. You can quickly tell the difference by looking at the Blog page of your theme or a Category page:

➤ **If you see the full content** of each Post, you can make excerpts show instead only by using the More button of the Content Editor.

➤ **If you see short excerpts** with wording such as Read More and a link to the full Post, the theme is using WordPress's automatic excerpt function. If you're not happy with the resulting text, you can create your own excerpts using the Excerpt meta box for each Post.

Now that you know when they can apply, walk through each of the three types of excerpting.

> **NOTE** *Excerpts apply only to Posts and not to Pages. There are, however, plugins that add the functionality to Pages, which are covered at the end of this lesson.*

The More Button

The idea of the More button is to place a marker where you want WordPress to end the excerpting process and create a Read More link. In Figure 9-3 A, you can see how the button creates a line in

Visual Mode, whereas Figure 9-3 B shows how it looks in Text Mode. Above the line is the excerpt.

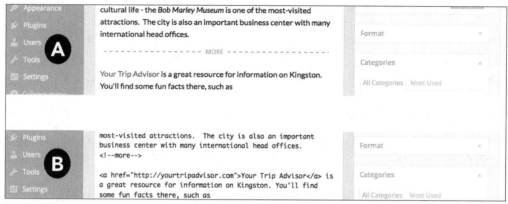

FIGURE 9-3

An important difference between the More button and the other two excerpting functions is that anything above the line is displayed: links, images, video, and so on—not just text.

Remember, this button functions only when the theme is not already using auto-excerpt; that is, when full Posts are shown in lists.

Automatic Excerpts

If a theme uses the WordPress excerpt function, this is the default behavior: Take the first 55 words of the Post (even if that means stopping in the middle of a sentence); add something like ellipses to indicate that the content continues; and finish with words such as **Read More** linked to the full Post. Figure 9-4 shows an example of an automatic excerpt.

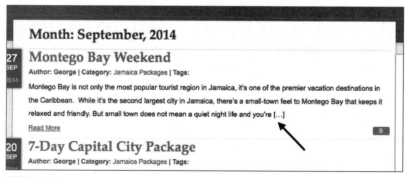

FIGURE 9-4

Notice I had to switch themes to show you this example because the default Twenty Fourteen theme does not use the excerpting function.

You need to understand that if there are links, images, video, or other nontext content in the first 55 words, only the text displays by automatic excerpting.

Themes can control aspects of this automatic excerpt function. They may choose more or less words for the excerpt, or even allow administrators to choose the amount. They can control the symbols and the wording that follow the excerpt, so the exact look and feel of excerpts can vary widely.

Remember, the More button does not override automatic excerpts; that's the job of the Excerpt meta box.

The Excerpt Meta Box

As mentioned earlier, this meta box is revealed through the Screen Options function, and from that point on, it shows on all Post screens (until you choose to hide it again). In Figure 9-5 you can see some text entered in Excerpt.

FIGURE 9-5

Whatever you enter here overrides the automatic excerpt created by WordPress, and there are two good reasons for doing that:

➤ No matter how well written your opening paragraph is, it's not likely a proper summary of your entire Post. With the Excerpt meta box, you can write exactly the summary you need.

➤ Although people understand the concept of cutting off a sentence in midstream and needing to click to see the rest of the article, it's still jarring to be cut off like that. Better to have a complete thought as your excerpt.

Although the Excerpt meta box is not large, the amount of text is not limited, and you can expand the size of the field. But you shouldn't need much room for a well-written, short excerpt. People don't want to see more than two or three sentences.

In Figure 9-6 you can see text in action in a theme that uses the WordPress excerpt function.

When I say "text," that's all you can put in this field—no HTML or any kind of code. That means links are not allowed and certainly no images. Some plugins are mentioned at the end of the lesson that can solve this, if it's an issue for your site.

And remember, putting text in this box will do nothing if your theme is not using the excerpt function. In other words, if it's showing full posts in its lists, the Excerpt will not have any effect.

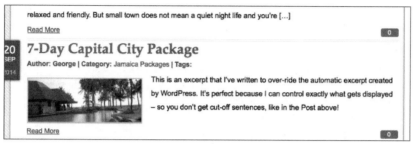

FIGURE 9-6

Send Trackbacks

This meta box is discussed in Lesson 25, "Connecting by E-mail." For now, keep this meta box hidden.

CUSTOM FIELDS

You rarely need to use the Custom Fields meta box, so keep it hidden. Just so you know, Custom Fields are used by developers to store additional information with each Post. To use the Island Travel site as an example, WordPress could be customized to store the contact information for each supplier Post in the suppliers Category.

The actual Custom Fields interface, as shown in Figure 9-7, is basic and potentially confusing to users.

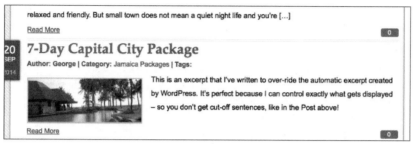

FIGURE 9-7

The potential for confusion is why developers typically create their own interface. Actually, you would rarely even know you're interacting with Custom Fields.

However, from time to time a developer may not bother with a custom interface, and when they tell you to enter something in Custom Fields, now you know where you would go.

> **WARNING** *If you do have the Custom Fields meta box displayed for some reason, be careful not to touch anything in it. The data you see may not always make much sense, but it will be vital to the operation of the Post. As mentioned earlier: Keep this meta box hidden.*

DISCUSSION

The Discussion meta box is the place where you can override two of the sitewide parameters under Settings ⇨ Discussion:

➤ Comments

➤ Trackbacks/pingbacks

By default, WordPress turns on both for all Posts or Pages, so unless you've changed anything in Settings, both boxes will be checked, as shown in Figure 9-8.

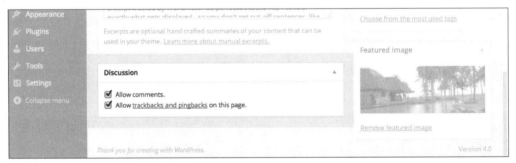

FIGURE 9-8

This is a box that I tend to keep open because it reminds me to check whether comments are on or off for the particular Post I'm working on.

> **NOTE** *You've probably seen blogs where it says that comments are now closed. Depending on how your theme is set up, that's the message you'll get if you uncheck the comments in the Discussion box for the post. Any comments made up to that point will continue to display, but no new ones can be entered. You can also have WordPress automatically close comments after a fixed period of time (see under Settings ⇨ Discussion).*

COMMENTS

While the Discussion setting controls whether the comments function is used on a particular Post, the Comments meta box displays the comments themselves, if there are any. As Figure 9-9 shows, you can see the details of each comment, and when you mouseover one, it shows a menu for all your options.

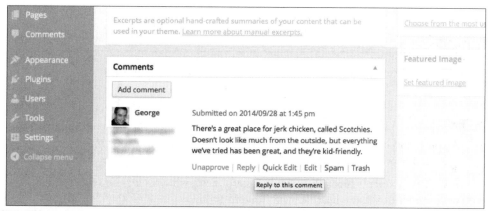

FIGURE 9-9

Although you can reply to a comment from that mouseover menu, you can also start a new one with the Add Comment button.

As you'll see in Lesson 23, "Managing Comments," there are several options for managing comments that do not involve having to go to the individual Post. This meta box can be handy for reviewing a Post's comments when needed, but typically I leave it hidden.

SLUG

There's little reason these days to use this meta box, as explained in Lesson 31, "Optimizing Behind the Scenes," when dealing with Pretty Permalinks. So, this is another meta box to keep hidden.

AUTHOR

If you're the only person writing Posts for your website, keep the Author meta box hidden. By default, WordPress assigns whichever user wrote the Post as the Author. If there are multiple users on a site, this meta box could be handy if you need to manually assign authorship. Each user's name appears on a drop-down menu.

If you do have multiple authors on a site, I would recommend not only displaying this meta box, but also moving it somewhere up near the Publish box, so you can quickly tell who has been assigned as author.

> **NOTE** *The username that shows up on the Author meta box menu, and ultimately is displayed on the website, is the one the user has chosen in her Profile under Display Publicly As. Make sure that the user's names shows as First Name or First Name–Last Name.*

PLUGINS

Plugins for Revisions are covered in Lesson 8, and plugins for Comments are covered in Lesson 23.

EXCERPTS

➤ **Advanced Excerpt** enables you to control the length of auto-excerpts, change the Read More text, and much more.

➤ **Rich Text Excerpts** turns the default Excerpt field, which is a plain text area field, into a rich text editor like the Content Editor.

➤ **Page Excerpt** is one of several plugins that add Excerpt functionality to Pages.

AUTHOR

➤ **Co-Authors Plus** enables you to have multiple authors for one post, and you can choose the order in which the authors appear.

Some themes display a box about the author of a Post, typically at the end of the content and usually showing the Profile picture and biography. There are many plugins that give you control over these boxes or even put in an author box where there isn't any now. Just search Plugins ➪ Add New for the author box.

TRY IT

In this lesson, you use the More button to create an excerpt for a Post.

Lesson Requirements

You need a Post with at least three or four paragraphs of text and the WordPress Twenty Fourteen theme as your active theme.

Step-by-Step

1. Make sure you're in the Visual mode of the Content Editor.

2. Place your cursor where you'd like the excerpt to end, but at least five sentences into the Post.

3. Click the More button on the top row of the button bar. A line with the word More should appear where your cursor is.

4. Click Update.

5. Navigate to the homepage of your site if it displays your posts, or if you've set a specific page to display blog posts, go there.

6. Find the Post you worked on. You should see a link with the words Continue Reading at the point where you put your More tag. You should also see any images or links that you may have within that text.

7. Click Continue Reading to test that you're taken to the full version of the Post.

> **REFERENCE** *Please select the video for Lesson 9 online at* www.wrox.com/go /wp24vids. *You will also be able to download resources for this lesson from the website.*

10

Adding a New Page

The process of adding a new Page in WordPress is virtually identical to adding a Post. Actually, it's simpler because you don't have to think about Categories and typically you don't need a Featured Image.

The common question people ask is, "What do I put on Pages?" Review Lesson 1, "Thinking Like WordPress," to get the answer to that question, which inspires the topic of a Page created during this lesson.

PAGES VERSUS POSTS

Posts are for content that will have many different instances under one or more Categories. For Island Travel, testimonials are perfect for Posts because each one can be about one or more different topics, and hopefully new ones keep coming in from clients forever.

Countries in the Caribbean, however, are limited in number and have a lot of relatively static information about culture, climate, and so on. That makes them good candidates for WordPress Pages. So let's make a Page about Jamaica. After that, this lesson describes the Page's unique functions.

ADDING A PAGE

Start by going to Pages ➪ Add New. The default screen does not look much different from Add New Post, as shown in Figure 10-1.

The Content Editor forms the bulk of the screen. (The second row of buttons display automatically because WordPress remembers that I revealed them earlier.) On the right side, you can see the Publish meta box with the Featured Image meta box at the bottom (not visible in Figure 10-1).

The Page Attributes meta box is new, which is discussed shortly. Its default settings are fine for the Page you are going to create.

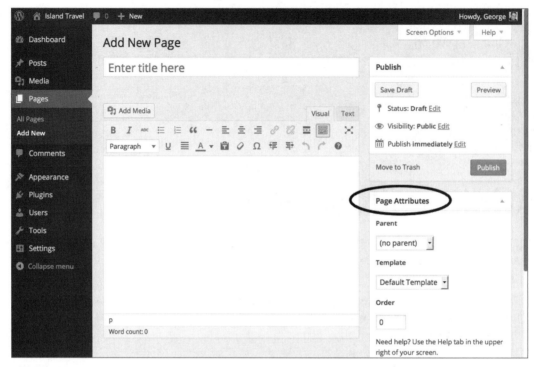

FIGURE 10-1

In the Title box enter **Jamaica**.

Then simply paste text into the Content Editor. I have a couple headings that I format as Heading 2. (Remember the Title of the Page automatically is set as Heading Level 1.) Now my screen looks like Figure 10-2.

And that's it. I'm ready to Publish. I'll be working on adding images in the next section of the book, but for now I'm done.

Notice in Figure 10-3 how this theme has automatically added my new Page to the main menu. My Posts get listed only in the sidebar.

This is all default behavior for this theme. You learn how to control it in later lessons. But now, let's discuss some of the options you have in the Page Attributes meta box.

> **NOTE** *As with Add New Post, the default screen doesn't show all the meta boxes available, but they can still be accessed through Screen Options at the top right. Because Pages don't have Categories or Tags or Trackbacks, the list of hidden meta boxes is shorter: Custom Fields, Discussion, Comments, Slug, Author, and Revisions.*

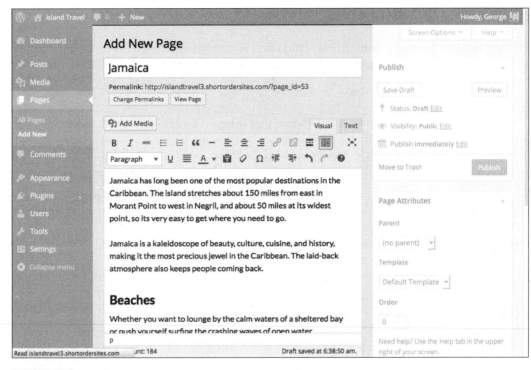

FIGURE 10-2

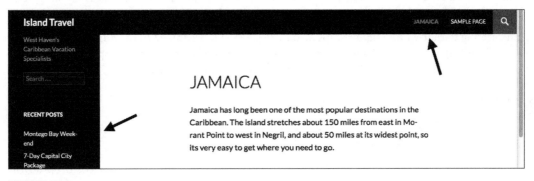

FIGURE 10-3

PAGE ATTRIBUTES

As in the Jamaica example, nothing in this meta box is mandatory for publishing a Page. Also, be prepared for other functions appearing here, depending on your theme and the plugins you activate.

Parent

The first option in the Page Attributes meta box is the Parent drop-down menu, as shown in Figure 10-4. It displays a list of all published pages on your site (drafts are not included), enabling you to make this new page a child of any one of them. A child is just another way of saying a subpage. By default, any new page is a top-level parent: That is, it isn't the child of any other page.

FIGURE 10-4

In the Jamaica example, there was no logical parent Page. But one option would be to create a Page called Destinations and make Jamaica and all the other country Pages children of that parent.

Whatever relationships you create, keep in mind that they do not commit you to having that same structure displayed on any menus you create. You can create child or subpages on a menu independently of the relationship you designate in the Parent box. (In fact, you can make anything a submenu item of anything else, which is covered in detail in Lesson 21, "Managing Widgets and Menus.")

Why use the Parent drop-down system? It may be important for having a clear URL structure because a child will have the parent in its URL. For example, if I create a Kingston page and make it a child of my Jamaica Page, its URL would end in /jamaica/kingston/ (depending on how I configure my Pretty Permalinks; see Lesson 31, "Optimizing Behind the Scenes"). How you relate Pages on your menu does not affect the URL; only the relationships created with the Parent drop-down are affected.

And creating Parent-Child relationships also helps keep you organized in the admin area. For sites with a lot of pages, it makes it much easier to find what you need by having subpages, such as all Pages related to Jamaica (see Lesson 18, "Managing Posts and Pages").

Template

Every theme has a default layout for Pages. Often the theme creates different layouts for various purposes by means of Page templates.

If a theme has any templates beyond the default, those appear in Page Attributes as a drop-down. The number of templates depends on the theme, but you could have dozens to choose from.

Usually, the name of the template is self-explanatory. The Full Width template in Twenty Fourteen, for example, prevents any sidebars from showing on a Page. Some templates create their own content; you simply add a new Page, give it a title, and then choose the template. For example, in Figure 10-5, you can see how the Contributors template produces a web page showing all authors for the site.

> **NOTE** *You aren't limited by what Page templates a theme might offer. You could create custom templates yourself if you're comfortable with HTML, PHP, and CSS, or you could hire a developer.*

FIGURE 10-5

ORDER

You can use the Order attribute to control the order in which WordPress displays Pages under certain circumstances. If your theme uses the default WordPress menu, you can bypass its alphabetical listing of Pages by specifying the order. Enter 1 for the first menu item, 2 for the second, and so on.

However, virtually all themes these days make use of the powerful WordPress menu building system (Appearance ➪ Menus). It enables you to put anything on a menu, not just Pages. And you can put Pages in whatever order you want. No matter what you put in this Order field, a menu you build yourself pays no attention to it.

So is there any value to the Order attribute? Definitely, because there are Page-related widgets and plugins, for example, that use a Sort By function, and Order is usually included in those Sort By drop-downs.

PLUGINS

If you want WordPress Pages to have some of the features reserved for Posts, here are a few plugins that make that possible:

➤ **Post Tags and Categories for Pages**—Makes the Tags and Categories you create for Posts available to use on Pages.

➤ **Next Page, Not Next Post**—Many themes use WordPress's Post navigation function to display links to the next and the previous Posts. This plugin enables you to do the same for Pages by using shortcodes.

➤ **List Pages Shortcode**—There are many ways to list Posts, but few themes have a Page listing function. This plugin enables you to put a list of all Pages, including the hierarchy of parent-child Pages, anywhere you can use shortcodes.

➤ **Bulk Page Creator**—Handy for when you set up a WordPress site or plan to add a large number of Pages to an existing site.

TRY IT

In this lesson, you practice making a new Page a child of an existing Page.

Lesson Requirements

You need at least one Page already in the system.

Step-by-Step

Following are the steps for making a new Page a child or sub-page of an existing Page.

1. Click Add New on the Page area of the Admin menu.

2. Enter a title and then some text.

3. In the Page Attributes meta box, select the Parent drop-down menu.

4. Choose a Page to be the parent.

5. Click Publish.

6. Refresh the homepage on your live site. Assuming that you have not created your own menu, the default menu should display your new Page as a drop-down item when you mouseover the parent.

7. In the WordPress admin area, go to Pages ➪ All Pages and you should see your new Page listed below its parent.

> **REFERENCE** *Please select the video for Lesson 10 online at* www.wrox.com/go /wp24vids. *You will also be able to download resources for this lesson from the website.*

SECTION IV
Working with Media Content

11

The Basics of Adding Media Files

Up to now, you've learned about entering, editing, styling, and laying out text content. In this lesson, you begin the same process for media files, which primarily means images, but also includes video, audio, and documents.

There are two scenarios for adding new media files to WordPress:

➤ Uploading and inserting them into the content of a specific Post or Page

➤ Uploading them to the Media Library for later use

Each of these is demonstrated with images because they're the most common media files you'll use, but the basics apply to other media types as well.

UPLOADING AND INSERTING AN IMAGE INTO A POST

Adding images to the content of a Post (or, of course, a Page) is a simple process that begins with deciding where you want the image to appear. Then place your cursor at that point in your text, as shown in Figure 11-1.

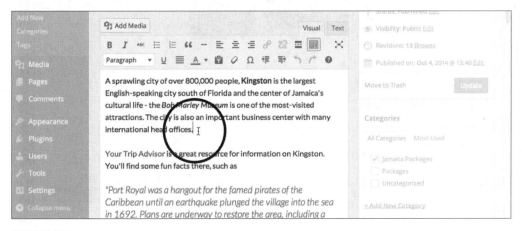

FIGURE 11-1

Don't worry if you change your mind about the location after uploading. Moving an image within the Content Editor is a matter of dragging and dropping it to a new spot.

Now you're ready to add the image by using the Add Media button located at the top left of the Content Editor, as shown in Figure 11-2.

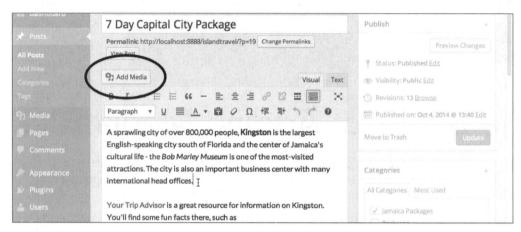

FIGURE 11-2

Click the Add Media button to produce a pop-up window known as the Media Uploader, as shown in Figure 11-3.

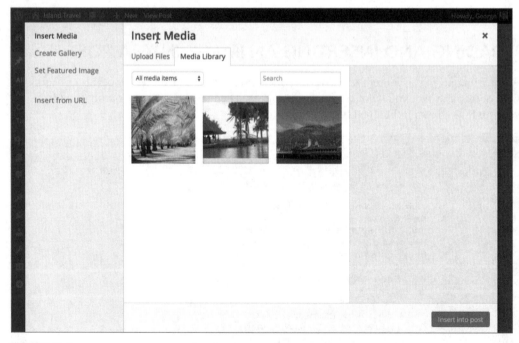

FIGURE 11-3

Make sure the title at the top of the Media Uploader says Insert Media. This window can perform a number of functions (see Lesson 12, "The Media Uploader Window"), which are listed at the left side. If the Insert Media title isn't showing, simply click its link on the left side menu.

In the center area of the Insert Media screen, you have two tabs representing the two choices you have for inserting media content into your Post:

➤ Upload Files—Choose new files from your computer.

➤ Media Library—All files already uploaded to WordPress.

In this case I'll be uploading a new image, so I click the Upload Files tab, and now the Media Uploader screen looks like Figure 11-4.

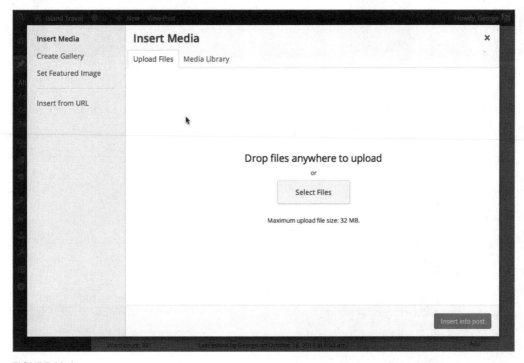

FIGURE 11-4

I can either drag my file(s) to the center area of the window or use the Select Files button and get the traditional pop-up window allowing me to choose from files on my computer.

You see a progress bar during the uploading process, and when that's complete, the screen shows two thumbnails of your image: one on the right side and one in the center area with a blue check mark, as shown in Figure 11-5.

That check mark confirms that this is the image you'll be inserting, so you're ready to click the blue Insert Post button at the lower right side.

FIGURE 11-5

Now there are a number of options on the right side of the Media Uploader screen (discussed in Lesson 12), but for the moment I'll click the Insert into Post button, and you see the result in Figure 11-6.

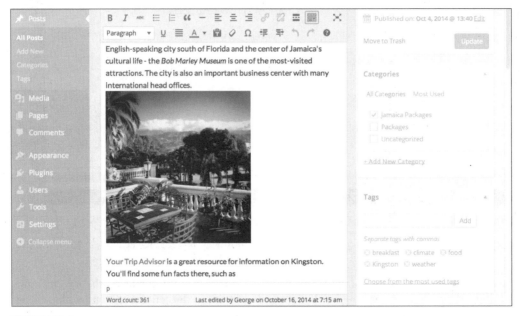

FIGURE 11-6

Although you can see the image in your content, remember you still need to click the Update button for WordPress to save the inserted image.

In Lesson 13, "Working with Images in the Content Editor," you can see more about how to position images exactly the way you want, but for the moment you can see how straightforward it is to place an image in your content.

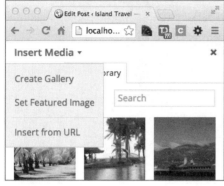

FIGURE 11-7

You can repeat this process to add as many images as you want for a particular Post. However, if you have a lot of them, you might consider creating a Gallery, which is covered in Lesson 15, "Working with Image Galleries."

For mobile users on a narrow screen, the Media Uploader screen looks a little different. The menu on the left is at the top left instead and toggles you between the various choices, as you can see in Figure 11-7.

In the previous example, I uploaded a new image and inserted it into a particular Post. But the image also became a part of the Media Library. In other words, the image can now be used elsewhere on my website. Any media file that gets uploaded to WordPress becomes a part of the Media Library, even if it was uploaded for use in a specific Post.

In some cases you'll have media files you think you may want to use in the future, but for which you don't have a specific place at the moment. This is when you can use the uploading function only.

UPLOADING AN IMAGE TO THE MEDIA LIBRARY

FIGURE 11-8

Adding media files to WordPress without inserting them into any specific Post or Page—uploading them only to the Media Library—can be done through one of two links: one in the main admin menu and the other in the tool bar, as shown in Figure 11-8.

Both links lead to the Upload New Media screen, as shown in Figure 11-9. You can see the familiar upload interface allowing you to drag and drop files or use a pop-up window to browse files on your computer.

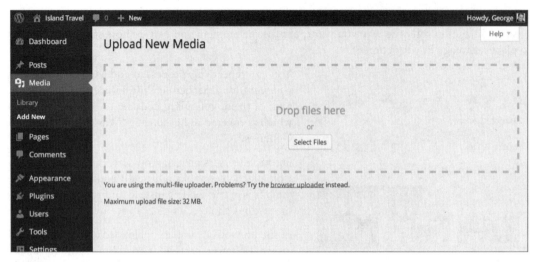

FIGURE 11-9

During the uploading process you see a progress bar on the right, as shown in Figure 11-10 A. When uploading's complete, a small thumbnail of the image appears on the left with an Edit link on the right, as shown in Figure 11-10 B.

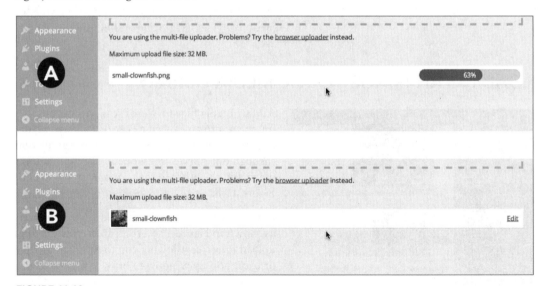

FIGURE 11-10

The Edit link takes you to all the details about the image, and offers the ability to actually crop, rotate, and resize it (which is covered in Lesson 14, "Using the WordPress Image Editor").

But for the moment there's nothing more you need to do. The image is now available for use anywhere on your site, which you can verify by going to the Media Library. In Figure 11-11 you can see the new image listed.

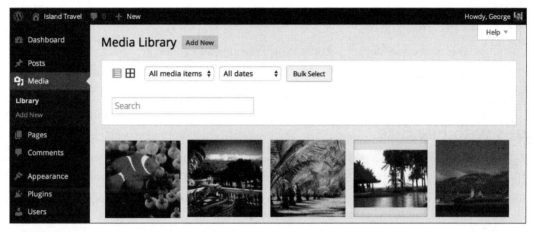

FIGURE 11-11

Having seen how to upload a single image to the Media Library, suppose now you have 30 images or other media files that you know you want to use at some point. Are you doomed to go through the upload process 30 times in a row?

Thankfully, the Add New Media screen enables you to upload multiple media files at one time. You simply drag or choose multiple files, and as with the single image in our example, you'll get a progress bar for every file (as shown in Figure 11-12).

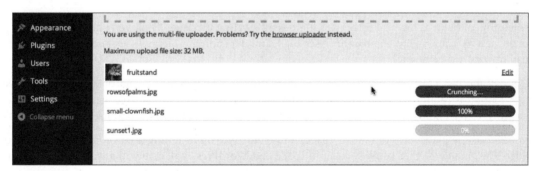

FIGURE 11-12

When each file is finished uploading, you'll see a thumbnail for images or an icon indicating the file type (video, audio, or document).

Keep in mind that uploading multiple media files at a time is only possible with the default Upload New Media screen. Sometimes, though, your browser does not allow you to use that screen, which can cause potential problems when uploading media files.

PROBLEMS UPLOADING MEDIA FILES

Every so often you may run into trouble when uploading a media file, and the four most common issues are:

➤ Your file is too large.

➤ Your browser does not support the WordPress upload method.

➤ Your file is of the wrong type.

➤ WordPress does not have permission to upload.

Issues with File Size

If you follow my advice about image sizes and don't try to upload anything more than 150 K, file size will never be an issue. But with other types of media, even when optimized, size can be an issue.

Your hosting company is actually in charge of how large files can be for uploading, and WordPress tells you what this limit is, as you can see in Figure 11-13.

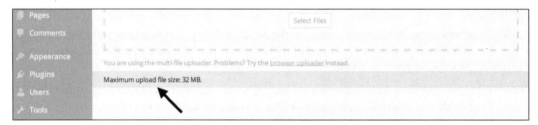

FIGURE 11-13

The limit could be as low as 2 MB or as high as 128 MB; it all depends on your hosting company's settings. You can ask it to change those settings, and depending on its policies and server set up, that may or may not be possible.

There is another way in which file size can be an issue: You may have run out of space on your hosting account. Although most hosting companies these days offer unlimited storage, there actually isn't any such thing. Now, most people would never reach that limit in normal use, but it is possible.

Not all hosting plans have unlimited space, however, so if you're adding a lot of large documents or video files, it may be that you'll run out of space and WordPress will give you a warning. This issue is discussed more in Lessons 15 through 17, when covering non-image media files.

No Browser Support for Uploading

Whenever you upload a file, WordPress displays the message shown in Figure 11-14.

Some older browsers may not play nicely with the methods WordPress normally uses for uploading files. Fortunately, there's a fallback option, which is to use your browser's upload function by clicking the browser uploader link. You can see the resulting screen in Figure 11-15.

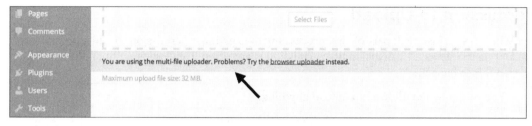

FIGURE 11-14

FIGURE 11-15

Unfortunately the upload function on this screen only allows you to select one file at a time. You can't even use keyboard commands to select several files at once.

> **NOTE** *When you switch file upload mode, WordPress remembers that mode the next time you go to Media ⇨ Add New.*

Incompatible File Types

Problems uploading files can also occur when the type of media file you're trying to upload is not supported by WordPress. Although the list of allowed types is not extensive, it covers the vast majority of people's needs, so normally this is never an issue. You can find an up-to-date list at http://codex.wordpress.org/Uploading_Files.

Keep in mind that your hosting company may have its own restrictions on file types, so even if it's on the WordPress list, you still may not be allowed to upload the file.

If you need to, there are ways to customize WordPress to allow a certain file type, including some plugins, which are mentioned at the end of this lesson.

No Permission to Upload

When WordPress is installed, part of that process involves giving it permission to add, edit, and delete files on the server. But occasionally permission is not given. Depending on the nature of the issue, two things happen:

➤ You're simply not allowed to upload anything.

➤ You have to provide login credentials every time you want to upload.

This can include not only uploading media files, but also trying to install new plugins or themes.

Clearly the first situation needs to be sorted immediately by calling your hosting company. The second situation, although it does enable you to upload, becomes annoying quickly. Again, you need to talk to your hosting company and get it fixed.

In all my years working with WordPress, I've seen permission issues only a few times. It's usually the result of someone doing a manual installation while he wasn't logged in with the right permissions. But once I encountered it because the hosting company saw restricted permissions as a way of maintaining security. Situations like that are extremely rare. If the hosting company won't change permissions for you, switch hosts.

PLUGINS

Many types of plugins deal with media files, but only those directly related to the uploading of images are covered here.

UPLOAD FILE SIZE

➤ **WP Image Size Limit.** Administrators set a limit on image size, and a notice of that limit is shown on the upload screen. If users try to upload an image that's larger, they get an error message.

➤ **Imsanity** automatically reduces the dimensions of images to a pre-set limit during upload, but can also be used on existing images.

➤ **EWWW Image Optimizer** optimizes your images as you upload them. It will even convert an image to a file type that's more efficient. It can also be used on files already in your Media Library.

Lesson 14 covers more about plugins that retroactively reduce existing files.

MANAGING FILE TYPES

➤ **WP Add Mime Types** shows you what file or mime types WordPress allows by default and then lets you add your own to the list.

➤ **Upload File Type Settings Plugin** lets you add new allowed file types to the default list in WordPress. Note: This plugin, along with a couple other file type changers, has not been updated for a few years.

continues

continued

USER UPLOADING

➤ **File Away** not only enables logged-in users to upload files from anywhere on the front end of your site, but it's a complete file listing and download manager as well. Useful for allowing users/members who don't have any back-end privileges to upload files.

➤ **WordPress File Upload** enables logged-in users to upload files from any front-end page on your website. You can limit file size and type. Can be used to allow the public to upload files, but that's not recommended.

FTP FILE UPLOADING

➤ **Add from Server.** Although you can add multiple files with the WordPress Media Uploader, adding hundreds at a time can be an issue. You could upload those files to your server using a file transfer protocol (FTP) program, but WordPress won't recognize them in the Media Library, even if you use the WordPress uploads folder. This plugin gets around that problem.

TRY IT

To combine the two scenarios described in this lesson, try uploading an image to the Media Library first and then inserting it into a Post.

Lesson Requirements

You need a new image to upload to WordPress and at least one existing Post with text.

Step-by-Step

Here are the steps for uploading an image to the Media Library and then inserting it into a Post.

1. Find the Add New link under the Media section of the main admin menu, and click it.

2. Click Select Files.

3. In the pop-up window, choose the image file to upload, and click Select. You should see a progress bar for the upload. When the upload is complete, you see a tiny thumbnail of the image.

4. To verify the image is in the Media Library, click Media ⇨ Library. You should see your image at the beginning of either the series of images or the list of images (depending on the screen setting of the Media Library).

5. Navigate to the Post where you want to insert the image. Click the Add Media button. You should see the images from your Media Library, but if not, click the Media Library tab.

6. Locate the image you just uploaded, and click it so that it displays a check mark. (You should also see it and all its details on the right side of the screen.)

7. Click the Insert into Post button at the lower right of the screen. The pop-up screen disappears, and you should see your image in the body of the Post.

> **REFERENCE** *Please select the video for Lesson 11 online at* www.wrox.com/go /wp24vids. *You will also be able to download resources for this lesson from the website.*

12

The Media Uploader Window

The Media Uploader window should be familiar to you at this point in the book. You saw it when setting the Featured Image of a Post and again when inserting an image into the content of the Post. So clearly this window does a number of tasks, and in this lesson you walk through some of the key ones.

Begin by refreshing your memory with Figure 12-1, which shows the Media Uploader window in its Insert Media mode.

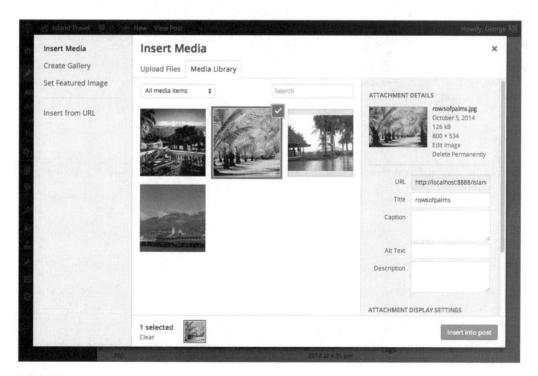

FIGURE 12-1

It's a pop-up window with the current admin screen grayed out behind it. In other words, it's not an admin screen itself or a new tab in your browser. That means you have to do something before returning to the admin screen, even if that's just to cancel out the window by clicking the X at the top right.

When you open the Media Uploader window, it shows you only what you need based on the button or link you used to open it.

If you clicked Set Featured Image, there is only one task you can perform: set the featured image. But if you clicked the Add Media button, the window shows the Insert Media function with a menu on the left side to switch functions, including Set Featured Image. This can be a bit confusing because people sometimes think these are different windows, but all versions of it are referred to as the Media Uploader window.

When you click Add Media, the window has a menu on the left side, as shown in Figure 12-2 A. In mobile mode, the menu is a drop-down at the top, as shown in Figure 12-2 B.

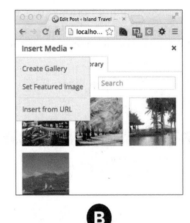

FIGURE 12-2

The four most common operations for the Media Uploader are:

➤ Insert Media

➤ Create Gallery

➤ Set Featured Image

➤ Insert from URL

There are two other operations: Create Audio Playlist and Create Video Playlist. But these appear only if there is at least one file of that type in the Media Library, and are covered in Lesson 16, "Adding Video and Audio."

The main four operations are discussed individually, but first consider one element of the user interface that applies to all.

The big blue button for taking action is always at the bottom right, and it remains inactive—you can't click it—until you make a choice or enter some information. You know the button is inactive because its colors are muted. As soon as you make a choice or enter information, the button lights up and you can click it.

> **NOTE** *The Add Media button can appear in numerous places throughout WordPress, not just on Posts or Pages, depending on your plugins and your theme. For example, there are plugins that create a widget with a mini Content Editor, and it will have an Add Media button.*

INSERT MEDIA

This is the most commonly used function of the Media Uploader: putting media into the content of Posts and Pages. It consists of two tabs: Upload Files and Media Library. As soon as you have at least one file in the Media Library, the default state of the Insert Media screen is to show the Media Library, as highlighted in Figure 12-3.

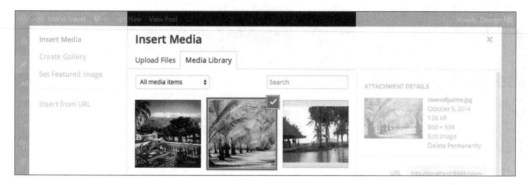

FIGURE 12-3

By default the Media Library tab shows all files in the library, but you can filter results by using the drop-down or the search function, as shown in Figure 12-4.

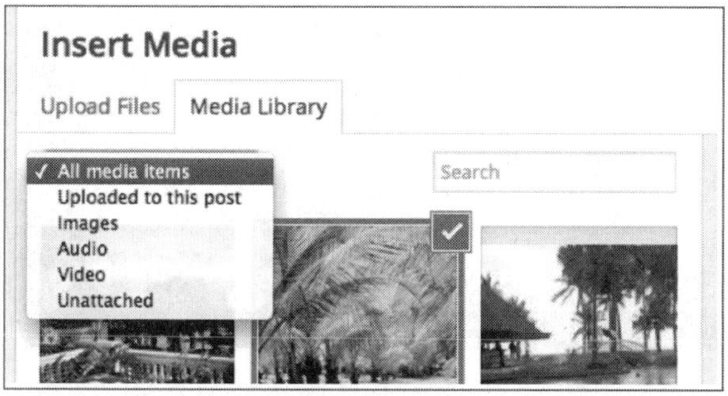

FIGURE 12-4

Unlike the Media Library admin screen, this Media Library area does not allow for filtering files by date. However, the ability to show only files that have been uploaded to the current Post is handy.

Whenever you upload a file while on a particular Post or Page, WordPress records that the file is "attached" to it. The file is still part of the Media Library and can be used on other Posts or Pages, but there's a special relationship to that original content. You can make use of that relationship here by filtering out all other files and showing only the ones you uploaded to this Post.

From the Media Library results, you can insert one or more media files at a time by clicking the files you want. You can verify what's going to be inserted by looking for a check mark on the thumbnail (or icon for non-images) and whether the file shows up in the Attachment Details area on the right, as shown in Figure 12-5.

FIGURE 12-5

But if you're uploading several files, they can't all show up on the right side, and if you have more than a few files in your library, they won't all show up at the same time within the window to see if they're checked. So how do you remember which ones you've selected? By looking at the little Selected area at the bottom of the window, as shown in Figure 12-6.

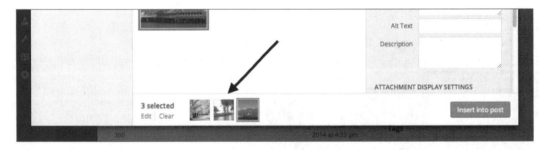

FIGURE 12-6

With images you have a tiny thumbnail and with other files you have an icon.

> **NOTE** *If you plan to insert more than one image file at a time, you'll likely want to use the Create Gallery function. I'll talk a bit more about that shortly, but cover it in depth in Lesson 15, "Working with Image Galleries."*

After you finish selecting, of course, you can click the Insert into Post button at the lower right. But before you do, in particular with images, it's important to check the Attachment Details.

On the right side of the Media Uploader, there's a gray section called Attachment Details, where you can find all of a file's details when you select it, as shown in Figure 12-7.

FIGURE 12-7

The unfortunate fact is that unless you have a tall screen, you don't see all the Attachment Details. Some of the most important information has to be accessed by scrolling, as shown in Figure 12-8.

FIGURE 12-8

So always remember to scroll down and check all details before inserting a file into your content.

In mobile mode, the situation with the Attachment Details presents a slightly different issue. When you click an image, the details box slides out from the right, as shown in Figure 12-9 A.

FIGURE 12-9

If you click the image again, the details slide back out of sight. But if the image you clicked was covered by the details box, you need to click a different image to make the box disappear. That's not such a big deal, but if you try to select multiple images, the Attachment Details remain in place, covering some of your images, as shown in Figure 12-9 B.

The Attachment Details area has three main functions:

➤ **List the file specifications**—Date uploaded, size, and so on.

➤ **Manage meta data for the image**—Title, caption, alternative text.

➤ **Settings for displaying the file**—Alignment and so on.

File Specifications

Here you can find a variety of file specifications, depending on the type of file. For images you get details like those shown in Figure 12-10.

FIGURE 12-10

Knowing the dimensions of the image you uploaded can be important, for example, in deciding if the full-sized version will suit a particular place in your content. Those dimensions also give you a sense of what smaller versions WordPress would have created automatically (an image that's only 125 pixels wide has no smaller versions, whereas one that's 1,200 pixels wide will have a Thumbnail, Medium, and Large version.

The file size specifications are also helpful in spotting images that are unnecessarily large (for example, a 1.5 MB image is far too big a file size) or deciding which of two versions of a PDF you accidentally uploaded is the one you optimized for the web.

When you do come across a file that should be deleted, there's a handy Delete Permanently link. And when it says permanently, that means the file does *not* go to the Trash with the possibility of restoring it later.

If you want to edit an image after uploading it, there's also an Edit Image link, and which is discussed in Lesson 14, "Using the WordPress Image Editor."

> **NOTE** *When you upload a file with the same name as an existing file, WordPress does not overwrite the original or ask if you want to overwrite it. Instead, it adds a number to the end of the new file's name.*

Attachment Meta Data

In the middle area of Attachment Details, you have the opportunity to add and modify several types of metadata about the file, as highlighted in Figure 12-11.

FIGURE 12-11

Following are the four options for metadata:

➤ Change the file Title (by default its filename)

➤ Caption

➤ Alternative (Alt) Text (for images)

➤ A Description

The file Title is an HTML attribute that is used as a kind of tooltip when you mouseover the file (whether linked or not). While WordPress automatically fills this field with the file's name, changing it does not change the filename.

Captions are used mostly for images but are available for use with other file types. How (and even, if) captions display depends on your Theme.

> **NOTE** *You can use basic HTML tags in the Caption box. So if you need to create line breaks or bold something, for example, you can. Don't know HTML? Open a new tab, start to Add New Post, and write your caption in the Content Editor. Then switch to Text Mode and copy the HTML. Exit the Post without saving it.*

Alternative or Alt Text was originally devised for web reader programs used by the visually impaired so that images could have a short description. However, it's also important for helping search engines understand what your image is about.

The Description displays on the Attachment Page. Every media file you upload to WordPress automatically has a web page assigned to it, which is known as the Attachment Page. As you'll see in the next section, this is one of your choices when deciding whether to link a media file or not. The Description may also be used in other situations, depending on your Theme.

Display Settings

This is one of the most-used sections of Attachment Details, but for browsers on most devices, it remains entirely or partially hidden, and you have to scroll to see the settings. Settings for an image are shown in Figure 12-12.

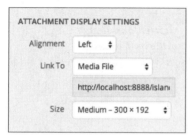

FIGURE 12-12

Up to three settings are found here, depending on the file type:

➤ Alignment (for images) relative to the surrounding text

➤ Whether, and to what, the file is being linked

➤ Which size (of image) is to display

Alignment means whether an image floats to the left or right of the surrounding text or whether it sits on its own line, either to the default left or centered in the content area.

Linking is a choice that's available for all files; though again it varies with the type. In Figure 12-13 you can see the choices for images, documents, and video/audio files.

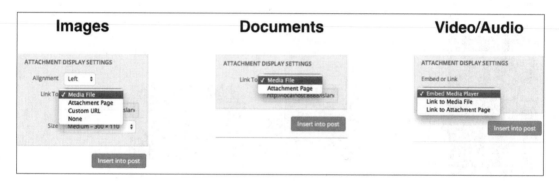

FIGURE 12-13

Attachment Pages were mentioned earlier, and these are complete web pages, with your header, footer, and so on, and the file and its description showing in the content area.

Linking to Media File is going be the usual choice for non-image files because you want visitors to download or play them, although you may want visitors to go to the Attachment Page and get more details before downloading or playing.

In most cases for images, I would recommend the None setting for Link To. It can be confusing for visitors to click an image and be taken to an Attachment Page—even more so if you choose Media File, because they'll simply see the full-size image in a blank browser window.

However, plugins that create pop-up lightbox effects from images typically need you to link to Media File, so watch for that.

The final choice for images under Display Settings is the size of image to be inserted. What options you have depend on the dimensions of the original image. If the original were smaller than WordPress's Thumbnail setting, you'll have only the choice of inserting the full-sized image. With large originals, you have a choice of Thumbnail, Medium, and Large.

> **NOTE** *WordPress remembers the last Display Settings you used and makes them the default for the next file you insert. But it's still important to always scroll down and check the settings before you insert. It's easy enough to correct, but save yourself some time.*

CREATE GALLERY

A WordPress Gallery is a collection of images that automatically is formatted through your Theme. By default, the Thumbnail versions of the images display, and on the Island Travel site look like Figure 12-14.

FIGURE 12-14

Galleries are created and managed through the Media Uploader window. Exactly how the screen looks for Galleries depends on the function you perform, but the Create Gallery link on the left menu produces the screen shown in Figure 12-15.

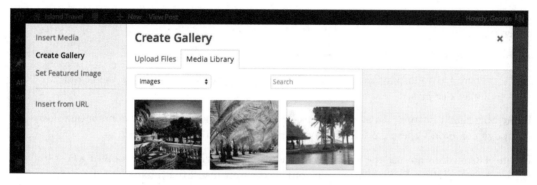

FIGURE 12-15

In Lesson 15 I'll walk you through the entire process of creating and managing a Gallery, but for the moment let me just say that it begins very much like choosing a group of images to insert into a Post. You click on each image you want and a checkmark is displayed to indicate your choices.

> **NOTE** *Even if you were planning to insert only a single image when you clicked Add Media, you can create a Gallery instead simply by using the left-side menu to switch the window contents. Or you could decide to set or change the Featured image by clicking that link in the left-side menu.*

SET FEATURED IMAGE

This link produces the same screen (Figure 12-16) you would get if you click the Set Featured Image link in the Featured Image meta box of a Post or a Page.

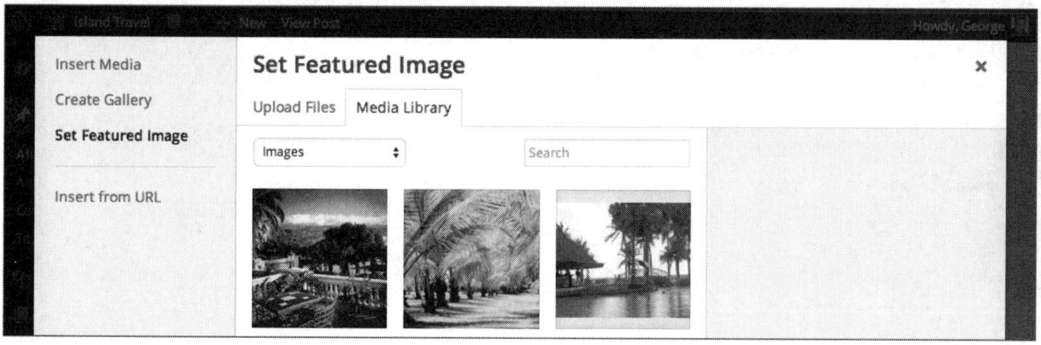

FIGURE 12-16

Although it's similar to the Insert Media version of the screen, there are two important differences:

➤ You can choose only one image.

➤ There are no display settings; your Theme determines where and how the Featured Image displays.

Remember that a Featured Image is not inserted by Themes into the actual content of a Post. Although commonly these days, it displays somewhere near the top of a Post.

If your Theme does not use the Featured Image when displaying the full version of a Post (most use it when displaying lists of Posts), you could separately insert that image into the body of the Post.

> **NOTE** *The technical name in WordPress for Featured Images is "post thumbnail." You sometimes hear that word used in plugin names or in documentation; it simply means Featured Image.*

INSERT FROM URL

To insert a media file into a Post or a Page, it does not have to be uploaded to WordPress. It could reside on a server separate from your website. For example, a manufacturer you deal with might have an image on its website that it allows you to link to. Or you might have a PDF for downloading that you store in a cloud account.

In cases like that you would use the Insert From URL link in the menu of the Media Uploader, as shown in Figure 12–17.

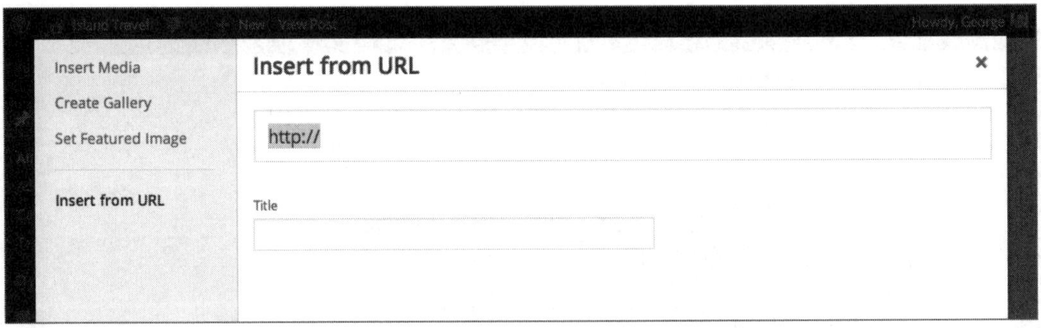

FIGURE 12–17

The first step is to enter the full URL for the file. Make sure the http:// is at the beginning. Give it a moment for WordPress to find the file to determine what type it is. If it's an image, for example, you'll see the image displayed along with various settings, as shown in Figure 12-18.

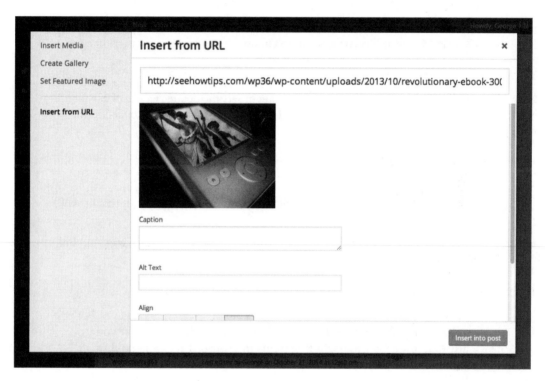

FIGURE 12-18

If you're linking to a video or audio file, WordPress displays it in a player if the connection is successful.

For a document such as a PDF, WordPress simply verifies that it exists (you'll see a spinning circle to the right of the URL); then you can enter the Title, which is the text to which the document is linked in your content.

> **WARNING** *Unless you control the location of the content you're inserting via URL, keep in mind that it could disappear at any time. And of course make sure you have permission to use the content.*

PLUGINS

Following are some plugins related to functions in the Media Uploader window, except for Galleries, which are covered in Lesson 15.

INSERT MEDIA

➤ **Media Manager Plus** enables you to choose files from sources other than the Media Library, such as Flickr and Instagram.

➤ **Default Media Uploader View.** The default view for the Media Library tab is to show all items in the library; this plugin sets the default view to Uploaded to This Post so you see only Media Library items that were uploaded to the current post.

DISPLAY SETTINGS

➤ **WP Image Size Selection.** Themes and plugins may create other image sizes, and this plugin makes them all available in the Size drop-down of the display settings.

➤ **Default Image Settings** allows you to control the default image alignment, linking, and size settings from Settings ⇨ Media.

SET FEATURED IMAGE

➤ **Require Featured Image** is for you if you want all Posts or all Pages or both to have a Featured Image. Handy when you have other authors or you just want to remind yourself. It prevents the Post or Page from publishing without a Featured Image. Only drawback is that you can't select specific Post Categories—it's all or nothing.

➤ **Auto Post Thumbnail.** Rather than requiring a Featured Image, this plugin checks if one has been set; and if not, it uses the first image uploaded to the Post or Page.

➤ **Instant Featured Image** enables you to both insert an image into content and at the same time make it the Featured Image. This is useful if your Theme does not make use of the Featured Image when displaying the full Post and you want that image in your content.

TRY IT

In this lesson, you practice inserting an image into a Post using the Insert from a URL link on the Media Uploader window.

Lesson Requirements

You need an existing Post and an image that's live on your website. (If you have permission to use an image from another site, great.) The goal is to use the URL for the image, so the simplest thing is to use one from your own site.

Step-by-Step

Following are the steps for inserting an image into a Post when that image is on another server.

1. Open a Post for editing.

2. Click the Add Media button.

3. Click Insert from URL over on the left menu.

4. In a separate tab of your browser, on the front end of your site, find the web page with the image you want to insert.

5. Right-click the image, and choose View Image or Show Picture. If neither is available, choose Properties, and highlight the URL in the pop-up window.

6. If View Image or Show Picture works, you see the image by itself in your browser; copy the URL in the address bar.

7. Back in your browser tab with the WordPress Media Uploader, paste the address for the image into the URL field.

8. Click anywhere in the Title field. A small, spinning circle displays beside the URL field, indicating that WordPress is checking your image is where you say it is. If the image is found, it displays along with a series of options.

9. You can finish entering information, such as the Alternate Text. This is what people see if there is no image, and is used by search engines.

10. Enter a Caption if you want one to appear in the post.

11. Alignment is the position of the image relative to the text around it. You can choose from None, Left, Center, and Right.

12. Choose whether you want the image to link to anything—simplest to just choose None.

13. Click Insert into Post.

14. Click Preview to see the image in your Post.

> **REFERENCE** *Please select the video for Lesson 12 online at* www.wrox.com/go /wp24vids. *You will also be able to download resources for this lesson from the website.*

13

Working with Images in the Content Editor

After you insert an image into a Post, there may be changes you want to make: alignment to the text, position on the page, and so on. This lesson looks at working with images after they're in the Content Editor, including some of the design considerations when laying out your content.

THE IMAGE DETAILS WINDOW

Much of your work with images in the Content Editor will involve changing settings, and you do that through the Image Details window.

When you click an image in the Content Editor in WordPress 4.0, two icons appear at the top left (Figure 13-1 A). As of WordPress 4.1 you'll see a bar with icons, as shown in Figure 13-1 B.

In WordPress 4.1 you have alignment icons, while in both versions, the X icon deletes the image (if you accidentally press this, just insert the image again) and the pencil icon leads to the Image Details pop-up, shown in full in Figure 13-2.

Much of this window accesses settings you worked with in the Media Uploader (you could add or change a caption here), but some are new. For example, you can access the image editor to perform cropping and other functions, which are covered in Lesson 14, "Using the WordPress Image Editor."

Aligning Images

When I inserted an image into the 7 Day Capital City Package, it was sitting by itself between two sections of text, as shown in Figure 13-3 A. That doesn't look great. It would be nice to have the text flow around the image, the way it does in Figure 13-3 B.

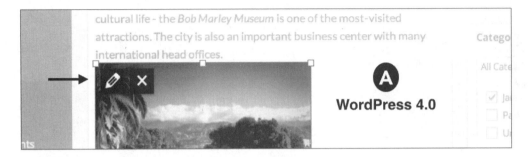

FIGURE 13-1

FIGURE 13-2

No Alignment   **Left Alignment**

FIGURE 13-3

That's where the Image Details window comes in. You simply choose your alignment, click Update, and it repositions relative to the text. If you need to actually move the image after aligning, that is covered shortly.

As noted above, as of WordPress 4.1, you can adjust the alignment without having to click through to the Image Details window. Simply click on the image and the alignment buttons are displayed.

Replacing Images

Sometimes, you may need to switch one image for another. Perhaps you have a new staff photo or an updated cover for a book.

WordPress has a Replace function in the Image Details window that can save a few steps instead of deleting the image and inserting a new one. The trick is to make note of the display settings for the image you're replacing.

When you click the Replace button, a Replace Image screen displays, which is basically the Insert Media screen, but the current image is checked and it's details are visible on the right, as shown in Figure 13-4.

If the new image needs to be uploaded, use the Upload Files tab, or if it's already in the Media Library, simply check the image.

Replicate the old image settings in the new image attachment display settings (alignment, size, and so on) and then click the blue Replace button at the lower right.

You return to the Content Editor, and the new image will have replaced the old in exactly the same position (assuming you used the correct settings).

FIGURE 13-4

NOTE *If you've been working with a non-WordPress website using FTP, you might be accustomed to replacing an image with a new version by giving the new file the same name, uploading it via FTP, and overwriting the old one.*

The problem with doing that in WordPress is that the original image may be changed, but all the smaller sizes created by WordPress would still look like the old image. That's why you should upload a new image from inside WordPress and use a feature such as Replace.

Now, suppose the image you need to replace has been used in several locations throughout your site. In that case the URL for each instance of the image would need to remain the same. (Unless you manually replace each image, but that's what you're trying to avoid.)

Because WordPress uses a year/month folder system for images by default, simply uploading a new image using WordPress would create a new URL. This is one situation in which manually replacing the original image via FTP, in its original folder, may be necessary. To take care of the smaller image versions, you could use a plugin that regenerates thumbnails.

Advanced Options

Most people won't need to touch these settings, and that's why they're hidden by default, as shown in Figure 13-5 A.

One setting that could be valuable in special circumstances is the ability to give the image a class, so that a designer (or you, if you know CSS) could write rules to style it.

You could do this for an individual image, but the real power is in assigning a class to, say, all images in Posts of a certain Category. Then, with that one CSS rule, you could change all the images in that Category.

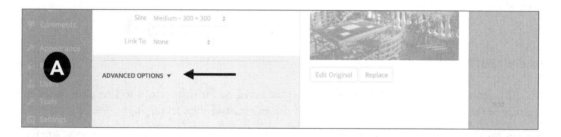

FIGURE 13-5

MOVING IMAGES

When inserting an image into a Post, it appears wherever you had placed your cursor. But what if you need to move the image after inserting? Fortunately, it's as easy as dragging and dropping.

The trick with moving an image is keeping your eye on the cursor to tell you exactly where you're moving to.

As you can see in Figure 13-6 A, when you click and drag an image, a transparent copy is made, and that's what you actually drag around.

I've zoomed in on Figure 13-6 B to show you that the text cursor follows along just in front of your mouse pointer while you drag. That's how you can tell when you've reached the exact point in the text where you'd like to have the image.

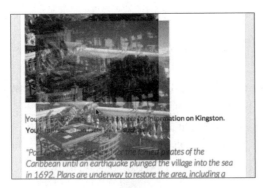

A **B**

FIGURE 13-6

The process is much easier to follow in a video that I created for this lesson, so I recommend watching that at the website URL given at the end of the lesson, and then trying it yourself.

Remember that whatever alignment setting you have for the image will continue to apply, so even if you think you're dropping the image at a certain point in the text, alignment may change it somewhat.

> **NOTE** *If you have trouble with the drag-and-drop method, it's almost as simple to delete the image, put your cursor where you'd like, and re-insert it.*

RESIZING IMAGES

You have three options for resizing an image that you've inserted into a Post:

➤ Choose a different version of the image.

➤ Use HTML to resize it in the browser.

➤ Physically resize the image, or crop it using the Image Editor.

Lesson 14 covers the Image Editor and the third option. Here the first two options are discussed.

Choosing a different version of the image means selecting one of the other sizes that WordPress automatically creates when you upload an image. To do that, you can access the Image Details window by clicking the image in the Content Editor and then the pencil icon at the top left. Then it's simply a matter of choosing from the available sizes, as shown in Figure 13-7.

The new version appears in the window, and you can just click Update and the image in the Content Editor is replaced.

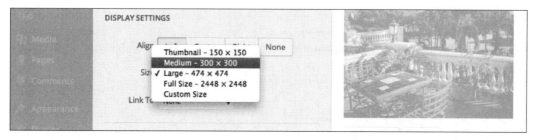

FIGURE 13-7

The second option for resizing an image is to specify a custom size in the Image Details window. It's the final choice at the bottom of the size drop-down in Figure 13-8 A. When you choose it you get the width and height boxes, as shown in Figure 13-8 B.

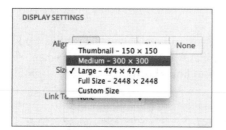

FIGURE 13-8

If you change the width, you'll notice that the same number automatically appears in the height box, and vice versa. You might think you're going to get a square image, but what you're actually telling WordPress is: Whichever is the longer side, make it this size and keep the other side proportionately large. That way there's no worries about distorting your image.

> **WARNING** *Do not use a Custom Size that's larger than the original image or it will look blurry or pixelated.*
>
> *If you've ignored my advice not to upload gigantic images, then do not use Custom Size. It will take a long time for the browser to download the huge file, then more time to do the re-sizing, and we know how visitors feel about slow-loading web pages.*

If you don't know exactly how large you want the image, simply try it, see how it looks, and then edit the size again until you get the effect you want.

You can custom-size your image directly in the Content Editor by using the drag points you see around the edges when you click on the image, as highlighted in Figure 13-9.

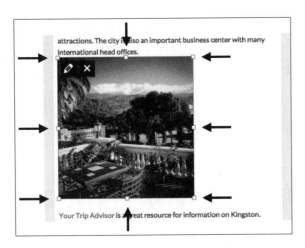

FIGURE 13-9

By clicking and dragging on any one of the tiny white boxes, you can resize your image live, and WordPress keeps the proportions of the image as you drag. That way you can better tell when you have the size you want. The sequence in Figure 13-10 illustrates how this works.

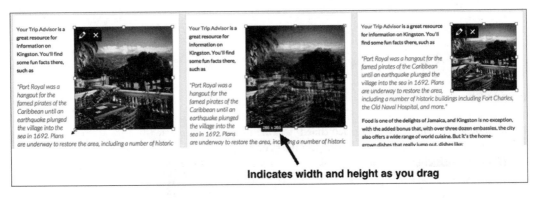

Indicates width and height as you drag

FIGURE 13-10

> **WARNING** *Most browsers keep the image's proportionality as you drag one of the points on the image, but some older ones may not.*

Now custom-sizing your image (either method) may be handy, but it's not ideal. It can cause two issues:

➤ The image may not look as crisp compared with displaying at its natural size.

➤ The browser has to work to resize the image as the page loads, and this can contribute to slower loading of the page (particularly if you have several resized images on the page).

These problems don't always arise, but you need to be aware of them.

DESIGN CONSIDERATIONS FOR IMAGE PLACEMENT

There are a few things to watch for when you're inserting images into the Content Editor, or you can end up with some messy-looking web pages. Luckily, the simplicity of working with images makes it easy to quickly correct such problems.

Often when you insert an image that's left-aligned or right-aligned so that text flows around it, you end up with a couple words dangling below the image, as shown in Figure 13-11 A.

By simply resizing your image slightly, you can get rid of those orphaned words, as shown in Figure 13-11 B.

FIGURE 13-11

If you have multiple images in a Post, try to give some breathing space between them. You can see how crowded things got in Figure 13-12 A, but simply by repositioning the second image, Figure 13-12 B is much easier on the eye.

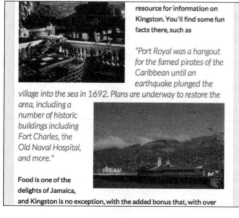

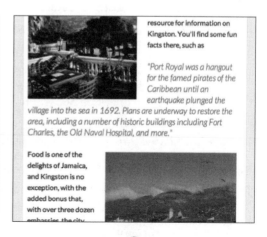

FIGURE 13-12

A third common issue is having an image that's too wide so that you end up with the kind of narrow column of text trying to flow around it in Figure 13-13 A. Again, a simple resizing of the image can relieve that (Figure 13-13 B). Or if you don't want the image any smaller, simply remove the left or right alignment so that the image is on its own line, as shown in Figure 13-13 C.

FIGURE 13-13

Finally, there's the question of putting two images side by side. It's a matter of setting the alignment of each to "left" and then dragging and resizing until they look good. (The video for this lesson demonstrates this more easily. See the end of the lesson for the URL to the videos.)

Another method that avoids resizing issues is to create a Gallery using the two images, set the columns to 2, and probably size the images to medium instead of the default Thumbnail. The Gallery styling takes care of lining up the two images side by side. Working with Galleries is covered in Lesson 15, "Working with Image Galleries."

PLUGINS

There aren't any plugins directly related to using images in the Content Editor, but some do deal with the image details window, and I give an example below.

There are two groups of plugins that deal with page layout, and therefore the positioning of images: shortcode and visual composition plugins. There is a special section for each of them in Lesson 36, "More Plugin Suggestions."

Advanced Image Styles enables the user to add padding and border width and color to each image through settings in the Advanced Options section of the Image Details window. Some people like this because it doesn't involve knowing CSS, but this kind of inline styling overrides any theme settings and that's not good practice. It's better to use the existing image class field and then write a CSS rule to style the image; then you just change the style sheet once when you change themes. Still, some people want this kind of control, so there's a plugin for it. Rant over.

TRY IT

In this lesson, you practice moving an image and then change its alignment.

Lesson Requirements

A Post with at least three paragraphs of text and at least one image already inserted somewhere in that text (does not matter what its alignment is).

Step-by-Step

This is how to move an image inside the Content Editor and then change its alignment relative to the text.

1. Find the Post on the All Posts screen, and click Edit.

2. Make sure you're in the Visual mode of the Content Editor.

3. Click the image you want to work with. Hold.

4. When you find a new location, let the image go and it should reposition.

5. Click the image again, and look for the two icons at the top left.

6. Click the edit icon to bring up the Image Details window.

7. Under Display Settings, choose a different alignment from the current one.

8. Click the Update button. Your image should now be repositioned relative to the text.

> **REFERENCE** *Please select the video for Lesson 13 online at* www.wrox.com/go /wp24vids. *You will also be able to download resources for this lesson from the website.*

14

Using the WordPress Image Editor

After you upload images to WordPress, you can make corrections using the built-in Image Editor. Although it provides only basic functions, they're enough to handle the three most common issues users face:

- ➤ Replacing the default Thumbnail created by WordPress
- ➤ Changing the dimensions of the full-sized version of the image
- ➤ Mirroring an image left or right so that it faces a new direction

You can use the cropping, scaling, and flipping tasks to see how the Image Editor works. But first, check out a map of how to get to the Image Editor from the grid view of the Media Library and from the list view, as shown in Figure 14-1.

You can also get to a version of the Image Editor through the Image Details window, as shown in Figure 14-2.

As you can see, the Image Editor looks slightly different depending on where it's used, but they have the same functionality. For consistency, the examples in this lesson are based on the Edit Media screen.

If your screen is wide enough, on the Edit Media version, the image Save box will be to the right of the Image Editor, and that can crowd things. You can easily move it by switching to one column using Screen Options.

On tablets and smartphones the screen automatically switches to a single column. But smartphone users beware: In portrait mode it's difficult to do anything more than enter numbers to scale or crop, as shown in Figure 14-3.

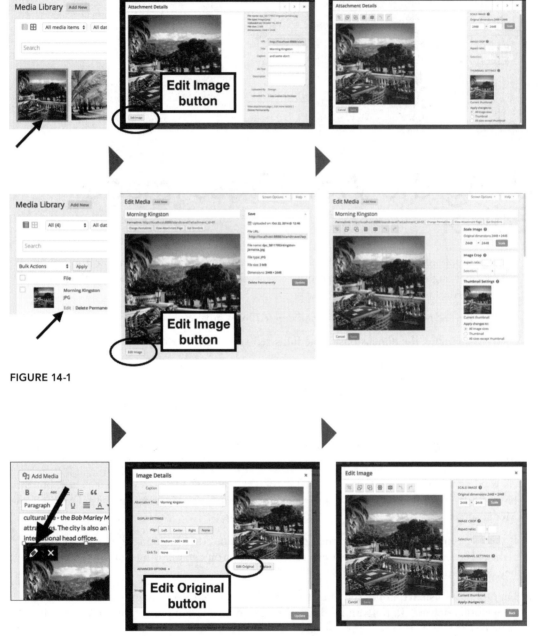

FIGURE 14-1

FIGURE 14-2

You need to understand the limitations of the Image Editor. It is not a mini-Photoshop. You can't adjust colors, remove red-eye, or add effects or text. These are all tasks you would need to perform before uploading an image to WordPress.

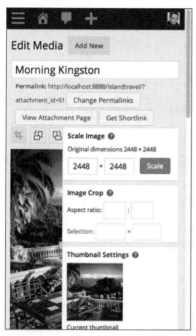

FIGURE 14-3

The "Plugins" section at the end of this lesson point you to some plugins that try to bring some of this added functionality to WordPress. However, you might be better off using a dedicated image program on your device or one online. Let WordPress do its job, and leave complex image manipulation to software built for that job.

Because of the nature of the tasks covered in this lesson, they're not easy to convey in words and images. Watching the videos online and simply trying out the Image Editor can make things clearer (see the end of the lesson for the URL to the videos).

> **NOTE** *Relax. No matter what you do in the Image Editor, the original image you uploaded is never changed, and you can always revert back to it. However, changes applied to the WordPress-generated copies of the original remain changed until you apply new changes.*

THE IMAGE EDITOR FUNCTIONS

Following is a full list of functions for the Image Editor:

➤ Crop

➤ Rotate Left or Right (counter-clockwise or clockwise)

> ➤ Flip Horizontally or Vertically

> ➤ Undo or Redo an operation

> ➤ Scale

Figure 14-4 shows a close-up of the function icons just above the image you're working with.

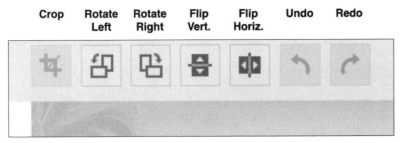

FIGURE 14-4

Scaling has its own button over on the right side, along with a box to adjust your cropping by dimensions, as shown in Figure 14-5.

If you click the blue question marks beside each box's title, explanations display, showing how the functions work.

CROPPING AN IMAGE

The default setting for the thumbnail-sized images created by WordPress is a 150 x 150 pixel area from the center of the original. In many cases, that works fine. But sometimes what's at the center is not what you want visitors to see as the thumbnail.

The Crop function of the Image Editor enables you to choose the area of the original to use for the thumbnail. Here's how it works:

Before doing anything else, check the Thumbnail Settings box on the right, as shown in Figure 14-6.

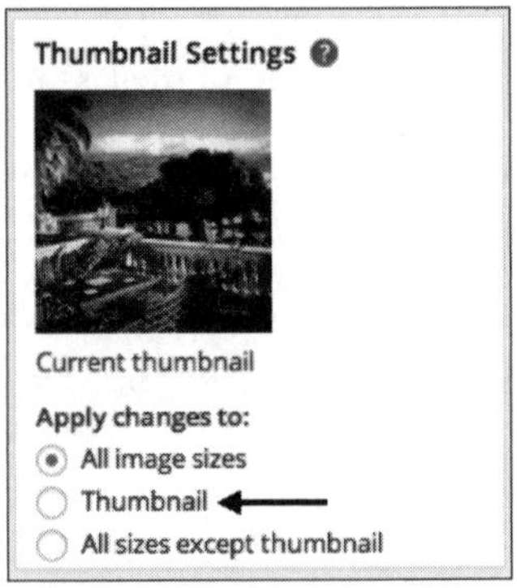

You see a picture of the current thumbnail and Apply Changes To setting. This determines to which images your cropping (or any other edits) will be applied. Make sure it's set to Thumbnail. If you don't, you'll end up cropping all sizes of the image, and that's rarely what you want.

Now you can start dragging your cursor anywhere in the image. This darkens the rest of the image and creates a box with an animated border and drag points or handles, as shown in Figure 14-7.

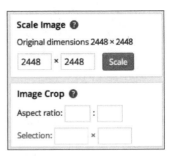

FIGURE 14-5

FIGURE 14-6

FIGURE 14-7

The default setting for WordPress Thumbnails is a square, so drag one of the handles on the box until it's roughly a square. On the right in the Image Crop box, you can see Aspect Ratio. Set that ratio as 1:1 and WordPress automatically adjusts the box to make it square.

> **NOTE** *Don't worry that the numbers in the Selection width and height do not change when you set the Aspect Ratio. All that matters is that the selection area on the image changes to match that ratio.*

You can also drag the edges of the box until the numbers in the Selection fields match. Or in cases in which you have a specific size you need to crop to, you can simply enter the values in those fields. However, you can't enter any numbers into the Selection fields until you click on the image and start a selection region. Then, when you enter values into the fields, the selection region resizes to match those values.

Placing your cursor inside the selection area allows you to move it around the image. Now that the box is square, as you move it around the image, you can see exactly what area would display as a thumbnail.

When you find a good spot, click the Crop button, which is at the far left of the icons on top of your image. At that point you see the cropped version, and the Save button becomes active. Before saving, it's a good idea to check again and make sure this change is going to be applied only to Thumbnails. When you're sure, click Save.

> **NOTE** *Some people become confused because when you first open the Image Editor, the crop button is grayed out and clicking does nothing. That's because the button is for completing the process, not starting it.*

You should now see the new version of the thumbnail in the Thumbnail Settings area. Of course, the new version is what you'll see throughout the back end of the site (say, the Media Library) and on the front end of the site (in a listing of blog posts, for instance).

SCALING AN IMAGE

In some cases the problem with an image is that its dimensions are too large in full-size mode. For example, many lightbox plugins automatically show the full-size image when you click a thumbnail, but if it's larger than the screen, that's a problem. Using the Image Editor to scale down the dimensions of an image is a great solution.

The Scale Image box at the right side of the Image Editor shows you the dimensions of the original and then has a box for the width and the height where you can enter a new value, as shown in Figure 14-8 A.

You cannot enter different values for width and height because you're scaling the existing relationship. This example has a square original. When you enter a value in one box, the other adjusts proportionally. And that's it; you're ready to click Scale.

FIGURE 14-8

Although it may seem that the scaling function is reducing the dimensions of the original image, WordPress is actually creating a new "full-size" image to be used in place of the original. As you can see in Figure 14-8 B, there's a Restore button after completing the scaling, and it will bring back the original image.

So if your intent is to get rid of an overly large image taking up space on the server, scaling with the Image Editor is not the answer. The original is still there, and you now have a new image on the server as well.

There are plugins that can change the dimensions of the original image, thereby bringing it down in file size as well. Some of these are mentioned at the end of this lesson.

CONTROLLING WORDPRESS IMAGE DIMENSIONS

With the Image Editor, scaling is limited to the full-size version of an image. But suppose you want to change the dimensions of the medium-sized version of an image or the thumbnail version? Although you can't do that for individual image sizes, you can do it for all images on the site.

Under Settings ⇨ Media you can find the sizings for the additional images that WordPress creates when you upload images, as shown in Figure 14-9.

In the case of Thumbnails, for instance, you might want smaller or larger square images throughout your site, or you might want a rectangular look. Adjusting the values for width and height determine the size and shape of the cropping.

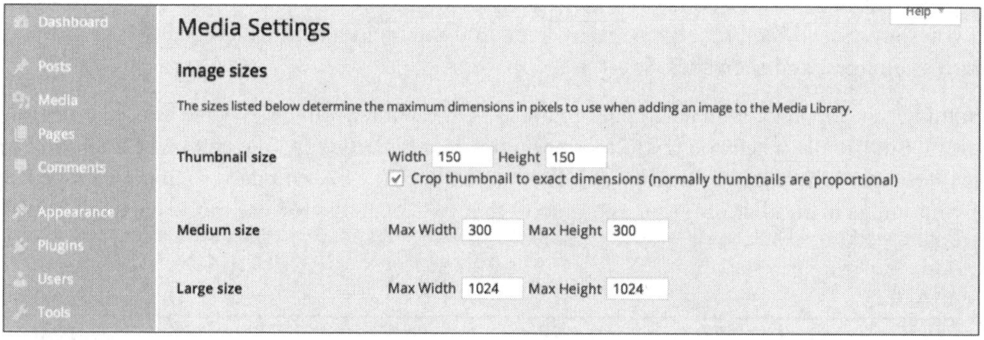

FIGURE 14-9

You can also remove cropping for the Thumbnail size altogether, at which point the numbers function like Medium and Large, and WordPress resizes the entire image by the number of pixels on the longest size. In other words, your thumbnails would no longer be a portion of the image but a small version of the whole image.

> **WARNING** *Changing the image size values in Settings ⇨ Media changes the dimensions of the versions created when you upload an image, but only for uploads going forward. In other words, changes made here do not apply to existing images in the system.*
>
> *To change images you've already uploaded to WordPress, you need a plugin to regenerate the various sizes. A couple of those are listed at the end of the lesson.*

FLIPPING AN IMAGE

You can flip an image either vertically or horizontally. A vertical flip is usually needed only when you've uploaded an image to WordPress and not realized that it was upside down coming out of your camera.

Just click the Flip Vertically button, and you see the change. Before you click Save, though, make sure the Apply Changes To is set to All Image Sizes because, of course, you want them all to be right-side up.

In the case of horizontal flipping, the most common scenario is when an image would look better facing the other direction. For example, you may want the face of a person looking in the direction of your text instead of away from it. It sounds like a little thing, but a visitor's eyes get drawn in a certain direction for many different reasons, and human gaze is a major one.

Again, you simply click the Flip Horizontally icon, and the image will be changed. Make sure it applies to all images, and then click Save.

Keep in mind that flipping an image applies to all sizes of the image, unless you've limited it to the Thumbnail. But usually when you try to mirror an image, it's already in a Post. Maybe you don't want all other versions of the image to be flipped horizontally. In that case, you need to make a flipped version of your image in another program and upload that to WordPress for use in the particular Post.

PLUGINS

Although I'm not aware of any plugins that modify the Image Editor, some create alternative functions or even alternative image editors.

IMAGE ALTERATION

➤ **Post Thumbnail Editor**—With the WordPress image editor, you can crop all image sizes together or just thumbnails; this plugin not only lets you crop individual sizes, but any sizes also created by themes and plugins.

➤ **Imsanity**—If you want to change the actual dimensions of the original image you uploaded, this plugin will do it. Even better, it can be set to reduce those dimensions automatically when you upload images (in case you forget to resize that 4,000 pixel-wide image from your camera).

REGENERATING IMAGES

➤ **Regenerate Thumbnails**—Re-creates all image sizes for a single image or all of them at once.

➤ **Ajax Thumbnail Rebuild**—If you have a lot of images to regenerate, it's possible to run out of time if your server is asked to run them all at one time. This plugin aims to solve that by individually regenerating images.

➤ **Regenerate Thumbnails Reminder**—This one alerts you if an image dimension has been changed in SettingsMedia or if a new image size has been introduced by a theme or a plugin.

IMAGE EDITORS

➤ **Edik**—Basic image manipulation like the WordPress Image Editor, but also has functions such as brightness, saturation, exposure, and some effects.

➤ **NIC Photo Editor**—You could call this a layering editor with the capability to have transparent backgrounds and export PNG images; you combine and arrange different images on separate layers and then export a single image.

➤ **Aviary Editor**—Integrates the online editing program Aviary (now part of Adobe) within the WordPress Media Library.

As said earlier, I don't think anything more than basic image manipulation belongs in WordPress, especially when there are so many good free or inexpensive programs for desktops and mobile devices, not to mention online image applications such as Canva, Sumo Paint, or Aviary.

TRY IT

In this lesson you practice flipping an image that you've already inserted into a Post.

Lesson Requirements

A Post with at least one image inserted.

Step-by-Step

The following steps explain how to horizontally flip an image within a Post:

1. Find a post with an image in it and click Edit.

2. Make sure you're in the Visual mode of the Text Editor.

3. Click the image so that you see the two buttons at the top left and the drag points around the edges.

4. Click the Edit button (the pencil). The Image Details window displays, and on the right, underneath the image, you should see an Edit Original button.

5. Click Edit Original, and the window changes to the Edit Image window.

6. Click the Flip Horizontally icon above the image. The image should now be facing in the opposite direction horizontally.

7. Make sure Apply Changes To on the right says All Image Sizes.

8. Click Save. You should now see that the image in the Post is also flipped horizontally.

9. Update the entire Post.

REFERENCE *Please select the video for Lesson 14 online at* www.wrox.com/go /wp24vids. *You will also be able to download resources for this lesson from the website.*

15

Working with WordPress Image Galleries

You've seen how WordPress makes it easy to upload and insert images into your posts, but what if you have a lot of images for a single Post? It would be nice to just show thumbnails of each picture and then have people click them to see the larger version. WordPress makes that easy, with the Create Gallery function in the Media Uploader window.

To be clear, this is a function built in to WordPress. Don't confuse this type of Gallery with the many photo gallery plugins or photo gallery functions built in to some themes. You don't need any extras to do what you see in this lesson.

CREATING AN IMAGE GALLERY IN A POST

Start by clicking the Add Media button. By default you get the Insert Media screen. Although you'll insert a Gallery, you first need to make one, which is why you need to click the Create Gallery link on the left menu (Figure 15-1 A) or from the drop-down menu in mobile mode (Figure 15-1 B).

FIGURE 15-1

What you see is all the images you have in your Media Library. Other file types are automatically excluded because they can't be used for a Gallery. And, of course, there's a tab for uploading new images.

> **WARNING** *It's best if you make the original of each Gallery image exactly the same size. That way, if you use full-size mode (as discussed this later in the lesson) or if you install a plugin that creates a pop-up lightbox or slideshow from your Gallery, the images will flow better.*
>
> *If you use images of different sizes, choose ones with the same width or close in overall dimensions. That will minimize the amount of visible difference in full-size mode. You can see the dimensions of each image as you click it in the Media Uploader, so that will help with choosing exact or close matches.*

As you click images and they display check marks, those are the images that will be included in your Gallery, as shown in Figure 15-2.

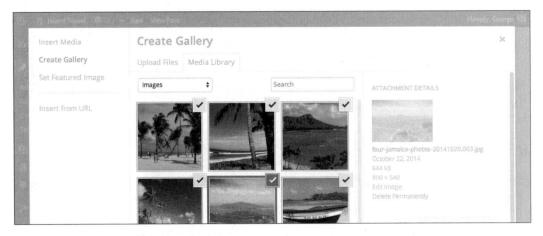

FIGURE 15-2

To remove an image from the Gallery, you have to click the check box. If you click only on the image, the check mark remains.

If you want to delete all items and start again, there's a Clear link below the tiny thumbnails on the Selected list at the bottom of the screen (Figure 15-3).

FIGURE 15-3

These tiny thumbnails can help keep track of what you've chosen because as you scroll through the Media Library, you can't see all the checked images at one time.

However, for mobile users, there are no tiny thumbnails—only the number of images selected and the Clear link. For desktop users, the number of images shown depends on the width of the browser window, and you cannot scroll through the thumbnails to see ones that are hidden.

If you click one of the tiny thumbnails, you can see all its details on the right side.

After you have all your images selected, you can click the Create Gallery button at the bottom right, resulting in the Edit Gallery screen in Figure 15-4.

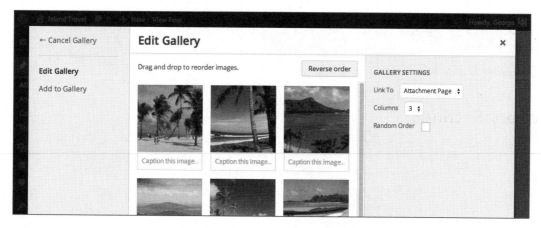

FIGURE 15-4

Here's where you can make all kinds of adjustments to the Gallery before inserting it in your Post. This is also the screen you'd come back to for editing after inserting the Gallery.

Order the images by dragging and dropping them, or simply reverse the current order using the Reverse Order button at the top right. As mentioned earlier, if you use the Random Order check box at the right side in Gallery Settings, any ordering you've done will no longer apply.

You can get rid of images at this stage as well with the tiny X at the top right of an image when you mouseover it (Figure 15-5).

In Figure 15-5 you can also see the Caption This Image box below each image. Clicking in there allows you to add wording that will appear, most commonly, below the image.

> **NOTE** *Be aware that themes display captions in different ways, so it's a good idea to try out a Gallery and preview it before going live. For example, the Twenty Fourteen theme I'm using for Island Travel displays the caption over the top of the image only when you mouseover it.*

FIGURE 15-5

Gallery Settings

When all your images are ready, it's time to check your Gallery Settings on the right (Figure 15-6).

FIGURE 15-6

These provide some control over display of the Gallery, so let me walk you through each of them.

LinkTo

The Link To setting determines where visitors are taken when they click an image in the Gallery. If you choose Attachment Page, the image links to a web page which is determined by your theme—often, this will be the default single post template. What displays depends on the theme template, but typically, this includes the image Title and Description fields.

Choosing Media File displays the full-size version of the image in an empty browser tab or window.

There are plugins for WordPress that will automatically create the nice lightbox pop-ups that have become so popular. Some of these are discussed at the end of this lesson. Often these plugins require that you set the Link To function as Media File, but you need to check with each plugin's documentation.

Your final choice for linking images is to have no link at all. If you use the Gallery in full-size mode (you see how to do that shortly), the None setting could be useful.

Columns

This sets the number of columns across the page—the default is 3. That's quite safe for most sites based on the default thumbnail size of 150 pixels. However, it depends on the thumbnail size and the width of your theme's content area—it's just a matter of experimenting, which is easy because you can switch the column quantity anytime.

Random Order

If you want the order of images in the Gallery to be randomized every time the page is loaded, check this box. Obviously, this overrides any order of images you made by dragging and dropping.

Inserting a Gallery

After you finish with settings, you can click the Insert Gallery button at the lower right of the Media Uploader window. You should now see the Gallery images in the Content Editor, as shown in Figure 15-7.

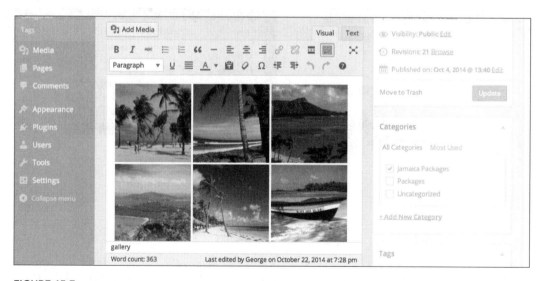

FIGURE 15-7

While it looks like a lot of individual images, you can confirm it's a Gallery by clicking any image. The entire group is enclosed in a gray box with an edit and delete icon at the top left (Figure 15-8).

FIGURE 15-8

You can drag this Gallery around the Content Editor as if it were a single image, although it will always be on its own line. In other words, you can't have text flowing around a Gallery.

Editing an Existing Gallery

Just as you can edit an image that's been inserted into content, you can do the same with a Gallery. Just click the pencil icon that appears at the top right when you click the Gallery in the Content Editor.

You'll get the Edit Gallery screen of the Media Uploader window but with a slightly different menu on the left, as shown in Figure 15-9 A.

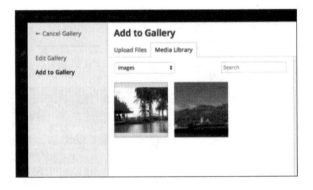

FIGURE 15-9

If you want to add images, just click the Add to Gallery link. A special screen called Add to Gallery (Figure 15-9 B) is displayed, which shows the Media Library and has an Upload Files tab.

If the Media Library looks a bit sparse in Add to Gallery, it's because none of the existing Gallery images are shown—only ones available to add to the Gallery display. You can choose as many as you like; then click the Add to Gallery button.

The new images are added to the end of the existing Gallery images. You can then play with the order as usual. And, of course, add captions, remove images, change the number of columns, and so on. When you finish, click the Update Gallery button.

Remember, even though you updated the Gallery, always click the Update button for the Post or Page.

MORE GALLERY OPTIONS

In Visual mode of the Content Editor, you've seen how a Gallery displays as a series of images, but in Text mode, it's actually just a bit of code—what's called shortcode—as you can see in Figure 15-10.

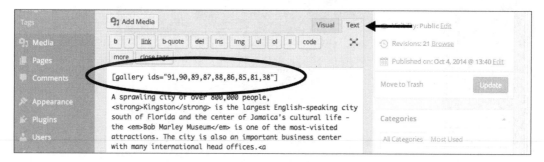

FIGURE 15-10

Using this shortcode, you can customize your Gallery in a number of ways unavailable in the Media Uploader. Now learn about a couple of them here.

Image Size

By default, Galleries display the Thumbnail version of an image, and unfortunately the Media Uploader does not provide a way of choosing a different size. However, by altering the Gallery shortcode in Text Mode, you can tell WordPress to use a different size:

```
[gallery ids="50,24,35,62,42" size="medium"]
```

You must be careful not to change anything else in the shortcode or it could break. If you put your cursor just before the final square bracket and start typing, everything should be fine.

> **NOTE** *If you do happen to break something—no worries. Just delete any remnants of the shortcode using Text Mode. Then it's fast to add the Gallery again from scratch.*

The other setting you need to change is the number of columns the Gallery will use. For Medium size images, you'll probably fit only two columns. It depends on your Settings ⇨ Media settings and your Theme.

Now you could edit your Gallery through the Media Uploader and change the columns, but it can also be done through the shortcode as well:

```
[gallery ids="50,24,35,62,42" size="medium" columns="2"]
```

You can see in Figure 15-11 what the Gallery looks like using this new sizing and just two columns.

FIGURE 15-11

You are seeing this at the front end of the site because the change of size is not reflected in the Content Editor—you'll still see thumbnail images. That's because in the Content Editor you're seeing placeholders for the Gallery, not the finished version.

Notice that the first image in the second row of the Gallery in Figure 15-11 is not quite as tall as the others. That's an example of why, in Galleries that are not using cropped thumbnails, you must make each image exactly the same size.

If your original images are sized according to the width of your theme's content area (usually between 600 and 800 pixels wide), you could use the full setting and only 1 column to produce a nice effect, as shown in Figure 15-12.

In this case, differences in height are not a problem because all the images are wide enough to fill this content area. That won't always be the case, so it's still best to make all images in a gallery the same width at least, and hopefully height as well.

> **NOTE** *The default sizes you can use in the shortcode are thumbnail, medium, large, and full, but if your Theme or plugins have created other image sizes, those can be used in the shortcode (lowercase names only).*

You can find a lot of advice on the Internet about changing the size of thumbnail images in Settings ➪ Media to get larger thumbnails in Galleries. Although this does work (and you have to regenerate all existing thumbnails using a special plugin), remember that it's changing all thumbnails everywhere on the site, and that's likely not what you want. The method used here is on a Gallery by Gallery basis.

FIGURE 15-12

Image Order

In the Gallery screens of the Media Uploader window, you saw how to order images by dragging and dropping them, but you can also order them through the shortcode method using the `orderby=` attribute.

```
[gallery ids="50,24,35,62,42" orderby="title"]
```

In this example, the Gallery would be ordered alphabetically according to the Title of each image. Another option would be to order by the date the image was uploaded:

```
[gallery ids="50,24,35,62,42" orderby="post_date"]
```

Keep in mind that this is just an example. The numbers in the `ids` attribute are random numbers I've picked for illustration. The Media Uploader generates those `ids` for you; I'm simply showing you where to add to the shortcode.

> **NOTE** *You can read all the details about gallery shortcodes in the WordPress Codex at* `http://codex.wordpress.org/Gallery_Shortcode`.

PLUGINS

Here are some plugins related to WordPress Galleries and for creating other types of photo galleries.

ENHANCED WORDPRESS GALLERIES

➤ **Cleaner Gallery**—Cleans up the HTML generated by WordPress Galleries and also enables default settings for all Galleries, including choosing file sizes other than Thumbnail and using Titles automatically as captions. Also integrates with lightbox scripts to create pop-up lightbox effects.

ADD A POP-UP LIGHTBOX EFFECT TO WORDPRESS GALLERIES

➤ **LightBox Plus Colorbox**—Creates a nice pop-up effect showing the full size image and enables you to scroll through all the images in the gallery. Works with individual images and other media files, too.

➤ **Simple Lightbox**—Same functionality as Lightbox Plus Colorbox.

There are many lightbox plugins for WordPress. The preceding two are among the most popular and ones I've worked with. But others will have different styling or different effects, so try out a few.

NON-WORDPRESS GALLERIES

➤ **NextGen** is the granddaddy of gallery plugins. It is for sites that have a lot of images that need heavy organization and ease of management.

There are a lot of basic gallery plugins for WordPress, and many of them were started when the built-in galleries weren't as easy to make. Be sure that a gallery plugin is doing something that WordPress Galleries can't, or there isn't any point in loading down your site with another plugin.

TRY IT

In this lesson, you practice inserting an image Gallery into a Post.

Lesson Requirements

You need a Post with text and at least six images in your Media Library (or available to upload).

Step-by-Step

Here's how to insert a WordPress Gallery into a Post.

1. Find a Post and click Edit.

2. Make sure you're in the Visual mode of the Content Editor.

3. Click Add Media.

4. Click Create Gallery.

5. Choose six images from the Media Library by clicking them (or upload some first).

6. Check the Selected area at the bottom of the screen to see what you have.

7. When you have six images selected, choose Media File from the Link To drop-down.

8. Set the columns to 3.

9. Click Insert Gallery. Thumbnails of your images should now appear in the Content Editor.

10. Click Preview Changes to see what the Post will look like.

11. Click Update.

> **REFERENCE** *Please select the video for Lesson 15 online at* www.wrox.com/go /wp24vids. *You will also be able to download resources for this lesson from the website.*

16

Adding Video and Audio

Changes in WordPress, combined with new HTML5 capabilities, mean that adding video and audio to your website is now as simple as adding images. That's good news because the popularity and importance of video continue to grow. And the potential for audio to enhance your site becomes truly practical. So the question now is not whether you can use video or audio in WordPress, but where to store and serve these sometimes numerous and large files.

VIDEO

This section shows you how to insert video that you host on another server, as well as video you upload to WordPress, and how to decide between each method. You also see how to resize videos to fit a specific location on your site.

Inserting Video Hosted with a Third Party

As a rule of thumb, you don't want to put video files on your (very likely, shared) hosting account. They'll slow down your site and potentially overload your server if you get any kind of traffic to them. So what do you do?

For most of us, the obvious answer is YouTube:

➤   Accounts are free.

➤   You can store and serve hundreds, even thousands, of videos.

➤   Public videos get exposure through the YouTube search engine.

There are other scenarios and other solutions (some are mentioned later) but let's use YouTube as an example so that you can see how simple the process of embedding external video is.

I've created a YouTube account and uploaded a video. (I won't go into details here because it's well-documented online.)

I copied the URL for the video from my browser address bar (Figure 16-1 A). I started a new line in my Content Editor and pasted in the URL (Figure 16-1 B). After updating my Post, I achieved the result in Figure 16-1 C.

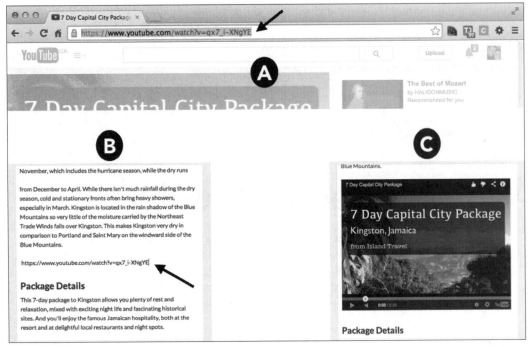

FIGURE 16-1

That's all there is to it. The same will work for videos on Vimeo, Blip, Animoto, and several other sites. You can find the most up-to-date list at `http://codex.wordpress.org/Embeds`.

Be sure to copy the full URL of the video, including the `http://`, or WordPress won't recognize it properly. And again, it must be on a line by itself in the Content Editor.

> **NOTE** *This embedding protocol, known as oEmbed, works for more than just video, as you'll see later in the "Audio" section. But it also works for image sites (such as Instagram) or article sites (such as iSnare), and many other types of content.*

Of course, you can do this with any publicly available video on any sharing site, so the video content you can include on your site is not limited to ones you create yourself.

> **WARNING** *There's always the possibility that a video or other content on a third-party site will be removed or made private at some point in the future. You need to keep an eye out for third-party videos on your site that no longer work. There are plugins that can help with this—see the end of the lesson.*

What about sites that don't support this special embed protocol? Say, for example, you host your videos in a cloud account, such as Amazon S3, which is inexpensive to do. Fortunately, adding such videos to WordPress is almost as straightforward.

Remember the Insert from the URL screen of the Media Uploader? If you paste the URL of a video file into that screen, WordPress can tell you if it's going to work by displaying the video in a player there in the uploader window, as shown in Figure 16-2.

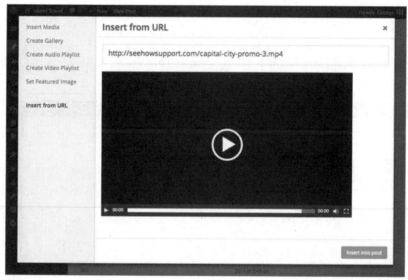

FIGURE 16-2

Then it's just a matter of clicking Insert into Post and the video player will show to your visitors.

> **NOTE** *To ensure a video will work with any browser or operating system, it should be in the mp4 format. And if the video is not your own, make sure you have permission to embed it on your site. Videos on public-sharing sites include that permission.*

Inserting Video Hosted on Your Account

Not every situation or even every video is best suited to using a service such as YouTube or Vimeo or any third party. If the video file is short enough and small enough, it's certainly feasible to upload it to WordPress and run it from your server.

For example, a 30-second introduction for your homepage, if formatted and saved efficiently at the production stage, may be no more than 2 or 3 MB. Many PDFs for download are that big. And a site introduction may not be great YouTube material anyway, because it's so specific in nature, but it is a good candidate for uploading to WordPress.

Inserting videos you've uploaded to WordPress can be done one of two ways:

➤ The first is to get the complete file URL from the Media Library and paste it onto its own line in the Content Editor, just like I did with the YouTube link. Make sure you're in Visual Mode, of course. Like a YouTube video, a player will appear, and visitors can watch your video in the body of the content.

➤ The second way is to use the Add Media button and either upload the video or choose it from the Media Library; then click Insert Into Post. Again, you get a video player in your content.

Although the result appears to be the same, there is an important advantage to adding the video through the Add Media button. You can edit the playing parameters of the video through the Video Details window shown in Figure 16-3.

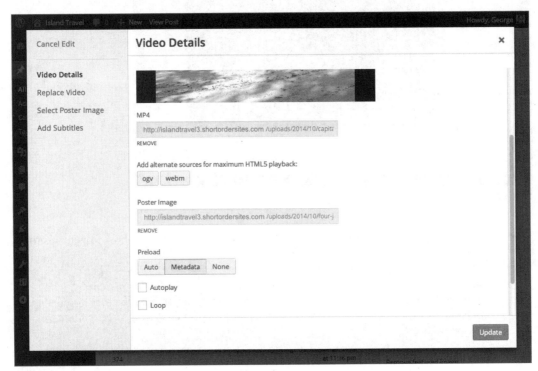

FIGURE 16-3

In a sense you can think of this as the Video Player Details window because the settings control how visitors will see and interact with the file:

➤ Put in a lower resolution video for mobile users.

➤ Remove existing or select a new Poster Image. (This is just another name for the Featured Image, and it changes for all instances of the file, not just this player.)

➤ Choose whether to preload video, featured image, or none.

➤ Choose whether the file should Auto Play.

➤ Choose whether the file should Loop.

➤ Add subtitles, chapters, or other meta data (by uploading a special text file in webvtt format).

You can see now why using the Add Media button for video makes the most sense. It gives you a lot of additional control. If you drop in the URL of an uploaded video, the edit icon just takes you to the Insert URL window, and the only option there is to change the URL.

If you edit the video file through the Media Library, you never get the Video Details window because in that case, the file is not played in a specific Post or Page; you're working with the file itself. What you can do on the Edit Media screen is add a caption and description for use on the file's Attachment Page, and you can also assign the video a Featured Image.

Featured Images for Videos

For video files you upload to WordPress, you can set a Featured Image. It's used in two key ways:

➤ The Featured Image displays in the video player that visitors see (Figure 16-4 A).

➤ In the Media Library Grid view, the Featured Image is shown instead of a generic video icon. (The video filename displays over the top, so it isn't confused with actual image files, as shown in Figure 16-4 B).

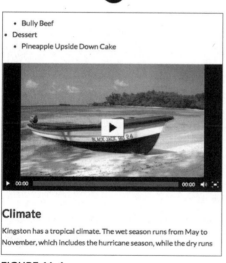

FIGURE 16-4

It also is used in Video Playlists, as you'll see shortly.

You can set a Featured Image only after you've uploaded the video file. Go into the Media Library and edit the video file. At the bottom of Edit Media, you see a Featured Image box, just like for Posts and Pages.

> **NOTE** *If you started running videos from your site and found that it was slowing down your site or causing issues, it's simple enough to load one or more of them to a YouTube account and then replace the insertions in your Post with the URL of the video.*

More Control with Shortcodes

Although it's easy to drop in a YouTube (or other embeddable third-party) URL, what you get is its video player. But what if you didn't want its player to show? WordPress has a shortcode for that:

```
[video src="put third-party video url here" width="200" height="150"]
```

This produces the same video player that's used when you insert a video you've uploaded to WordPress. That means you could style it using CSS, plus you could use a number of shortcode options to control the video.

Now these options are essentially the ones you saw in the Video Details window when I inserted a video from the Media Library. WordPress just takes what you tell it in that window and creates a shortcode with the information.

But one option that's not in Video Details is the size of the video. Using your own shortcode, though, you can specify the width and height of the video player.

```
[video src="put third-party video url here" width="200" height="150"]
```

This sets the maximum size of the video player. In this example, if I put this shortcode in a place with a width less than 200 pixels, the video would just be the width of that place.

> **NOTE** *Although shortcodes can be used by default in Posts and Pages, you need a plugin to use them in other places, such as Widgets. See the end of the lesson for such a plugin.*

Video Playlists

Video Playlists are groups of videos and can be created from the Media Uploader by clicking the Create a Video Playlist link on the left menu. Don't see the link? That means you haven't uploaded any video files to the Media Library.

After you upload some video, creating a playlist is almost exactly like making an Image Gallery: You click the videos you want to show on the list and then click the blue Create a Video Playlist button. Like a Gallery, you're then taken to an Edit screen where you can order the videos, change the titles, or delete files, as shown in Figure 16-5.

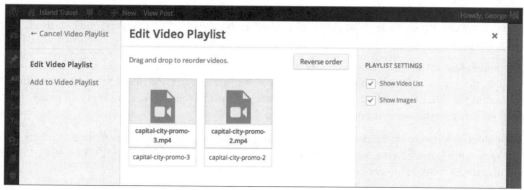

FIGURE 16-5

The big difference is in the settings. There are no columns to choose and no Link To function. Instead, you choose between showing the list of videos, showing an image for each video, or both.

By default, the title displayed in the video list is the filename, but you can change it to whatever you want in the Create or Edit Gallery screens. They look like the caption settings for Image Galleries.

But what are these images that you can show or not show? No explanation is given in this window, but the answer is: the Featured Image for each video. As you saw earlier, this image can be set when you edit a video file in the Media Library.

> **NOTE** *If you're wondering about using third-party videos in Playlists, the answer is no. You cannot put a YouTube or Vimeo video into the Media Library, so it can't be part of a Playlist. However, there are plugins that let you create third-party playlists (see the end of this lesson).*

AUDIO

Audio files are handled in almost exactly the same way as video files. You can drop the URL for an mp3 file directly into the Content Editor, and it will produce an audio player, as shown in Figure 16-6.

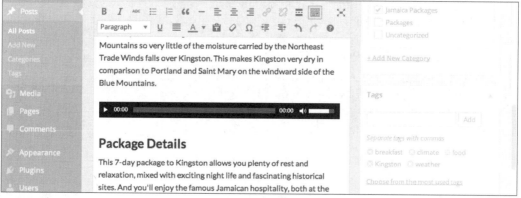

FIGURE 16-6

You can create Audio Playlists (but only if there are any audio files in the Media Library). Auto-embedding from some third-party music and audio sites also works. And you can use Featured Images with audio files.

There are some differences, however. The Featured Image shows up for visitors only on an Audio Playlist, not on an individual player. Typically, the Featured Image for music would be the album cover, but for other types of audio, you could have a photo of the speaker or create an image representative of the content and the topic of the audio.

The colors of buttons on the default audio player (or video player) may get picked up from your theme, so they'll match your site colors automatically. You could do more with CSS styling, or there are plugins to provide fancier player interfaces.

Audio tends to be overshadowed by video these days, but keep in mind that visitors can continue to listen to your audio even if they're doing something else. So, for example, recording a reading of your blog Post and putting the audio player near the top is a great way of engaging your audience.

PLUGINS

While WordPress can handle the basics of players and playlists, you may need more features for video and audio files, and there are plenty of plugins to help with that.

VIDEO PLAYERS

There are a lot of video player plugins in the Plugin Directory, many left over from the days when it wasn't so easy to embed video. These days, you do not need a plugin to play videos in WordPress.

However, some player plugins offer added features, such as easily styling the video player, tracking YouTube stats, or tying into marketing tools. Following are some examples:

➤ **WordPress Video Player**—Also called Spider Video Player, you can easily custom design your player and even watermark the videos.

➤ **Video Analytics for YouTube, Vimeo, and Dailymotion Embeds by VidAnalytic**—The title says it all; see how many people are viewing which videos on your site.

THIRD-PARTY VIDEO PLAYLISTS

You can automate the process of showing videos from third-party sources, like YouTube, using plugins like these. Show the latest from a channel or a search term, show the most popular ones, and so on.

➤ **TubePress**—Work with individual videos, playlists, channels, and search results from YouTube and Vimeo; their website has dozens of examples of shortcodes to use and how they'll look.

➤ **WordPress Video Gallery**—Organize both third-party and your own videos with a huge number of settings; includes widgets to show video lists of most popular, most recent, and so on.

VIDEO LOADING

➤ **Lazy Load for Videos**—By default WordPress does not load its videos until someone starts to play them, but the same is not true of third-party videos, such as YouTube. This plugin replaces those videos with an image and only when someone clicks the image is the video loaded. This helps keep your pages loading quickly.

AUDIO PLAYERS

As mentioned with video, you do not need a plugin to play audio. But there are a lot of audio player plugins sitting around. If you're considering one, make sure it does something useful for you besides playing the audio (and that includes being able to control the styling).

➤ **HTML5 jQuery Audio Player**—Nice out-of-the-box templates for playlists in particular.

➤ **Compact WP Audio Player**—This player is handy if you want to do audio versions of your blog posts and don't want an obtrusive audio player on every page; this plugin uses a tiny Play button that you can easily position; has other player skins, too.

➤ **Blubrry PowerPress Podcasting plugin**—Helps integrate both audio and video podcasts into your WordPress site. One of the most popular of the many podcasting-oriented plugins available.

TRY IT

In this lesson, you practice embedding a video from YouTube.

Lesson Requirements

You need a Post with text and a video from YouTube that you would like to embed (does not have to be one you've uploaded—just relevant to your Post).

Step-by-Step

Here are the steps for embedding a YouTube video in a Post or a Page.

1. Find the Post you want and click Edit.

2. Make sure you're in Visual mode of the Content Editor.

3. Position your cursor where you want the video to appear, and make sure you're on a new line. Press Enter if you're not sure.

4. Go to `YouTube.com` and find a video you'd like to embed.

5. When you're on the page for that video, find the address bar of your browser. (You'll see a URL beginning with `https://www.youtube.com`.)

6. The URL may be highlighted already, but if not, highlight it using Ctl+A, and then copy it (Ctl+C).

7. Back in your Content Editor, paste the URL, making sure there's nothing on the same line as it.

8. Update your Post, and you'll see a video player in the Content Editor. To see how it will look on the site, click Preview Changes or View Post.

> **REFERENCE** *Please select the video for Lesson 16 online at* `www.wrox.com/go/wp24vids`. *You will also be able to download resources for this lesson from the website.*

17

Adding Documents

It's often easier to make information available to visitors in the form of documents rather than trying to re-create the information on a web page. Plus, they have something to "take away" with all your contact information on it as well. So easily uploading and linking to documents is important, and WordPress enables you to do this.

UPLOADING AND INSERTING A DOCUMENT

A common type of document on a website is a press release. I've created a Category for Island Travel press releases and added a Post about a new destination being added to the travel roster, so now I'm going to add the PDF of the press release.

Linking Text to Documents

I begin by placing my cursor where I want the link to appear in my text and then clicking Add Media.

In this case, I'm adding the PDF from my computer, so I use the Upload Files tab of the Media Uploader window. When the upload is complete, my document is highlighted in the Media Library, and the Attachment Details are on the right side, as shown in Figure 17-1.

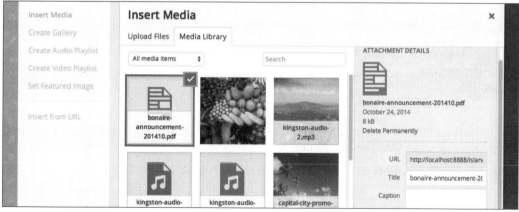

FIGURE 17-1

The key to inserting documents is to remember that WordPress uses the Title as the text linked to the document.

Now by default the Title is the name of the file, but even if you have a good descriptive filename, it still needs to be altered to fit the context of your content. You could, of course, change the link text later in the Content Editor, but it's always a bit faster to do it from here. So in the Title field, put the text you want the visitor to read.

The only other thing to watch for when adding a document from your computer is to be sure the file's URL shows properly in the Link To setting of the Attachment Display Settings, as shown in Figure 17-2:

FIGURE 17-2

Remember, this area of the Media Uploader is often not visible, so be sure to scroll down. If, for some reason, it does not say Media File and show the URL of the document, just drop down the menu and choose Media File.

I'm now ready to click the Insert Into Post button. The link displays in the Content Editor, as shown in Figure 17-3.

FIGURE 17-3

If the wording of the link isn't right, you can, of course, change it in the Content Editor without going back and reinserting the document.

When you finish, remember to Update or Save Draft, or Publish.

> **NOTE** *If you change the wording of a document link, be careful not to erase all the wording or you'll lose the link. But if it does happen, you simply reinsert the document.*

Linking Images to Documents

There may be occasions in which you want people to click an image to download a document. Maybe you have a cool graphic to attract their attention to the download and you want the file to be accessed when they click the graphic.

Normally, when you insert an image, you either link it to itself or to nothing at all. But there is the option in the Media Uploader to link to a Custom URL, as shown in Figure 17-4.

FIGURE 17-4

This is where you would paste the URL of your document after getting it from the file's edit link in Media Library.

> **NOTE** *Sometimes you don't want a document to be publicly accessible. A simple solution in that case is to insert a document and then password-protect the Post or Page.*
>
> *Keep in mind that this method is not entirely secure: anyone who knows the URL of the document could still access it, and unless you use a plugin to hide the page and document from search engines, it could get indexed.*

DOCUMENT FILE TYPES

You can upload all sorts of document files into WordPress, such as PDFs, PowerPoint presentations, Word documents, spreadsheets, and so on, but you should always be guided by the needs of your visitors. They want material to be accessible and safe.

Do visitors have the program to open the file and can their version read the document?

My preference is to always post documents as PDFs if possible, because they're universally accessible (most browsers today include a PDF reader) and visitors are sure to see the exact formatting and layout you created.

WordPress has a wide range of document file types that it enables, including most types of Microsoft Office files, OpenOffice formats, WordPerfect, and the Apple iWork format. If there's a specialized file type that you're having trouble with, there are plugins that enable you to change the allowed types. Some are mentioned at the end of this lesson.

UPDATING A DOCUMENT

In some cases, you'll want to update an existing document that you've inserted into a Post. How you do that depends on whether you need the existing URL of the document to remain the same.

If it isn't important to maintain the original URL, the process of updating is simple: Erase the old link in the Post; then upload and insert the new document as previously done. If you don't need to keep a copy of the old document, you can delete it through the Media Library.

If you linked to the old document elsewhere on your site, here's how to update those links:

1. Place your cursor on the new link you just created.

2. Click the link button on the top button bar of the Content Editor. (It should be highlighted.)

3. Copy the URL from the pop-up box.

4. Wherever there's a link to that document on your site, you can go into the Post, edit the link, and paste in this new URL. Then all the links will reference the new document you uploaded.

If it's important that the URL of the new document be exactly the same as the old file, things are a little more complicated. Usually, you update a document long after the date of the original, which means that even if you uploaded a file of exactly the same name, WordPress would put it in a different folder, thus creating a different URL. So here's what you can do:

1. Make a note of the file's name and location by checking the link in the body of your Post. The exact location depends on what pathways you set up, but by default, WordPress puts all uploaded files into `wp-content/uploads` and typically organizes them by month and year. However, you may have customized that as well.

2. Name the new version of the file exactly the same as the old file.

3. Open your FTP program and log in to your server. Navigate to the location of the new file on your computer (usually the left side of the screen) and to the old file on the server.

4. Highlight the new file and click the Upload button. The new file overwrites the old version. To verify, you can check the date of the file on the server, and it should now say "today" or today's date.

Fortunately, unlike images, WordPress doesn't make different copies of documents, so you have only the one to replace through this FTP method. If you're not comfortable with FTP, there are plugins that can help with this issue. (Some of the plugins are mentioned in the sidebar on plugins.)

In some cases, the answer of old versus new documents is easily solved because you can keep both versions in the Media Library. Even if you remove the link to the old one, its URL would still work if you haven't deleted it from the Media Library.

> **WARNING** *Erasing a link in a Post to a document you no longer want anyone to see does not get rid of the document or the original URL. If the document is still in your Media Library, anyone with the URL can read it. Delete any documents you want to remove from public access.*

PLUGINS

Following are some plugins directly related to documents and document management.

REPLACING FILES

➤ **Enable Media Replace**—If you need to replace an existing document with a new version but not change the original URL, this plugin can do it all for you. Also this does other scenarios of media replacement.

ADDING FILE TYPES

➤ **WP Add Mime Types**—If you deal with document file types that are not on WordPress's allowed list, you can add them to the list using this plugin.

FILE ORGANIZING AND DOWNLOAD TRACKING

➤ **Download Monitor**—Organize and display files and then track how many times they're downloaded.

➤ **WP-Filebase Download Manager**—Another plugin for categorizing your documents and tracking downloads.

➤ **File Away**—Another plugin for categorizing your documents and tracking downloads.

TRY IT

In this lesson, you practice uploading a PDF into a Post.

Lesson Requirements

A Post with text and a PDF file for uploading.

Step-by-Step

Here's how to upload a document into a Post and create a link to it.

1. Find the Post you want and click Edit.

2. Make sure you're in the Visual mode of the Content Editor.

3. Place your cursor where you want the document link to appear.

4. Click the Add Media button.

5. Choose the Upload Files tab.

6. Click Select Files, locate your PDF, and click Open.

7. When the file finishes uploading, you should see it highlighted in the Media Library and its Attachment Details on the right.

8. In the Title field, enter the name of the document. (This will be the text in the link that WordPress creates in your Post).

9. You can fill in Caption and Description if you want.

10. Make sure there is a URL displayed under Link To, and if not, choose Media File from the drop-down.

11. Click Insert into Post. You should see a link in the body of the Post.

12. If you want to change the wording of the link, you can do so.

13. Click Update.

> **REFERENCE** *Please select the video for Lesson 17 online at* www.wrox.com/go /wp24vids. *You will also be able to download resources for this lesson from the website.*

SECTION V
Managing Your Content

18

Managing Posts and Pages

Up until now, you have been working with individual Posts and Pages, but what about managing them on a site-wide basis: finding materials, making large-scale changes, importing content, and so on? That's what this lesson is all about.

On the Island Travel site, for example, I might want to see which Posts are in the Jamaica Packages category, but scrolling through hundreds of items would be time-consuming. Or suppose I want to add a Tag for the name of an airline to every Post that mentions that airline. If dozens and dozens of Posts meet that criterion, to open each one, add the tag, and then update would be a painfully long process. But in this lesson, you learn how to perform tasks like these with a single action.

FINDING POSTS AND PAGES

If your site is new or relatively small, finding Posts isn't too much of a problem. But as you add more content, it can be a hassle to find items, especially 2 years later.

By default, WordPress displays listings of Posts and Pages in reverse chronological order—the newest items first—and it shows you 20 items at a time. Though you can increase the number of items displayed at one time using your Screen Options button at the top right, more efficient strategies exist for finding material than simply scanning long lists.

Finding Posts

The starting point for finding posts is the Posts ⇨ All Posts link on the main admin menu. You already know that this brings up a list of your Posts, but look closely at the top area of the screen, as shown in Figure 18-1. You can see a menu containing all or some of the following: All, Published, Draft, Private, Pending, and Trash. (If there's nothing to show, the menu item won't be there.)

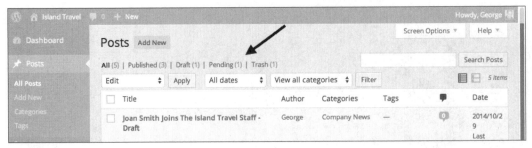

FIGURE 18-1

These menu items are filters for choosing what's displayed on your list of Posts. The numbers in brackets, of course, refer to how many there are of that type. Maybe you want to see only your Drafts or you need a list of what's in your Trash. If the number next to "All" does not equal the total of the others, it's because Trash is not included.

On any list of Posts, you can re-order them by clicking the title of certain columns. The default order is by date, with the newest posts first, but you can sort by Title, Comments, or Date, either ascending or descending.

Often you'll want to find a listing of all Posts in a particular Category. There are two ways to do that:

➤ In the Categories column, if you click the name of a Category, you'll get a list of only the Posts in that Category. You can do the same with Tags.

➤ At the top of the screen is a drop-down to View All Categories, and from it you select the one to view. Click the Filter button when you've made your choice.

You can also restrict your list to Posts from a certain month. That's the drop-down next to Categories. Again, you need to click Filter after choosing a month.

If you know the name or part of the name of a Post, you could use the Search function to find it. It searches only the titles of Posts, not the body or tags and so on. Also, the search is performed on only the Posts you've included through any filtering. So, if you're viewing posts in a particular category, the search is performed only on those posts.

> **NOTE** *If you want to return to your search results after editing one of the posts you found, use your Back button until you get back to the original listings screen. If you click Posts on the side menu, you'll get all posts, and not your search results.*

Just below the Search box are two icons. The one on the left produces the List View that you see by default. The one on the right is Excerpt View, and it displays a short excerpt from each Post, which is helpful if you can't remember what a Post was about. However, mostly I don't use it because the excerpts take up a lot of space, and you end up doing a lot of scrolling.

For mobile users with narrow screens, the listings page is greatly simplified, as you can see in Figure 18-2.

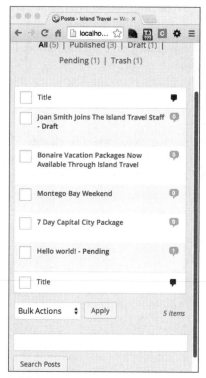

FIGURE 18-2

In addition to the general filters at the top, there is still a search function, but at the bottom of the list.

Finding Pages

Finding Pages is slightly different from Posts because there are no Categories or Tags to choose from, as you can see in Figure 18-3.

FIGURE 18-3

You also don't have the Excerpt View option.

There is still a drop-down date filter, and you can filter pages by their status—Published, Draft, and so on. You can sort the results on the screen by title, author, and date, and you can perform a search for words or phrases.

There are plugins that enable you to customize what information is shown on both the Post and Page listings screens; some are mentioned at the end of the lesson.

USING QUICK EDIT

There's a very powerful feature on Post and Page listing screens that enables you to change parameters—title, author, status, allowing comments, and so on—without going into the actual Post or Page. It's called Quick Edit, but it's only visible when you mouseover a list item, as shown in Figure 18-4.

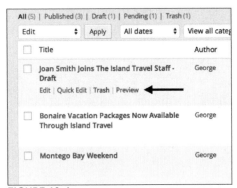

FIGURE 18-4

When you click Quick Edit, it opens up an area within the list item, as shown in Figure 18-5 A (Posts) and Figure 18-5 B (Pages).

There's quite a lot you can change through Quick Edit. Remember to press Update on the right after you make any changes.

For mobile users, Quick Edit has all the functionality available on wider screens, but just stacked vertically, as Figure 18-6 demonstrates.

> **WARNING** *Although you can edit the slug of a Post or a Page, keep in mind that you'll be changing the URL that people may have used to link to you. That means their link will no longer work unless you take additional action to redirect to the new link. Lesson 31, "Optimizing Behind the Scenes," discusses this when covering Permalinks.*

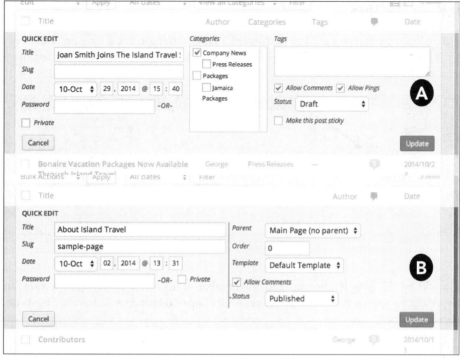

FIGURE 18-5

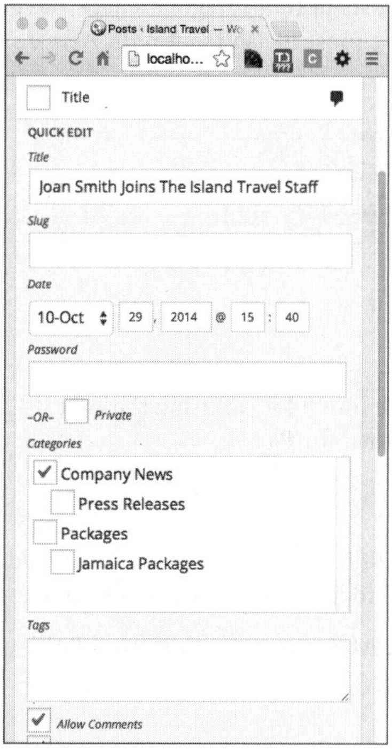

FIGURE 18-6

USING BULK ACTIONS

There will be many times when you need to perform the same action on a few or even dozens of Posts or Pages. That's when Bulk Actions comes in handy. It's the drop-down at the top left of listings' screens, as shown in Figure 18-7.

FIGURE 18-7

Bulk Actions works by checking the box next to any number of list items, choosing an action, and clicking Apply. And this applies to mobile devices as well. The two choices you have for Posts and Pages are Trash and Edit.

Move to Trash

If you have to clear out a lot of items at one time, this is handy. Suppose Island Travel stopped offering any packages to a particular country. I could filter all Posts in that category, check the box next to Title, and all of them would be selected. Then I can just choose Trash from Bulk Actions and click Apply.

> **NOTE** *Remember, items you Trash are still sitting in WordPress and can be restored within 30 days before being automatically deleted.*

Edit

The advantages of the Quick Edit feature are available in a more limited form using the Edit function of Bulk Actions. Here's how that works for Posts and then for Pages.

Bulk-Editing Posts

Suppose you create a new Category under Packages for the city of Kingston and you want to add all relevant Posts to that Category. With Bulk Edit you do not need to leave the Post listings screen.

Check the box next to each Post you want in the new Category. After choosing Edit from Bulk Actions and clicking Apply, you see the screen in Figure 18-8.

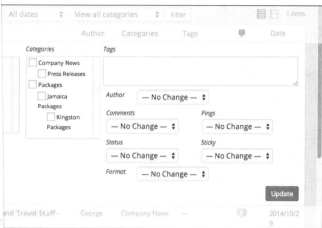

...rea is a list of all the Posts you checked. Beside each is a ...ves the Post from the edit, so there's still time to change

...gston Packages under Categories, click Update, and you're done. ...ow be in the new Category. Keep in mind that for the Categories and Tags, you can add them only to Posts using Bulk Actions; there is no bulk removal.

Following are the Bulk Edit functions you can simultaneously perform on a group of Posts:

➤ Assign to one or more categories

➤ Add one or more tags

➤ Change the author

➤ Allow or disallow comments

➤ Change the publishing status

➤ Allow or disallow pings

➤ Stick or unstick

➤ Change the Post Format

> **NOTE** *The functions you can perform by editing through Bulk Actions may be different depending on your plugins and theme. These can also affect the possible actions available in the Bulk Actions drop-down.*

Bulk-Editing Pages

The Bulk Edit feature on the Pages screen is more limited than the one for Posts, as you can see in Figure 18-9.

FIGURE 18-9

Following are the possible parameters you can bulk edit for Pages:

➤ Change the author

➤ Assign a parent page

➤ Assign a page template

➤ Allow or disallow comments

➤ Change the publishing status

If you wanted a section of your site to have a different look, you can also assign the Pages of that section to a specific page template you create. Lesson 1, "Thinking Like WordPress," discusses having thousands of web pages use a different header. Bulk Edit, along with a customized page template, is the means for making such a large change fairly simple.

IMPORTING CONTENT FROM ANOTHER SITE

It may be that you've been running a blog on a popular blogging platform such as WordPress.com (the hosted version of WP), Blogger, Typepad, and others. Even if it's just a dozen or so posts, that's a lot of material to be copying and pasting to your new WordPress site.

Fortunately, WordPress has a powerful set of import tools, which you can find under Tools ⇨ Import on your admin menu, as shown in Figure 18-10.

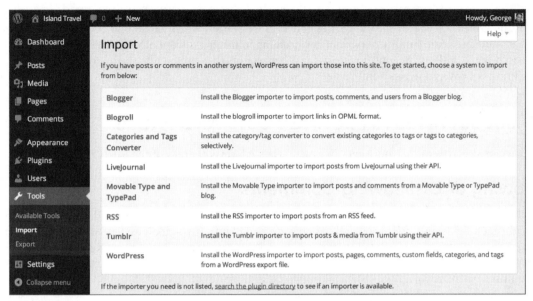

FIGURE 18-10

Following is the full list of current tools:

➤ Blogger

➤ Blogrolls (sets of links from other sites)

➤ Categories and Tags Converter (for within your own site, which Lesson 20, "Managing Post Categories and Tags," discusses)

➤ LiveJournal

➤ Movable Type and TypePad

➤ RSS

➤ Tumblr

➤ WordPress (other self-hosted installations of WordPress or from `WordPress.com`)

When you click any of these, you're asked to install a plugin, which is easy—just click the Install button.

At that point, you'll have a set of instructions, which includes details of how to prepare your content on the old site or blog for importing. For example, on `WordPress.com` blogs, there's an Export button that produces a text file that you save to your computer.

The Import function on your new WordPress site prompts you to find whatever file was created by the export process on the old site and upload it. At that point, you'll be asked some questions about how you want to import the data; for example, do you want the authors created if they don't exist already or do you want to map an author to an existing author?

I won't go into the details of each of these import functions—they all run roughly the same way as just described, except for the Categories and Tags Converter, which Lesson 20 covers. The point is that you have a fair number of options for bringing in materials from other sources. You can also search the WordPress plugins directory for other plugins that can handle the import process for sources not covered in this admin screen.

ADMIN SETTINGS AFFECTING POSTS AND PAGES

You can also affect Posts and Pages in general through several areas of the Settings menu.

Allowing or Disallowing Comments

This setting was mentioned in Lesson 5, but it's worth repeating here because it directly affects Posts and Pages. By default, WordPress allows comments on both. If you look under Settings ⇨ Discussion near the top, you see a check box that says Allow People to Post Comments on New Articles (Articles is just another way of saying Posts and Pages). This check box is active by default, but you can turn it off any time.

> **NOTE** *Be aware that a change to the site-wide comments setting takes effect only from the moment you do it. If it's 3 months into your site and you disallow comments, it will apply only to Posts or Pages from that time forward.*

There's a reminder with this setting telling you that, no matter what you do here, comments can be controlled on an individual basis for each Post or Page. In other words, if they're turned off for the site as a whole, you can turn them on for individual Posts or Pages and vice versa.

Some themes have options enabling you to control comments separately for Posts and Pages. There are also plugins that offer this more fine-grained control, as mentioned at the end of the lesson.

> **NOTE** *My rule of thumb for this setting is: If your primary form of content is meant to generate a response from visitors, keep comments turned on.*
>
> *If your primary form of content is more informational, such as a traditional site where you don't want people commenting on the 15 types of tax service you provide, turn off comments globally and turn them on individually only when you need them.*

Assigning Your Home and Blog Pages

By default, the homepage or front page in WordPress consists of the 10 most recent posts from all categories. However, you can change that on the Settings ⇨ Reading screen, which is shown in Figure 18-11 A.

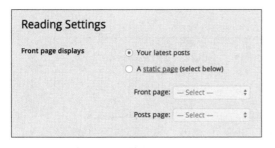

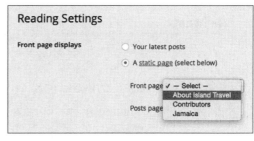

FIGURE 18-11

You can see the default setting for the front page is Your Latest Posts. The other choice is to make one of your WordPress Pages the site's homepage, by clicking A Static Page and choosing from the drop-down menu next to Front Page (as shown in Figure 18-11 B).

Although it's clear enough what choice you're making for Front Page, it may not be obvious what the second drop-down—Posts Page—is for. If you think about it, when you choose one of your Pages to replace the default homepage structure, there's no longer a place for people to find all your latest blog posts in one location. That's what the Posts Page drop-down is for. It takes the Page you choose from the menu and replaces it with your most current blog entries.

> **NOTE** *If you have existing content on the static page you choose as your Posts Page, be aware that WordPress will no longer display that content—it shows only blog posts. You need to create a new page with whatever title suits it best—Our Blog, Blog Posts, Company News, or whatever—and leave the Content Editor blank; then publish the Page. Now, when you choose that page from the Posts Page drop-down menu, no content is going to be hidden.*

Other Admin Settings for Posts and Pages

On the Settings ➪ Writing screen, you can change the following:

➤ Default Post Category.

➤ Default Post Format. If your theme supports these, a list of available formats display here, and you can choose which one will automatically be used for new Posts. Of course, you can still change the format for any individual Post.

On the Settings ➪ Reading screen, you can change the following:

➤ Blog Pages Show at Most. The default is 10 posts. Keep in mind that this setting affects not only the homepage (if it shows Posts) or the Posts Page if you've set that, but also any listing of Posts showing anywhere.

PLUGINS

A lot of plugins relate to managing Posts and Pages; following are a few:

POST AND PAGE LISTINGS

➤ **Admin Columns**—Gives you wide-ranging control over what displays in columns of any admin listing screens, not just Posts or Pages. You could show what page template is used, when an item is on a menu, how many words are used, and much more.

➤ **CMS Tree Page View**—Works on Pages and Custom Post Types but not Posts. Creates a tree-view structure and enables actions such as adding multiple pages at one time, ordering pages as you want them to appear in lists, and more.

➤ **Advanced Page Manager**—Powerful Page management enabling you to view Pages according to your own hierarchy, whether your Page is visible on the site, and more.

➤ **Color My Posts**—On the Posts listing page, this colors the background depending on various criteria, such as format, status, and so forth.

BULK ACTIONS

➤ **WP Ultimate CSV Importer Plugin**—Import any CSV file to create thousands of Posts or Pages at a time; uses mapping to let you connect your csv fields to the fields in the WordPress database.

➤ **Bulk Delete**—Bypass the Trash and permanently delete Posts or Pages based on numerous conditions, such as their status, how old they are, and more.

➤ **Convert Post Types**—A bulk conversion tool for changing post types, such as changing Posts to Pages; can work by category and other criteria.

➤ **Page Comments**—Keeps comments for Posts but turns them off for Pages. (You can still turn on comments for an individual Page.)

INDIVIDUAL ACTIONS

➤ **Post Duplicator**—Makes a copy of a Post or a Page, including elements such as categories and custom fields. Does not duplicate comments.

➤ **Post Expirator**—Allows Posts and Pages to expire automatically; can be handy for pages that you set up for special occasions, for example.

TRY IT

In this lesson, you practice changing the status of a number of Posts.

Lesson Requirements

You need at least four or five Posts.

Step-by-Step

To change the status of a number of Posts, follow these steps:

1. Go to Posts ⇨ All Posts.

2. Choose four Posts and check the box next to the title of each.

3. Drop down the Bulk Actions menu at the top or bottom of the screen, and choose Edit.

4. Click Apply.

5. In the menu of Posts with circled Xs beside them, remove one of the Posts.

6. On the Status drop-down on the right, choose Draft.

7. Click Update. All the selected Posts should now show Draft next to their titles.

8. Now check the box next to each draft Post, and go through the process of switching them all to Published.

REFERENCE *Please select the video for Lesson 18 online at* www.wrox.com/go /wp24vids. *You will also be able to download resources for this lesson from the website.*

19

Managing Media Files

You learned earlier that all media files you upload to WordPress are listed in the Media Library. This lesson shows you how to work with the library, both sorting and finding media files, as well as editing and deleting them. You also learn about some administrative settings for media files.

THE TWO FACES OF THE MEDIA LIBRARY

You've been introduced to the Media Library while uploading and inserting media files in Posts. A version of it appears in the Media Uploader window as a grid of images and icons, as shown in Figure 19-1.

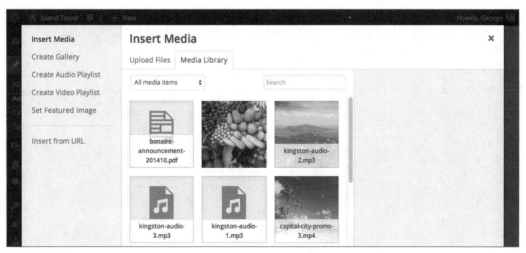

FIGURE 19-1

This same grid view can be accessed from the Media ➪ Library link of the main admin menu. You may need to click the grid view icon (highlighted in Figure 19-2) to access it.

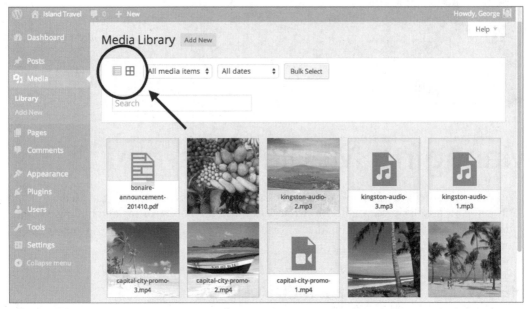

FIGURE 19-2

The Media Library screen offers two different views. Grid view is the first and the second is a list view similar to Post and Page listings, as shown in Figure 19-3.

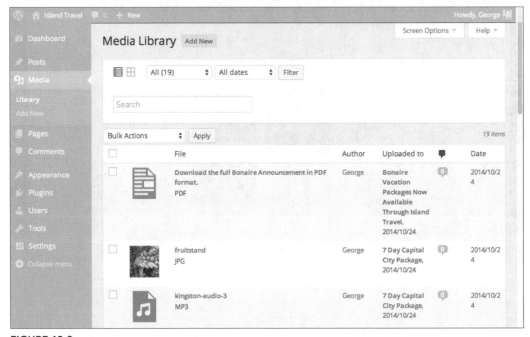

FIGURE 19-3

WordPress remembers the last view you chose and displays it the next time you click Media ➪ Library. So if you prefer one over the other, you need to choose it only once and you'll see it automatically until you switch to the other.

What are the advantages of each view?

In grid view you see more files at one time, and it works with a continuous scroll, so you never need to set the number of files to be shown on a page. Another big advantage of grid view is that it pops up a window showing the details of the file you selected, as shown in Figure 19-4.

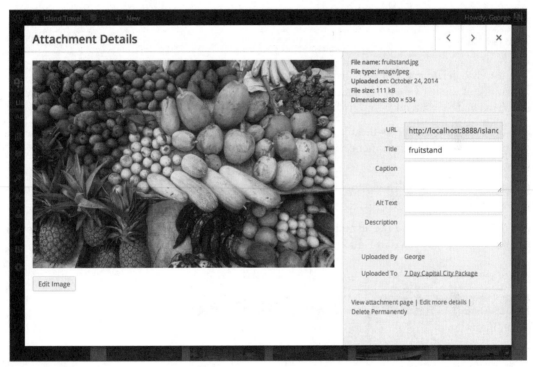

FIGURE 19-4

In this Attachment Details window, you can use the arrow buttons at the top right to quickly go to the details of the next or previous file in the library. You don't need to go back to the Media Library and click the next file to edit it.

One advantage of list view is that you can see some details about every file on the screen. (And the number of files shown can be adjusted through Screen Options.) In particular, you see immediately which Post a file may have been uploaded to or attached to, and you can click through to that Post as well, as shown in Figure 19-5 (Arrow 1).

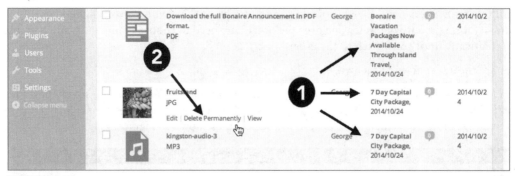

FIGURE 19-5

You can also delete items directly from the list view (Arrow 2), which brings us to another advantage of the list view: bulk actions. Like Posts and Pages, you can check a box next to each item in the list and then perform an action on them.

The only action available by default is deleting the selected files. However, many plugins make use of bulk actions to perform functions on large numbers of files at one time, which are discussed at the end of this lesson.

One other advantage of list view is that you can sort the list by each of the columns: File name, Author, Uploaded To, and Date.

For mobile users, some of the advantages of list view are lost because you don't have all the columns of desktop view, as shown in Figure 19-6 A.

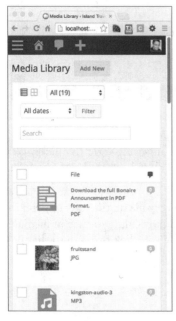

FIGURE 19-6

Grid view in mobile mode (Figure 19-6 B) still shows a lot of files at one time (even if they're a bit smaller) and retains its continuous scroll. Overall it's probably better suited to the touch-screen environment.

Whichever view you prefer to use for most of your Media Library work, they both enable you to filter and search the library the same way.

FILTERING AND SEARCHING THE MEDIA LIBRARY

At the top of both the grid view and list view is an area for filtering and searching the Media Library, which differ slightly, as shown in Figure 19-7.

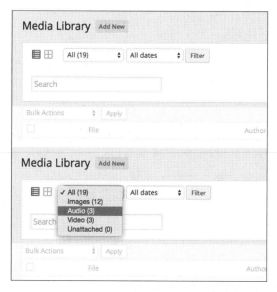

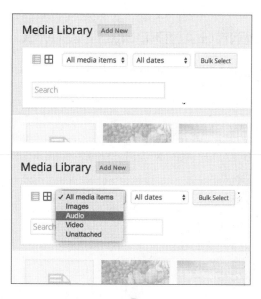

FIGURE 19-7

In grid view (Figure 19-7 B) there's a Bulk Select button because there is no check box system for selecting multiple items. Instead of a Filter button, you simply use drop-down menus to filter results.

In list view you're shown the total number of files for a particular media type.

The default mode for the Media Library screen shows all media types, but you can filter the results using the drop-down menu at the top. You may have noticed in the example that although I have a PDF in the library, there is no filtering choice for PDFs or documents in general.

The search function of the Media Library operates only on the titles of files and only on the file types you're currently displaying. You would need to add a plugin to search through captions or other details, as mentioned at the end of the lesson.

One of the advantages of list view is that you can sort results alphabetically according to their title, which can help narrow your search for a file even if you've filtered results. Keep in mind that even though it looks as if the File column is sorting by filename, that's only because WordPress automatically uses the filename for the title unless you give it your own title.

> **NOTE** *Remember that in list view, when you've made a choice with the drop-down menus, you still need to click the Filter button or nothing will happen.*
>
> *And if you expect to see a particular file or set of files and you don't, check to see that you haven't excluded their file type through filtering.*

EDITING AND DELETING MEDIA FILES

To edit a file in list view of the Media Library, just click its name. Or when you mouseover the row for that media file, a text menu appears enabling you to Edit, Delete, or View the file. In grid view, you simply click the thumbnail or icon of the file.

You saw earlier that clicking a file in grid view brings up the Attachment Details window. For list view, however, clicking the name or the Edit link takes you to the Edit Media screen — the screen for images as shown in Figure 19-8 — where you see the file and the options to edit its details.

FIGURE 19-8

What you can do on this screen varies depending on the file type, but just as you can see in the image here, you could play a video or audio file.

> **NOTE** *Changes made in the Media Library to elements, such as captions or titles, do not change what you may have entered during the insertion of that file into particular Posts or Pages.*

Clicking the Edit Image button brings up the Image Editor window you looked at in detail in Lesson 14, "Using the WordPress Image Editor." There, you can crop, rotate, and resize the actual image or just its thumbnail.

In mobile mode, these edit screens and Attachment Details windows work quite nicely, arranged vertically, of course, but editing images on a smartphone remains awkward at best.

As you saw earlier, if you need to delete a media file in list view of the Media Library, simply mouseover the title of the file, and click Delete Permanently from the menu that appears. If you need to delete large numbers of files, check the box on the left of the relevant files, choose Delete from the Bulk Actions drop-down at the top or bottom of the screen, and click Apply.

With grid view you need to click the file and do the deletion from the Attachment Details window. However, if you use the Bulk Select function, you can delete one or more files directly from the screen.

> **WARNING** *If you delete a media file that's been inserted into posts, the links remain in place and show on the website as broken. You need to go into each Post and eliminate the code that's trying to find the deleted file. All that means is finding the empty box in the Visual Content Editor and clicking it; you see the familiar X icon for deleting.*
>
> *For images displaying in a Gallery, deleting them from the Media Library does not leave a broken link; the image simply won't display next time the visitor loads the page.*

ADMIN SETTINGS FOR MEDIA

You can change some site-wide media file parameters under the Settings ➪ Media link on the admin menu. The screen for that page is shown in Figure 19-9.

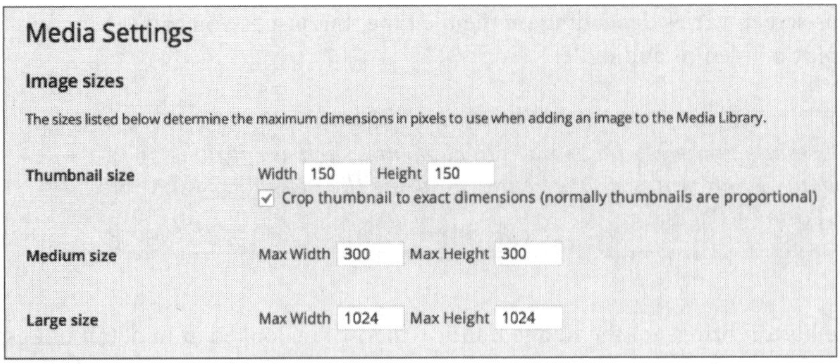

Media Settings

Image sizes

The sizes listed below determine the maximum dimensions in pixels to use when adding an image to the Media Library.

Thumbnail size   Width 150   Height 150
                       ☑ Crop thumbnail to exact dimensions (normally thumbnails are proportional)

Medium size   Max Width 300   Max Height 300

Large size   Max Width 1024   Max Height 1024

FIGURE 19-9

The Image Sizes settings control the dimensions that WordPress uses when it creates as many as three different versions of images you're uploading: Thumbnail, Medium, and Large. These additional versions are created only if the longest side of the uploaded file is larger than the maximum dimensions set on this page.

For example, if the maximum width or height for Medium is 300 pixels (the default WordPress setting) and the image uploaded is 400 pixels wide by 270 pixels high, no Large version would be created, only a Thumbnail and a Medium.

For Medium and Large versions, WordPress keeps the proportions of the original and makes the longest side whatever is set as the maximum width or height. For Thumbnails, you have a choice. With the default it is to hard crop the image, taking a 150 by 150 pixel portion from the middle of the image. If you uncheck the box, it would create a thumbnail that's 150 pixels on the longest side.

For most people, these settings are fine; though with wider content areas these days, you may bump up the Medium setting (the one most typically used when inserting images into Posts). Of course, it all depends on how much space your theme gives to the main content area.

Keep in mind that themes and plugins often create their own image sizes to be used for specific purposes. For example, an e-commerce plugin may have an image size for displaying the catalogue and another for viewing individual products. Sometimes, you may be given control over these sizes and whether they hard-crop an image. But rarely are you given control over what portion of the image is hard-cropped. For that you need a plugin, as mentioned next.

> **WARNING** *Changing any Image Size settings affects only images uploaded after the change is made. If you make the change on a new site before any images are uploaded, there's no issue, but if you've already uploaded some images, you need to regenerate the versions created by WordPress. And for that you need a plugin, as mentioned here.*

PLUGINS

A number of plugins dealing with images in general have been covered, so the following focuses on the Media Library and related functions.

MEDIA LIBRARY ENHANCEMENTS

➤ **Media Library Assistant**—Creates an alternative Media Library screen, same in styling as list view, but with more information shown. Enhanced search capabilities. Also works with the WordPress Gallery shortcode to give it expanded capabilities.

➤ **Admin Columns**—The Media Library is just one of the listings screens you can manage with this powerful plugin. For example, I like to display image dimensions and file size in list view.

➤ **Media Search Enhanced**—Broadens the fields through which the Media Library search function searches, including caption, alternative text, description, and more.

➤ **Image Cleanup**—We all accumulate images in the Media Library that we're no longer using—here's the answer. Many options for selecting possibly candidates for cleanup, but you can edit the list before deletion occurs.

REGENERATING AND EDITING THUMBNAILS

➤ **Post Thumbnail Editor**—This plugin enables you to change the cropping of any image size, including those created by themes and plugins. Creates a link in the menu of each image in the Media Library's list view.

➤ **Regenerate Thumbnails**—Re-creates all image sizes for a single image or all of them at once. Creates a new Bulk Action in the Media Library, and in list view there's a direct regeneration link for each image.

TRY IT

In this lesson, you practice uploading an image to the Media Library, placing it in a Gallery, and then deleting it from the Media Library.

Lesson Requirements

An image you don't need and an existing image Gallery in a Post.

Step-by-Step

How to upload a media file, insert it in an image Gallery, and then delete it.

1. Click Media ⇨ Add New on the main admin menu.

2. Select an image from your computer and upload.

3. Edit the image and give it a title you'll remember.

4. Click Update.

5. Find the Post with the image Gallery where you'll place the new image, and edit that Post.

6. Click the edit icon for the Gallery.

7. Click Add to Gallery and locate the image you just uploaded.

8. Select the image and click Add to Gallery. You should see the image in the Gallery list, so click Update Gallery. Check that the image shows in the Gallery box of the Content Editor.

9. Click Update.

10. Preview the Post and you'll see the new image among the thumbnails.

11. Click Media ⇨ Library.

12. Switch to list view and locate the new image.

13. Mouseover the row with the image, and click Delete Permanently on the text menu that appears.

14. Confirm the deletion by clicking OK in the pop-up window.

15. On the live site, refresh the Post, and the image will be gone from the image Gallery.

> **REFERENCE** *Please select the video for Lesson 19 online at* `www.wrox.com/go/wp24vids`*. You will also be able to download resources for this lesson from the website.*

20

Managing Post Categories and Tags

As your website grows and evolves, you may need to add a group of new sub-Categories, or you may decide that a particular Tag should be changed into a Category. This lesson shows you how to manage all aspects of your Categories and Tags.

MANAGING CATEGORIES

Lesson 6, "Adding a New Post: An Overview," covers how to add a new Category from the Add New Post Screen (or the Edit Post screen). You also saw in Lesson 18, "Managing Posts and Pages," how to add and remove Categories for a Post through Quick Edit and how to add a Category to multiple Posts at one time with Bulk Edit. Now it's time to look at managing the Categories.

You access the Categories admin screen, as shown in Figure 20-1, by way of the Posts ⇨ Categories link on the main admin menu.

The left side of the screen is for adding new Categories, and the right is for editing or deleting existing Categories.

In smartphone and smaller tablet formats, the existing Categories list displays first with the Add New Category section below it. To save room, the existing list does not display Category descriptions. There is no jump link to take you to Add New Category, so if you have a lot of existing Categories, you need to do a bit of scrolling.

The only disadvantage on this size of screen is that the search function is at the bottom of the page rather than at the top near the list of existing Categories.

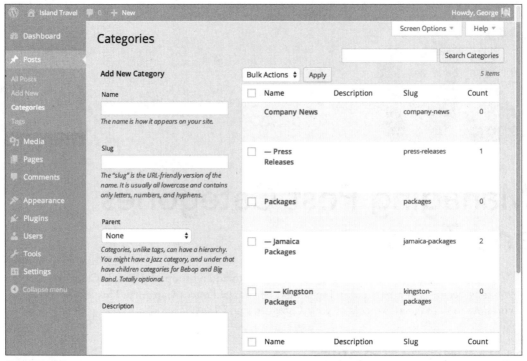

FIGURE 20-1

Adding a New Category

You can enter four parameters for a new Category:

➤ Name

➤ Slug

➤ Parent

➤ Description

The Slug is the wording used in the URL for the Category, but **you rarely need to enter anything in here.** WordPress automatically creates a Slug using the Name you give to the Category.

Normally, a WordPress URL for a category would be something such as `http://www.yourdomain.com/?cat=4`, but if you have friendly URLs turned on using the Permalinks settings (see Lesson 25, "Connecting by E-mail"), it might look like `http://www.yourdomain.com/category/jamaica-packages`. The `jamaica-packages` part is the Category Slug.

In some situations you might want a long Name but keep the Slug short. In that case make sure your Slug is all in lowercase and uses a hyphen instead of spaces between words.

> **WARNING** *If you've had your site public for even a short time, it's not good to mess with existing Slugs. If someone has linked to your Category with a friendly URL and you change the Slug, the link will be broken.*

Choosing a Parent for your new Category is just another way of saying that it will be a sub-Category of the Parent. The drop-down menu shows all Categories hierarchically. The Parent does not need to be a top-level Category; it can be a sub-Category of another Category.

The Description might be used by a theme at the beginning of a Category page, for example, or you could customize your theme to make use of it. However, it can also be useful when you have several people working on a site and you need to make clear what belongs in a particular Category.

When you finish entering information for your new Category, remember to click Add New Category at the bottom left of the screen.

Editing or Deleting Categories

On the right side of the screen, you see a list of all your Categories, by default, in alphabetical order. The four columns displayed are Name, Description, Slug, and Count (the number of Posts in the Category).

If you have a lot of categories, remember that under Screen Options at the top, you can change how many display at one time. (The default is 20.) If you have sub-Categories, they display with a dash beside them and in alphabetical order underneath their parent category. If you have sub-sub-Categories, each level is represented with an additional dash.

You can reorder the list of Categories by clicking the title of a column; clicking a second time toggles between ascending and descending order.

Finding Categories is also aided by a search function at the top right.

Like other admin listings screens, an options menu appears below the name of a Category by mousing over its row. The four options are Edit, Quick Edit, Delete, and View. The Quick Edit feature enables you to change the name and the Slug in the list.

If you don't see the Delete option for a Category, that's because it's the Default Category.

Clicking the View link shows you a Category page on the front end of the site, displaying its Posts in whatever way your theme has chosen to display them.

If you click Edit or the title of the Category, a new screen displays, as shown in Figure 20-2.

This is where you can change not only the name and the slug, but also the description and, most important, the parent.

Think of changing the parent as a kind of moving process, whether it's to a new sub-Category of the parent, to a new parent, or to the top-level categories.

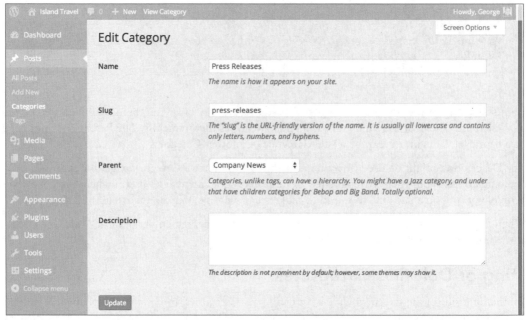

FIGURE 20-2

The final option for managing Categories is to delete them. Don't worry about the Posts, however. You're deleting only the Category and not the Posts that belong to it.

However, for Posts that belong only to the Category you're deleting, WordPress automatically assigns them to the default Category. If you don't want that to happen, then before deleting go through the Posts in the Category and assign them to the Categories you want; then proceed with deletion.

NOTE *Sometimes, a theme may ask you for the ID of a Category (or Page or Post). That information does not display in the categories listing (though there are plugins to do this), but you can still find it by mousing over the title of the category and looking on the status bar of your browser. You'll see something like this:* `http://www.yourdomain.com/wp-admin/categories.php?action=edit&cat_ID=5.`

That number at the end is the ID. You can find the ID for Posts and Pages the same way, though they won't necessarily be at the end of the URL.

Managing the Default Category

Lesson 6 mentions that posts must be in at least one category and that WordPress comes with one category that can never be erased—if you forget to assign a category to a post, WordPress automatically assigns it to this default category. Though you can never eliminate this category, you can change its name from the default Uncategorized to whatever you like.

After you add at least one additional category, you can also change the category used by WordPress as the default when you forget to categorize a Post. You do this under Settings ⇨ Writing, where you see a drop-down menu for Default Post Category.

MANAGING TAGS

Tags are managed in almost exactly the same way as Categories via the Posts ⇨ Tags link on the main admin menu, as shown in Figure 20-3.

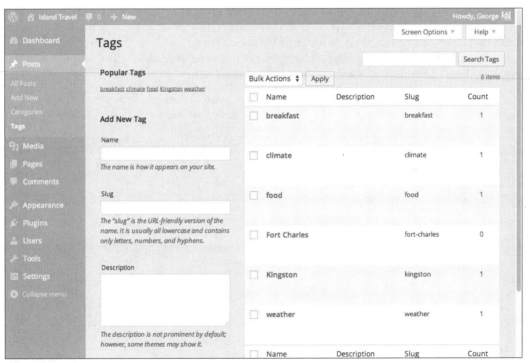

FIGURE 20-3

The only difference between the two is that Tags can't be hierarchical—no parent-child structure—so you don't have a Parent drop-down menu here.

You also see what's called a Tag cloud at the top left. It shows the most popular Tags on your site, using size to represent the level of popularity. You can display this same Tag cloud on your site using a Widget that comes with WordPress.

Another important difference between Tags and Categories is what happens when you delete Tags. Posts do not need at least one Tag, so when you delete a Tag from this screen, it simply disappears from any Posts that used it; Posts for which that was the only Tag will not be assigned some default Tag.

> **NOTE** *If you delete a Tag from a particular post, and that was the only Post to which the Tag had been assigned, the Tag remains in the system. You can see it in Post Tags, and it appears if you start to enter the first few letters in the Add Tag window of a Post.*

CONVERTING CATEGORIES AND TAGS

Categories and Tags aren't different in their function except that Categories are usually general in nature whereas Tags are specific. You may find at some point that a Category is too specific and you prefer that it is a Tag or vice versa. WordPress has a Categories and Tags Converter, which you can access from the list of options shown under Tools ⇨ Import or from either the Category or Post Tags screens—there's a text link to the converter at the bottom right.

The converter is actually a plugin, so the first time you try to use it, you'll be asked to install the plugin, which takes only a couple clicks. When that's done, you see the screen shown in Figure 20-4.

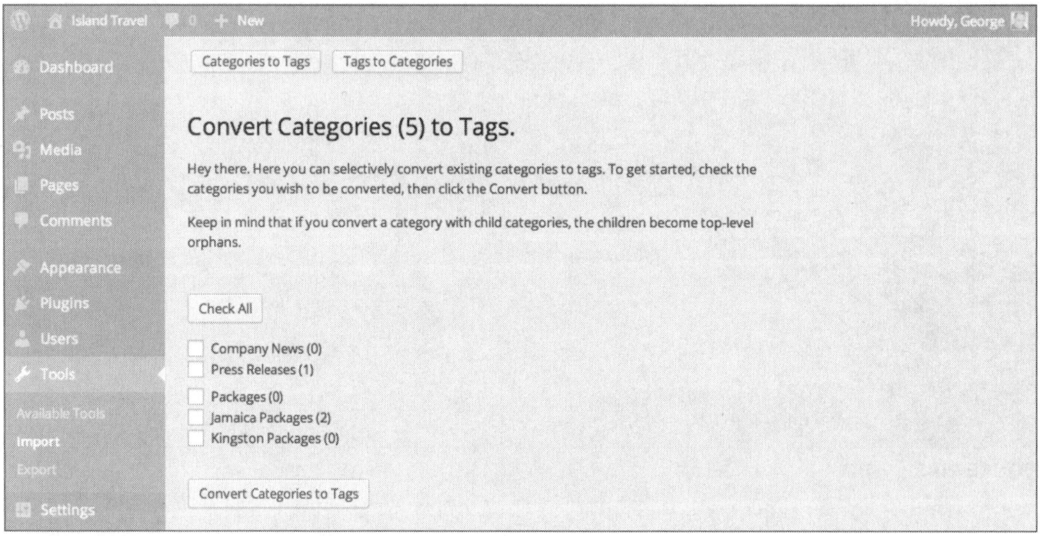

FIGURE 20-4

Simply select the Categories that you want to convert and click Convert Categories to Tags.

WordPress reminds you that if you convert a Category that has children, those sub-Categories will become individual top-level Categories. So, if you were relying on hierarchy to include a Post under several Categories, you need to rethink your Category structure or assign the relevant Posts to the additional Categories you need.

To change Tags into Categories, you need to click Tags to Categories at the top of the screen. This displays a list of all existing Tags, and again, you can either use the Check All button or select only the Tags you want to convert.

> **WARNING** *Sometimes, people think converting Categories to Tags is a way of just creating Tags with the same names as the Categories you select. No; you're actually changing them into Tags and the Categories no longer exist.*

PLUGINS

Following are some plugins that modify the way Categories and Tags work.

CATEGORIES

➤ **Category Checklist Expander**—If you have a lot of Categories, the meta box on Post screens will scroll. If you don't want to scroll to find Categories, this plugin expands the meta box to show all categories at once.

➤ **Media Library Categories**—Makes Post Categories available to use for media files. Displays the Categories for a file in the Media Library's list view, and you can sort by category in both list and grid view.

➤ **Category Icons**—Adds an icon to a variety of places where a Category is listed, such as on a Post or in a sidebar.

➤ **Author Category**—If you want to limit the Categories that users can choose for their Posts, this plugin creates a section in each users' profile where an administrator can make the restriction. Could even restrict them to a single category.

➤ **Category Pie**—Adds a pie chart to your Categories and Tags admin screens so that you can see which are most used. Okay; not a necessity but a nice visual aid.

TAGS

➤ **Auto Add Tags**—Checks the existing Tags, and if they're in the Post's content, automatically adds those Tags when you save the Post. Does not suggest new Tags.

continues

continued

➤ **Media Tags**—Adds tagging function to media files. Uses a separate set of tags from the WordPress Post Tags.

➤ **Tag Sticky Post**—When you display an archive for a particular Tag, this ensures the designated Post stays stuck at the top of the list.

BOTH

➤ **Category Tag Pages**—Enables Pages to use Categories and Tags. This means that when you list everything from a particular Category, it displays both Posts and Pages assigned to that Category.

➤ **BulkPress**—Makes it easy to add a large number of Tags or Categories at one time. You can also add Posts and Pages in bulk as well.

➤ **Categories to Tags Converter**—Alternative to WordPress's built-in converter.

TRY IT

In this lesson, you practice changing an existing Category by giving it a different name and assigning it to a parent Category.

Lesson Requirements

At least four or five existing Categories.

Step-by-Step

To change the name and relationship of a Category, follow these steps:

1. Click Posts ⇨ Categories on the main admin menu.

2. Locate the Category you want to modify.

3. Click the title or the Edit link of the mouseover menu.

4. Change the name of the Category.

5. Change the Slug to match the new name. (Remember to keep it lowercase with hyphens between words.)

5. From the drop-down menu, choose a parent Category.

6. Click Update. You return to the Categories page.

7. Check that your renamed Category shows below the parent.

8. You can verify that all your posts in the modified Category display under the new name by going to Posts ➪ All Posts and searching for the Posts under the renamed Category.

9. Change things back if you were just experimenting.

> **REFERENCE** *Please select the video for Lesson 20 online at* `www.wrox.com/go` `/wp24vids`*. You will also be able to download resources for this lesson from the website.*

21

Managing Widgets and Menus

In the preceding lessons you worked with content that appears in the main body of your website, but WordPress makes it easy to control the content in the sidebar and other areas of the layout without having to know HTML or other coding. That's the purpose of *Widgets*. This lesson shows you how widgets work and how they can work for you.

WordPress recently added a menu system that makes creating and managing navigation areas as simple as using widgets. This lesson shows you how to create new menus and then manage the items on those menus.

WIDGETS AND WIDGET AREAS

Widgets are elements outside the main content area of a web page that users can easily add, delete, and move around. A Widget might produce a list of all your blog categories; another might be a text box where you can update all your contact information; and yet another could contain the coding your mailing list manager provides for inserting a sign-up form.

Some Widgets come with WordPress, some are created by your theme, and still others appear when you install a plugin. There are literally thousands of possible free Widgets available through the Plugin Directory at WordPress.org and many more through paid plugins.

Widgets vary widely in complexity. Some have dozens of settings, whereas others you simply turn off or on. But no matter how complex the Widget, they appear in your administration screen as a simple box that you just drag and drop. You drop them into *Widget Areas* that are coded into your theme files—in the sidebar, the header, the footer, and any other spot theme developers can dream up.

For that reason, the available Widget Areas can vary depending on your theme. Some themes and plugins even enable you to create your own custom Widget Areas.

If a Widget Area is empty, most themes collapse that part of the screen. However, for a sidebar, if the theme layout calls for a sidebar, there will be a space where an empty Widget Area exists. Some themes show placeholder widgets if you don't include any.

> **NOTE** *Because Widget Areas are dependent on themes, if you switch themes, they are replaced by new Widget Areas. WordPress attempts to keep existing Widgets in place, but typically you need to move them to where you need them. WordPress does remember a theme's settings, so if you restore the theme its Widget Areas and Widgets are restored as well.*

The Widgets Screen

Widgets are controlled through the Appearance ⇨ Widgets link on the main admin menu. You're presented with the screen shown in Figure 21-1.

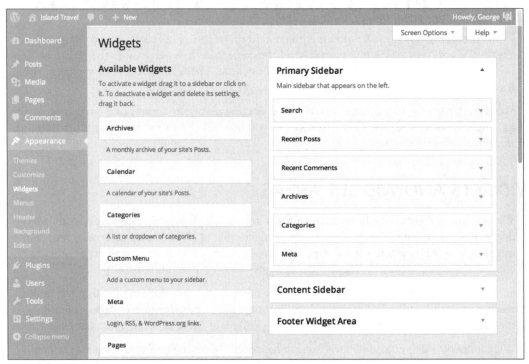

FIGURE 21-1

The left side of the screen shows the available Widgets, and the right side shows the Widget Areas that your particular theme has created anywhere on the website.

Referring to Figure 21-1, you can see the Twenty Fourteen default theme comes with three widget areas: one each for a left and right sidebar and one for the footer area of the site. Widgets you see on the left are some of the default ones that come with WordPress (they extend below the visible screen), but the list on your site will vary depending on your theme and what plugins you have installed. And for this theme, a number of the WordPress Widgets come pre-installed in the Primary Sidebar area on the right.

There are actually two lists of Widgets on the left, Available and Inactive (which is not visible in Figure 21-1), and the difference between them is covered in the final section of this lesson.

Activating Widgets

Following are two methods for activating a Widget:

➤ Dragging and dropping into a Widget Area

➤ Using the Add Widget button when you click a Widget

Dragging and dropping a Widget works well if the Widget Area you want is already open and if the two aren't too far apart on the screen. If you have a lot of Widgets, dragging a Widget all the way up the screen can sometimes be a bit tricky—and if the Widget Area is not open, it can be frustrating. That's why the fairly recently introduced Add Widget button is much handier.

The Add Widget button appears along with a list of all possible Widget Areas whenever you click a Widget in the Available Widgets area, as shown in Figure 21-2.

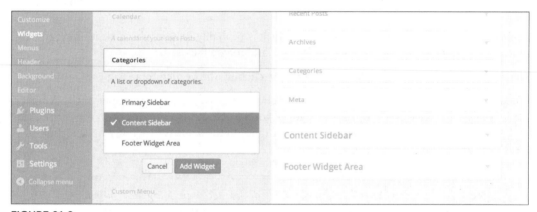

FIGURE 21-2

You simply check the Widget Area you want, and then click the Add Widget button. You can choose only one Widget Area at any one time and it's automatically opened, and the Widget is inserted and opened, ready for you to configure.

Mobile users with wider screens have the two-column layout for Widgets, but at smartphone size, the structure collapses to a single column, with Available and Inactive Widgets showing first and Widget Areas at the bottom. It's still possible to use drag and drop here, but the length of the screen makes Add Widget the better choice.

There is no Save button for the Widget screen; each Widget has its own. After you place a Widget into a Widget Area, you must click that Save button to fully activate it. Even Widgets that have no user-configurable settings usually have to be saved when you first place them in a Widget Area. Whenever you make changes to the Widget, you also need to save it.

When you move Widgets within the Widget Area or if you remove them, there is nothing to save. WordPress automatically records the action.

Saving a Widget does not close it, as shown in Figure 21-3.

FIGURE 21-3

You have to click the highlighted Close link, which is probably handiest because it's next to Save, or you can click the highlighted Widget header area and toggle it closed.

You can open and close the Widget Areas only by clicking the header area.

When you finish editing, you can click Close or click the down arrow at the right of the Widget header bar. (That same arrow opens the Widget, too.) You can also close or open the entire Primary Widget Area using the down arrow on its header (and do the same for each if you have multiple areas in your theme).

> **NOTE** *By default, WordPress shortcodes do not work in Widgets. You need a plugin to activate that functionality, as mentioned at the end of the lesson.*

Moving or Removing Widgets

Re-ordering Widgets within or moving them between Widget Areas is as simple as dragging and dropping. Click and drag from the header area of the Widget. If the Widget is currently open, it automatically closes.

As you drag, an outline of the box appears. As you move the Widget, the outline moves to where the Widget would next be placed, so you can easily see if you're targeting the correct spot, as shown in the sequence in Figure 21-4.

Removing or deactivating Widgets is as easy as dragging them from the right side back to the left—they instantly disappear from the Widget Area. Instead of dragging, you can also click Delete if the Widget is open. In either case, there's nothing for you to save after making the deletion; WordPress automatically records the change.

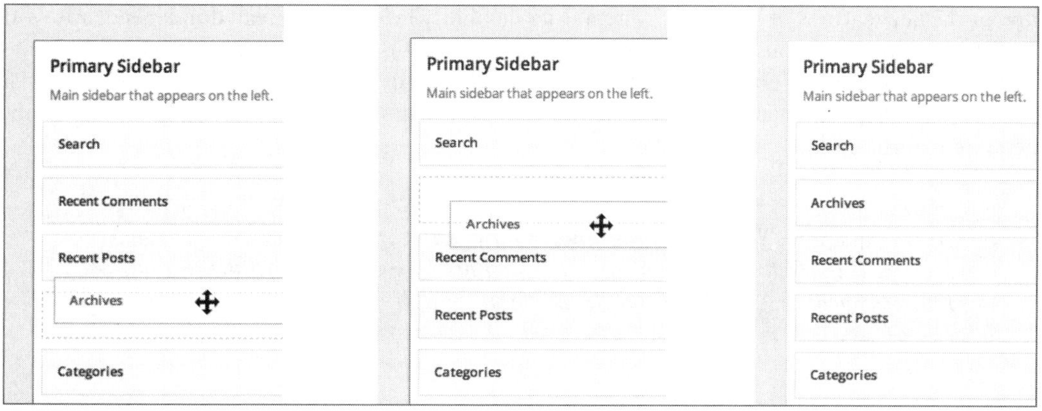

FIGURE 21-4

However, you need to think carefully about where you drag a Widget when removing it from a Widget Area:

➤ If you drag a Widget to the Available box, it loses all its settings and text.

➤ If you drag a Widget to the Inactive box, it keeps all its settings. This is handy, particularly if there are complicated settings such as URLs or specific wording that you might want later.

It's easy to forget about the Inactive box because it's often far down the screen. It's also difficult to drag Widgets back and forth from that box, again because it's so far down the screen and your browser doesn't always want to move nicely with your mouse. An easy answer is to collapse the Available Widgets box so that it brings Inactive closer to the top of the page.

Using the Delete link only removes a Widget; it does not enable you to choose to put it in the Inactive category.

> **NOTE** *Some older browsers may not enable you to move Widgets by dragging and dropping (or if you have JavaScript turned off). If this happens, there's a backup method, which you can find under Screen Options at the top right. There's a link that says Enable Accessibility Mode, and clicking it disables the drag-and-drop feature, replacing it with text links on all widgets—either Add if it's not in a Widget area or Edit if it is.*

THE WORDPRESS MENU SYSTEM

WordPress has a powerful built-in menu system that makes it simple for a user to create menus, add almost any type of content to those menus, order the menu with drag-and-drop functionality, and assign menus to various locations on the site.

One of the key features of the menu system is its flexibility. Menus are created independently of the possible locations of menus, so you can quickly assign or re-assign menus. How Pages, Categories, Posts, and Tags relate to one another is completely open. In other words, even if you made one Page a child of another, they could display side by side on the menu, or the parent Page could be a sub-menu item of the child.

> **NOTE** *It's possible that an older theme may not support the WordPress menu system. If that's the case, you see a warning message at the top of the screen under Appearance ⇨ Menus, at which point, you should get a different theme.*

Creating a Menu

Menus are all located in the right column of the Menus screen. When you first install WordPress there are no menus set up, and, as shown in Figure 21-5 A, there's a text box on the right side labeled Menu Name.

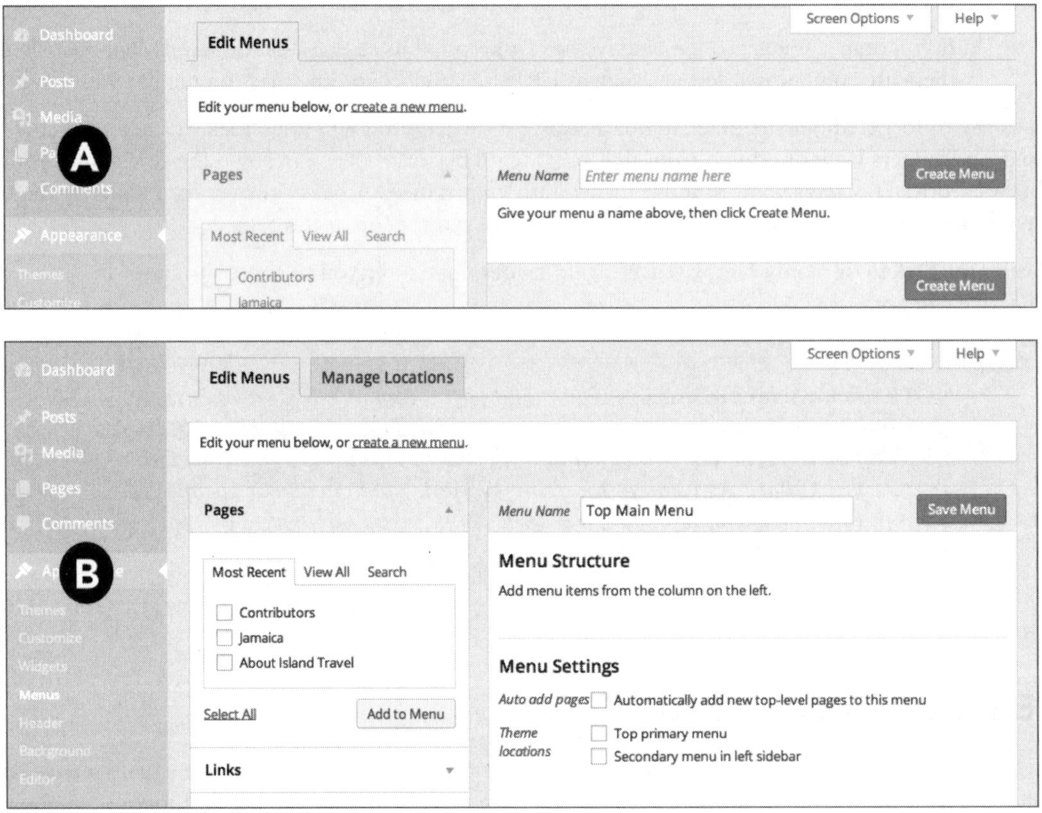

FIGURE 21-5

By giving the menu a name and clicking Create Menu, not only do you get a success message and a new tab called Manage Locations at the top of the screen, but also the set of drop-downs on the left become active instead of grayed out, as shown in Figure 21-5 B.

Only one menu can display at a time, and you can access any others via the drop-down menu below the two tabs at the top. That's also where you go to create a new menu: Simply click the little tab with the plus symbol.

> **NOTE** *Make sure you name menus clearly so that anyone can understand their purpose. For example, if you have a menu for the footer area, clearly label it as such.*

Adding Menu Items

After you name your menu and save it, you can start adding items to the menu. In this case, I've created a menu called Top Main Menu. It's going to be my primary navigation for the site, so I want all my key content pages up there.

Available Menu items are in the left column of the Menus screen, as shown in Figure 21-6.

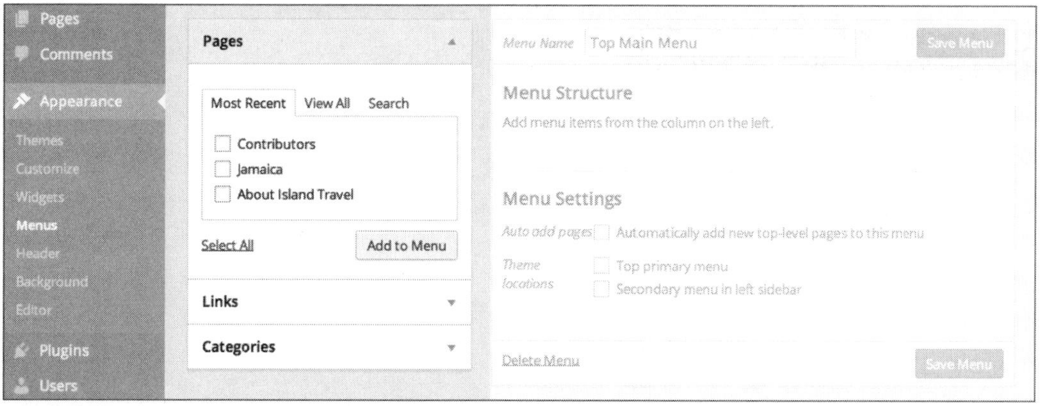

FIGURE 21-6

By default, the Pages section is open, but if you clicked on Links or Categories, the new one would open and the old one close.

More menu items are available, but you need to activate them using Screen Options at the top right. Hidden by default are Posts, Tags, and Format, but depending on your plugins, your theme, and any customizations you may have made, there could be many more choices. In other words, virtually any type of content can be a menu item!

One thing that can be a little confusing is that the drop-downs listing possible menu items all default to Most Recent. That's good in one sense, because usually when you add something to a menu, it's an item you recently added to WordPress. However, if you try to add something not so recent, it looks as if the item isn't available. Simply switch the tab to View All or use the Search tab.

But how do you get these menu items onto a menu? Simply check the box beside one or more menu items, and then click the Add to Menu button. Make sure, of course, that the menu you want to add to is displayed on the right. A rounded rectangle that looks like a Widget then shows up in the Menu area for each of the menu items, as shown in Figure 21-7.

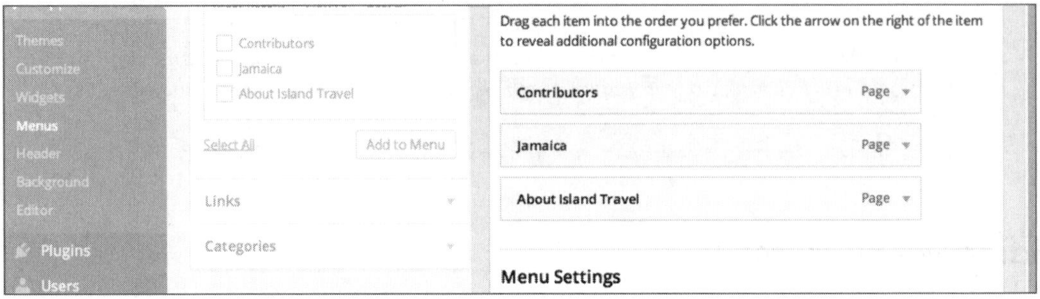

FIGURE 21-7

Smartphone users and smaller tablet users have a single column on the Menus screen rather than two, as shown in Figure 21-8.

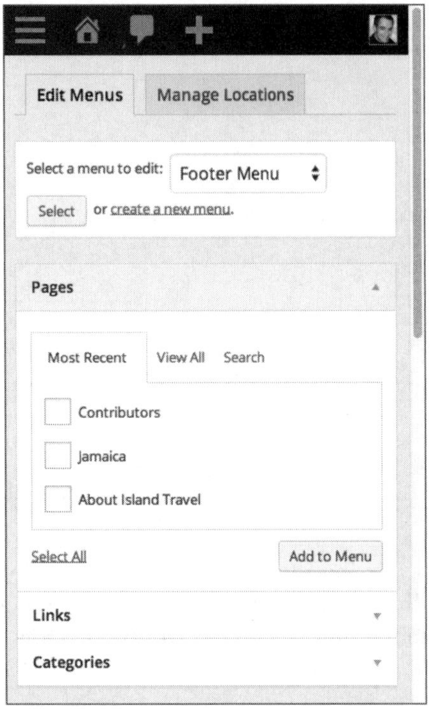

FIGURE 21-8

Because the menu currently being edited appears at the bottom of screen, you need to watch the menu select drop-down at the top of the screen to know where you are at the moment. One other difference for mobile users is that Screen Options is not available, so you cannot reveal any hidden menu item lists.

> **NOTE** *When you add a new top-level Page to WordPress (not a child or sub-Page), it automatically is added to any menu you've created. You can change this behavior by unchecking the Auto Add Pages box at the bottom of each menu. (This is how I prefer to work.) It does mean having to manually add Pages, but it also avoids having Pages show up that you don't want on a particular menu or on any menus.*

Assigning a Menu to a Location

Where you can place Menus is defined by your theme. Some themes might have six menu locations, whereas another has only one. If the theme documentation didn't tell you the possible locations, you can easily see them all by creating your first menu. At that point, you get a tab on the Menu screen that shows you possible locations, as shown in Figure 21-9.

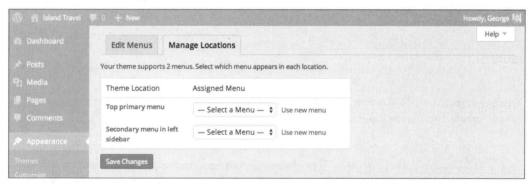

FIGURE 21-9

From here you can assign any menu to any menu location.

Menu locations are also shown at the bottom of each menu, from which you can also do the assigning, as you can see in the highlighted section of Figure 21-10.

WordPress tells you if any other menu is already assigned to an area, in which case it's unavailable.

You can also assign menus to any Widget Area using the Custom Menu widget. You're given the choice of naming the menu and choosing which menu to assign from a drop-down list, as shown in Figure 21-11.

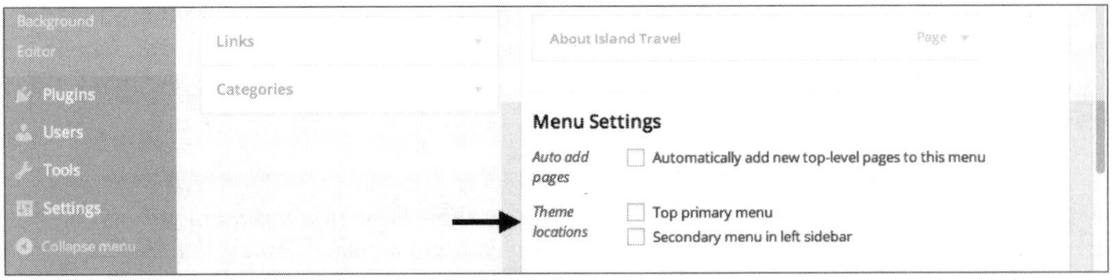

FIGURE 21-10

FIGURE 21-11

Notice that there's still a Custom Menu Widget showing in the Available Widgets area on the left. You can create and use multiple menus in Widget Areas.

> **NOTE** *The default theme in WordPress supports additional navigation areas, and you'll notice that even though no menu has been created, nor assigned to that navigation area, the site still displays a navigation menu. That's because the theme author coded in a default menu that kicks in if no menu has been assigned. Typically, these default menus simply show a list of all published WordPress pages, the order of which can be altered using the Order field on each page's admin screen (or via plugins that are available). However, you want to use the WordPress menu system—trust me.*

Managing Menus

After you have items added to a menu, you have a lot of options. One of the most important is the ability to rename the item using the Navigation Label field, which you can do by clicking the down arrow on the right side of the menu item box, as shown in Figure 21-12.

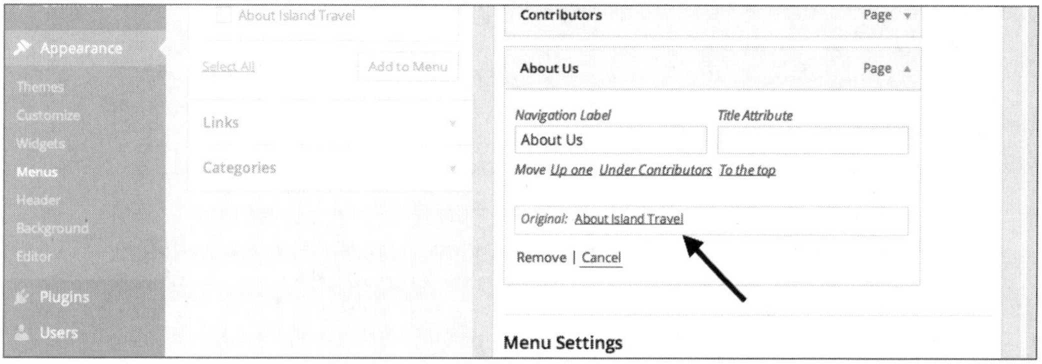

FIGURE 21-12

This is particularly important if something has a long name that needs to be shortened for use on a menu. Even when you change the name, you're reminded what the original name of the menu item was (highlighted in Figure 21-12).

You can delete a menu item by using the Remove link. There is no system of dragging off menu items to delete them.

Dragging and dropping does work, however, if you want to change the order of menu items. Unlike Widgets, though, *you must click Save Menu every time you make any changes*. If not, the changes won't appear on the site and will be lost if you leave the screen.

Creating submenu items (assuming your theme supports them, and most do) is as easy as changing the order. The only difference is that you need to drag a submenu item to the right and below its parent item, as shown in Figure 21-13.

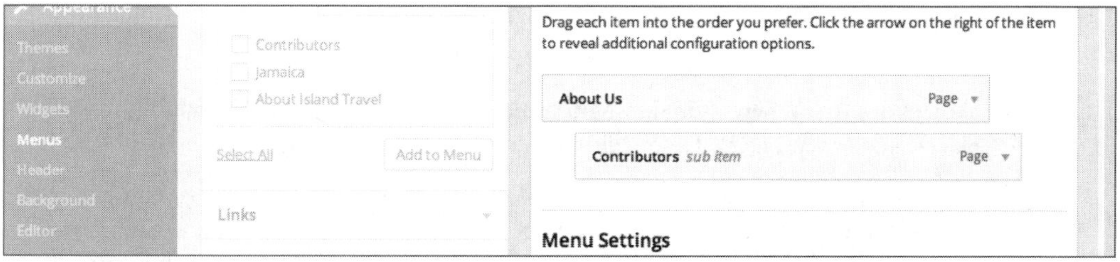

FIGURE 21-13

You can have sub-submenu items and so on, provided that the theme supports more than one level of submenu items.

If you want to delete a menu, there's a delete link at the bottom of the Menu Structure section. If you delete a menu and don't replace it with another in the location where it appeared, most themes simply collapse the area, assuming the menu was the only element in that area.

> **NOTE** *If you create a child or sub-Page in WordPress and then add it to a menu, it does not automatically show up as a submenu item of the parent. You need to manually make it a sub-item by dragging it below the parent menu item and slightly to the right.*

> **WARNING** *If you have a lot of menu items on a single menu—more than 100 for example—you can run into memory issues when trying to save the page. WordPress will not save entries past a certain point. You can either reduce the number of menu items or get your host to increase the max_input_vars setting for PHP.*

PLUGINS

It's common for plugins to create new Widgets, but the following plugins modify the way Widgets work. There are also some Plugins that add functionality to the Menu system.

WIDGETS

- ➤ **Display Widgets**—By default, Widgets display on every web page where their Widget Area displays. This plugin enables you to choose exactly where each individual widget will show up. You can choose between Hiding and Showing, and then select individual Pages, particular Categories, and more.

- ➤ **Custom Sidebars**—Great for making Widget Areas distinct, and they can then be assigned to specific Pages, Categories, Post types, and so on. That way you know if you drop the Widget in there that it will appear at a particular point on the site. A different approach from Display Widgets.

- ➤ **Shortcodes AnyWhere**—Enables you to use shortcodes in nontraditional places, such as Widgets, Description fields for Categories, Tags, and more.

- ➤ **Remove Inactive Widgets**—If you accumulate a lot of inactive Widgets or if you switch themes a few times and the old Widget Areas that WordPress has so helpfully kept in memory are beginning to pile up, this is the plugin for you. It creates a Remove Inactive Widgets button that can clear them all at once instead of having to delete them one at a time.

- ➤ **amr shortcode any widget**—Enables you to insert Widgets or whole Widget Areas into Posts, Pages, and so on.

MENUS

- ➤ **Auto Submenu**—WordPress allows top-level Pages to be automatically added to menus, but what about child or sub-Pages? This plugin automatically adds those child pages as submenu items if the parent Page is on the menu.

➤ **Duplicate Menu**—Sometimes you need to duplicate a complex menu—for example, you want a menu just for members and you want to replicate an existing menu.

➤ **Power Menus**—Adds a variety of additional controls to WordPress menus, including the ability to restrict a menu item to logged-in users or to users of a particular Role, such as Authors or Editors.

➤ **Menu Image**—Adds an Image field to all menu items so that you can load an icon or other image that displays next to the menu text. You can also upload a second image to create a mouse-over effect for a menu item.

➤ **Menu Icons**—Makes it easy to add common font icons to your menu items. Supports popular font icons such as Font Awesome, Genericons, Dashicons, and more.

➤ **Custom Menu Wizard Widget**—Enables you to customize how the Custom Menu Widget works by offering a series of filters and controls. For example, you can display only portions of an existing menu or portions based on the current page of the site, and much more.

TRY IT

In this lesson, you practice moving a Widget to a Widget Area and then making it inactive.

Lesson Requirements

A Widget-enabled theme. If you use the default theme, you're okay. At least two or three Categories are set up.

Step-by-Step

To move and activate a Categories widget, follow these steps:

1. Take a look at the sidebar on the front end of your site and note what's currently there, if anything.

2. Click Appearance ➪ Widgets on the main admin menu.

3. Locate the Categories widget on the left side.

4. Determine which of your Widget Areas controls a sidebar on your site. On the Twenty Fourteen theme, the Content Sidebar is the one for the main content area. If the name does not clearly tell you, drop down the Widget Area and read the short description.

5. Click the Categories Widget, and select the right Widget Area; then click Add Widget.

6. The Categories Widget should now be in the Widget Area and opened.

7. Enter a title, such as **My Blog Categories**.

8. Click Save.

9. Take a look at the front end of your site again and see how the sidebar has changed.

10. Back in the Widgets screen, collapse the Available Widgets area by mousing over the header and clicking. You should now see the Inactive Widgets area.

11. Drag the Categories widget you just activated from the right side to the Inactive box on the left. You should now see the Categories Widget, still with the title you gave it.

12. Look at your live site again, and the old sidebar should be visible once more.

> **REFERENCE** *Please select the video for Lesson 21 online at* www.wrox.com/go /wp24vids. *You will also be able to download resources for this lesson from the website.*

SECTION VI
Making Your Site Social

22

Connecting To Social Media

It's absolutely crucial these days to connect with your audience through the social media networks it uses the most. You don't need to be on ten different social media sites; only use the ones you need to reach your visitors.

You can connect your website to social media in four ways:

- ➤ Helping visitors *follow* you on your accounts
- ➤ Letting visitors *share* your content through their accounts
- ➤ *Posting* directly to social media from your website
- ➤ Displaying your social media *feeds* (your activities) on your site

Although entire books are written on each of these topics, this lesson covers them briefly, showing you how they work in WordPress.

HELPING VISITORS FOLLOW YOU

Social media networks want you to bring traffic to your page or profile, so they make it easy to include *follow buttons* on your website. The individual terminology may vary, but the idea is that you want visitors to follow what you do on that particular network: liking a Facebook page, following a Twitter account, or joining a Google+ circle, and so on.

Twitter is used for the example here, but the process is similar no matter what network you use.

The first thing you need to do is log in to your account so that the resulting button is tied to your credentials. Then look for a link that says something such as Promote, Resources, or Widgets (not to be confused with WordPress Widgets).

From the available tools, you want the one that typically says "follow" or some similar terminology. Figure 22-1 shows several buttons options for Twitter.

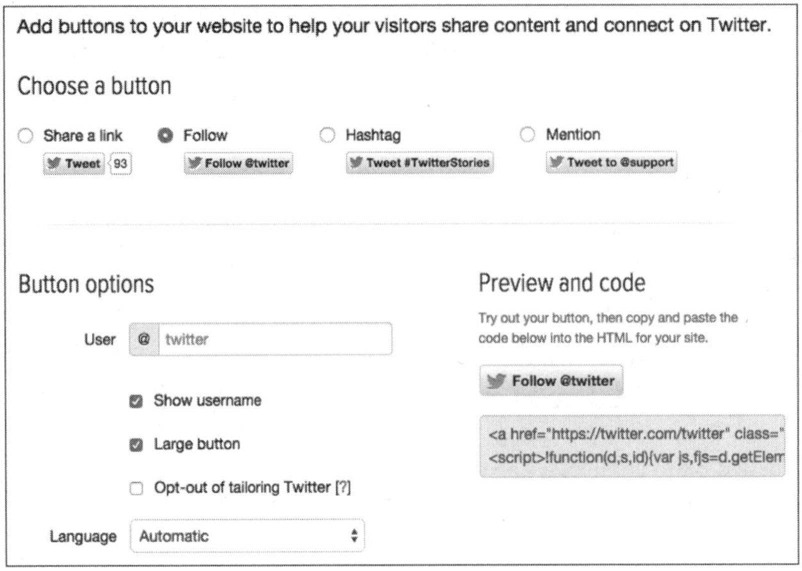

Add buttons to your website to help your visitors share content and connect on Twitter.

Choose a button

○ Share a link   ● Follow   ○ Hashtag   ○ Mention
🐦 Tweet 93   🐦 Follow @twitter   🐦 Tweet #TwitterStories   🐦 Tweet to @support

Button options

User @ twitter

☑ Show username

☑ Large button

☐ Opt-out of tailoring Twitter [?]

Language Automatic ▲▼

Preview and code

Try out your button, then copy and paste the code below into the HTML for your site.

🐦 Follow @twitter

`<a href="https://twitter.com/twitter" class="`
`<script>!function(d,s,id){var js,fjs=d.getElem`

FIGURE 22-1

You can set a number of parameters, including the look of the button. Figure 22-1 offers only a choice of size, but the options could include colors, logo type, and more.

As you set the parameters, the HTML code changes accordingly. When you finish, simply copy that HTML and return to your WordPress site.

Under Appearance ➪ Widgets you can find the Text Widget on the left side. Click it, and select the Widget Area where you want it to display. The box opens and you can paste it in, as shown in Figure 22-2 A.

Of course, you can then add more follow buttons from other social networks, but for the moment, you can see what the resulting button looks like on the front end of the Island Travel site in Figure 22-2 B.

And that's all there is to it. Exactly what happens when you click a follow button depends on the network. For Twitter, visitors would be given the opportunity to follow Island Travel on Twitter.

For plugins that enable you to display follow buttons for social networks, they typically send visitors to your page or profile on the particular network, where they can like, follow, or whatever that network may do.

Adding follow buttons on all pages of your site is fine when it's just you to be followed. However, what if you have one or more authors or staff members, for example, with their own social media accounts?

WordPress Profile Pages do not have built-in social media fields that enable each User to enter their own social contact information. Fortunately, there are plugins that add social media fields to the

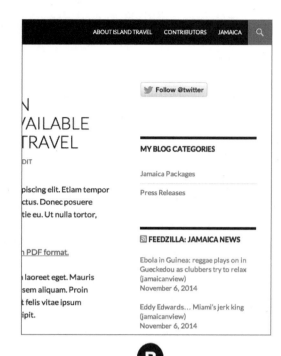

FIGURE 22-2

Profile Page and then display those links in Author boxes. (A couple are mentioned at the end of the lesson.)

LETTING VISITORS SHARE YOUR CONTENT

People enjoy sharing something fascinating, funny, or unusual. Assuming you give visitors that kind of content, make it easy for them to share it with friends via social media.

Like the follow button, most social networks offer the capability to embed a share button on your site, but you might ask, "Do I need to create a new button for every Post or Page?" After all, you want visitors to share the unique URL of the web page they're on. Fortunately, share buttons are smart and can find the URL automatically.

The process for creating a share button is virtually identical to creating a follow button. For Twitter, you create them from the same screen. In Figure 22-3, you can see the share button version of the Twitter screen.

As with the follow button, I put the generated HTML into a Text Widget in the sidebar of Island Travel, but notice in Figure 22-4 that the title Share This with Your Friends makes it clear what the button does.

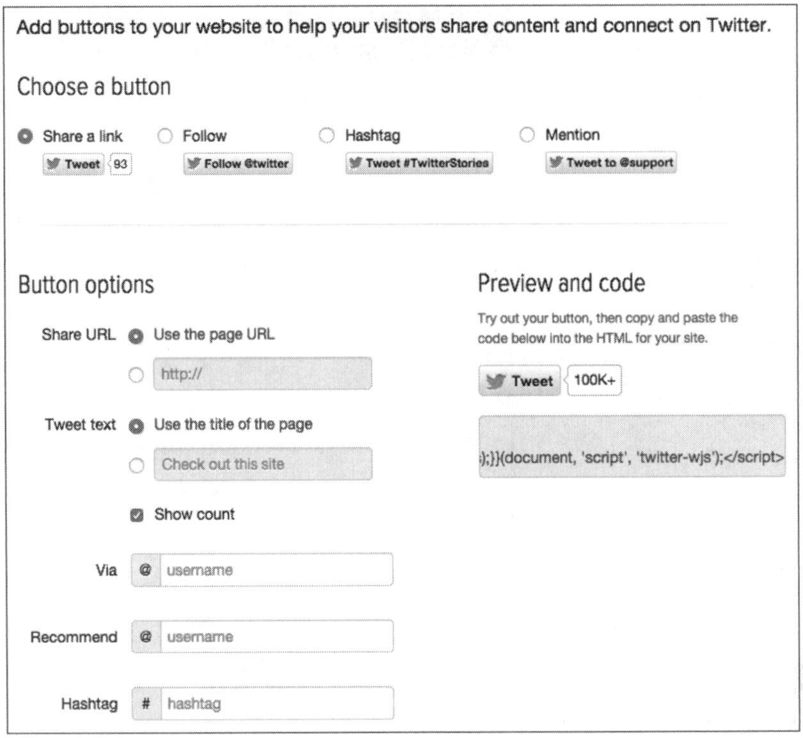

Add buttons to your website to help your visitors share content and connect on Twitter.

Choose a button

◉ Share a link   ○ Follow   ○ Hashtag   ○ Mention

🐦 Tweet 93   🐦 Follow @twitter   🐦 Tweet #TwitterStories   🐦 Tweet to @support

Button options

Share URL   ◉ Use the page URL
            ○ http://

Tweet text ◉ Use the title of the page
            ○ Check out this site

            ☑ Show count

Via   @ username

Recommend @ username

Hashtag   # hashtag

Preview and code

Try out your button, then copy and paste the code below into the HTML for your site.

🐦 Tweet 100K+

);}}(document, 'script', 'twitter-wjs');</script>

FIGURE 22-3

Content Sidebar   ▲

Additional sidebar that appears on the right.

Text: Share This With Your Friends   ▲

Title:

Share This With Your Friends ←

```
<a href="https://twitter.com/share" class="twitter-share-
button" data-size="large">Tweet</a>
<script>!function(d,s,id){var
js,fjs=d.getElementsByTagName(s)
[0],p=/^http:/.test(d.location)?'http':'https';if(!d.getElement
ById(id))
{js=d.createElement(s);js.id=id;js.src=p+'://platform.twitte
r.com/widgets.js';fjs.parentNode.insertBefore(js,fjs);}}
(document, 'script', 'twitter-wjs');</script>
```

FIGURE 22-4

And on the front end of the site, you can see in Figure 22-5 the resulting pop-up boxes on two separate web pages, allowing me to share the URL of the particular page. The button has automatically inserted the URL, so I need only one button.

FIGURE 22-5

Of course, you could add more share buttons to this Widget, depending on how many social networks you want your visitors to have access to. And with a plugin that enables you to choose where a Widget appears, you could restrict this share Widget to just Blog web pages.

Now the sidebar isn't the best place for share buttons; putting them at the beginning or end of Posts, for example, is handier for visitors. In the case of the Island Travel theme, I don't have Widget Areas in either of those locations. Other themes may offer those, or there are plugins so that you can create your Widget Areas where you want.

> **NOTE** *For share buttons, you don't want to restrict visitors to social networks you're active on. You can get share buttons from any major social network without needing an account. However, with so many possible networks, it may be easier to use a share plugin. (Some are mentioned at the end of the lesson.) These plugins also make it easy to place share buttons where you'd like, including at the sides of browser windows and so on.*

POSTING DIRECTLY TO SOCIAL MEDIA

When you create a new Post on your website, it would be nice not to have to stop and log in to various social media accounts to let people on those networks know about your new Post. If you could automatically post to one or more social media accounts when you press the Publish button in WordPress, that would be a huge timesaver, which means it's more likely to actually get posted.

Unlike follow or share buttons, this kind of functionality is best handled with a plugin, as discussed at the end of the lesson. That's because there's integration required with WordPress Post and Page screens, and that gets complicated.

In the end, what you'll have, depending on the plugin, is the ability at the time of publishing a Post or a Page to choose whether and what text/imagery to send to one or more social networks. An example of a meta box that gets added to your Posts is shown in Figure 22-6.

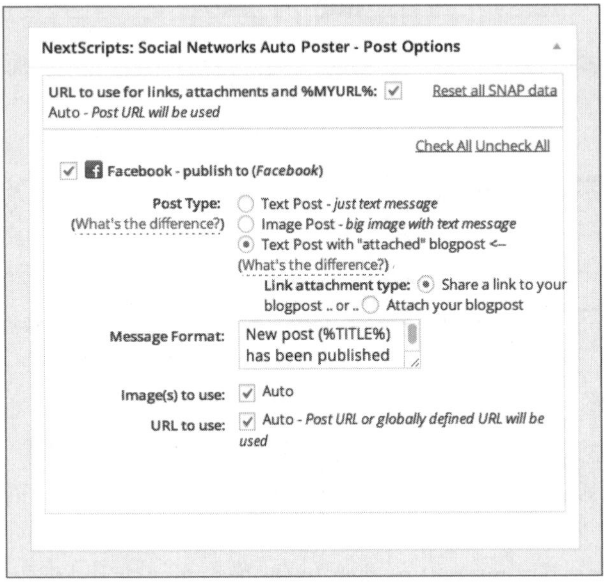

FIGURE 22-6

Notice how you have control over what is published, in this case, to Facebook. (This varies depending on the plugin.) You need to customize what is sent out so that you can personalize it for the particular network you're sending to.

DISPLAYING SOCIAL MEDIA ACTIVITY

Another way to involve visitors with social media is to display feeds from your social media accounts or from the accounts of others.

Feeds from Your Accounts

If you're active with your social media accounts, such as Twitter or Facebook, the content you generate on those sites could be useful on your WordPress site. Luckily, you can select simple ways from WordPress, out of the box, to display social media feeds on your site. At the end of the lesson you see some plugins that can make the process even simpler, or add functionality.

To get your Twitter feed (or timeline) on to your site, the process is similar for most social media tools. As with the follow and share buttons, you need to navigate to where your social network provides tools or resources for promoting your account. Look for a tool that displays your account activity (or feed, profile, and so on).

Many sites make it easy, as Twitter does in Figure 22-1 A, to customize how the feed looks on your site, how many items it displays, and so on. When you finish customizing, click something such as Finish & Grab Code or Generate Code, and you're presented with the HTML you need to paste into WordPress.

Simply go to Appearance ➪ Widgets, and using the Text Widget, assign it to the Widget Area you want; then paste in the HTML. When you save the Widget, your Twitter timeline displays on your site just as in the preview when you set it up. Figure 22-7 shows a sample feed.

Some social networks offer different versions of feeds or show thumbnails of some of your followers or the latest images from your account. You want to think about what will be most intriguing for your visitors.

For example, I always enjoy seeing that friends on Facebook have liked the same website that I like or that someone well known in a particular field has liked it. That's all part of what people mean when they talk about "social proof."

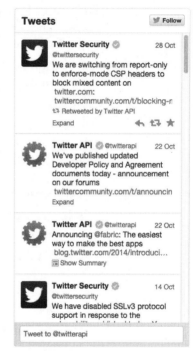

FIGURE 22-7

Feeds from Other People's Accounts

With many social networks, you're not limited to displaying your own feed. Any publicly available feed is an option as well. So you could display the Twitter timeline of a related industry association or a writer you admire. For Twitter, you can embed four types of timelines:

➤ **User Timelines**—The public tweets of any user

➤ **Favorites**—Shows all tweets that a user has favorited

➤ **Lists**—Public compilations of user tweets you create or you subscribe to

➤ **Searches**—Shows customized real-time search results from Twitter

Be aware that you're opening yourself up for all sorts of content with a search feed: possibly from competitors or possibly offensive. The more likely scenario for this kind of feed is when your organization or business uses a hash tag, such as *#ourconference*. The feed would pull in any tweets that use that tag.

Again, this is meant to give you only a sense of what's possible. Other social networks have their own versions of these or other kinds of feeds.

PLUGINS

Literally hundreds of social media plugins are available for WordPress, but following are a few to get you started. Although you can get plugins targeting individual social media networks, these focus on ones that cover multiple networks at one time.

FOLLOW BUTTONS

➤ **Simple Social Icons**—Creates a Widget in which you can add follow icons for the major social networks and easily customize the color of the icons and the hover effect color, as well as adjust the size of the icons.

➤ **Simple Follow Me Social Buttons Widget**—A follow buttons widget that uses font icons instead of images to improve loading speed and flexibility.

➤ **Social Media Widget**—Creates a Widget for putting your follow links to social media.

➤ **Follow Buttons by AddThis**—Like the sharing version by the same company, this creates follow buttons.

FOLLOWING INDIVIDUAL AUTHORS

➤ **Starbox—the Author Box for Humans**—Fancy author box with a lot of styling options and the capability to show author social media follow links.

➤ **WP About Author**—Adds an author box at the bottom of Posts, and along with biographies of authors, you can have their social media follow links.

SHARE BUTTONS

➤ **Simple Share Buttons Adder**—Adds share buttons to your Posts or Pages. You can use your own custom icons as well.

➤ **Custom Share Buttons with Floating Sidebar**—As the name suggests, these sharing icons float over at the side of your browser and remain in place as the Page scrolls. An example of the kind of styling that a sharing plugin can offer.

THIRD-PARTY SHARING SERVICES

➤ **ShareThis: Share Buttons and Social Analytics**—Share buttons can display in a number of ways. Because it's a third-party service, the choice of sharing sites is always updated on their end and can track statistics of clickthroughs.

➤ **Share Buttons by AddThis**—Another third-party service providing a wide range of possible sharing sites, along with statistics.

➤ **Share Buttons by AddToAny**—A third-party social media sharing plugin.

COMBINATION SHARE AND FOLLOW

➤ **Shareaholic | share buttons, related posts, social analytics & more**—As the name suggests, this plugin does a lot of different social media functions, including follow and sharing. It also offers analytics, related content linking, Pinterest image sharing, and more. Used to be known as Sexybookmarks.

➤ **Social Media Feather**—This is both a follow and a sharing plugin, and the feather part refers to being lightweight in terms of adding to the load time of the Page.

➤ **Ultimate Social Media and Share Icons** (Twitter, Facebook, Google+, Instagram, Pinterest, and such)—Both a follow and a sharing plugin that has 16 different icon styles, or you can use your own.

ACTIVITY FEEDS

These plugins tend to go by individual social networks, so just search the WordPress directory for the particular network. Or just use the coding that your network provides, as shown in this lesson.

POSTING TO SOCIAL NETWORKS

NextScripts Social Networks Auto-Poster Enables you to post to several social networks at one time whenever you publish a new Post or Page. You control exactly what is sent to each social media site.

WIDGET AREA PLUGINS

If you want a social media Widget to go somewhere other than in the Sidebar or Footer areas, you can use these plugins to create extra Widget Areas.

➤ **Simple Page sidebars**—Add your own Widget Areas to various places on a web page. You can then add share buttons to any point on the Page.

➤ **Custom sidebars**—Great for making Widget Areas distinct, and they can then be assigned to specific Pages, categories, Post types, and more.

TRY IT

In this lesson, you practice adding a social media share button to your website.

Lesson Requirements

You need at least a couple Posts or Pages on your site.

Step-by-Step

To add a share button to your sidebar or footer, follow these steps.

1. Go to Twitter, Pinterest, Digg, or any social network where people share website links.

2. Find the Resources or Promotion section or type **share** into the search function, or Google **share button** and the name of the network.

3. Follow the instructions for creating a share button, and when you finish, copy the HTML provided.

4. On your website go to Appearance⇒Widgets and click Text Widget.

5. Choose a Widget Area, probably a Sidebar or Footer area, and click Add Widget.

6. Paste the HTML into the Widget, and enter a title that tells visitors what the button is for.

7. Click Save.

8. On the front end of your website, make sure the button displays.

9. Click the share button and make sure the URL of the current web page displays. Try one or two other web pages to prove that the correct URL is found each time.

> **REFERENCE** *Please select the video for Lesson 22 online at* www.wrox.com/go /wp24vids. *You will also be able to download resources for this lesson from the website.*

23

Managing Comments

One of the best ways to interact with your visitors is to allow them to leave comments on your site, and because WordPress was developed as blogging software, it has an extensive comments system. This lesson shows you how WordPress handles comments and the ways you can manage them.

ALLOW COMMENTS?

WordPress offers two ways of deciding whether visitors can leave comments: on a sitewide basis and on a per-content basis. Both of these are mentioned in earlier lessons on site administration (Lesson 5, "Basic Admin Settings") and on creating Posts and Pages (Lesson 9, "Advanced Post Functions"), but it's worth repeating here.

How you control your settings depends on the kind of content you have on your site. If it's the kind that cries out for comments, such as a personal blog or a newspaper/magazine style site, it makes sense to turn on comments so that they're activated by default each time you create new content. Then, you simply turn them off in those situations that don't call for comments (such as your Privacy Policy Page).

If your site is more informational—not talking about issues, controversies, opinions, and so on—you probably want comments off by default, turning them on only when you need them.

The important point is that you need to consider the purpose of your website and how the WordPress comment function might fit in. Every site will be different, and every area on your site needs to be considered separately as well.

ADMIN SETTINGS FOR COMMENTING

You can find the sitewide settings for commenting on the Admin menu under Settings ➪ Discussion. By default, WordPress sets up the following parameters:

➤ The comment form and existing comments appear on any Post or Page.

➤ To post a comment, visitors must fill out their name and e-mail address.

➤ The ability to comment is always open—there's no time limit on the comments for a particular Post or Page.

➤ All comments are held for approval unless the commenter has been approved before.

➤ The e-mail address listed in WordPress administration will be notified if any comments are posted or if any comments are held for moderation.

➤ Any comment is held for moderation if it contains more than two links.

➤ No words or web addresses are blacklisted.

➤ Avatars (small graphics or photos) display with each comment, and a default avatar is selected if the visitor doesn't provide one.

When comments are active, these are standard settings, so in most cases, you won't need to make any changes. The key setting you need to decide on is the ability to comment on every Post and Page, as shown in Figure 23-1, under Default Article Settings. ("Article" just means Posts or Pages.)

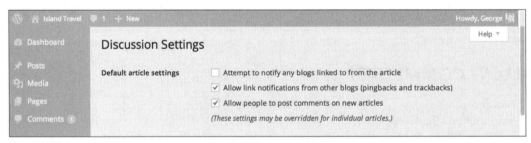

FIGURE 23-1

If you turn off commenting for every Post and Page, you still have the ability to allow commenting on any particular one. WordPress reminds you of this when it says, "These settings may be overridden for individual articles."

In the past, WordPress showed the Discussion settings for individual content at the bottom of every Post or Page Edit screen, so it was there to refresh your memory and check the status for that item. Now, however, the Discussion box is hidden by default, and you need to choose it under Screen Options if you want to make any changes.

> **NOTE** *If you've had sitewide commenting turned on and then turn it off, all Posts up to that time continue to allow comments unless you manually turn them off. For new posts, commenting will not be available unless you manually turn it on for a specific post.*

One other useful option under Settings ⇨ Discussion is the ability to automatically have comments close after a specified period of time, say, 60 days. Existing comments continue to show; there just can't be any new comments.

Some people use this feature if they have trouble blocking spam comments, but they want to allow a bit of time for legitimate comments to be made. Others don't want to deal even with legitimate comments on old topics. With this feature, you don't have to remember to manually turn off commenting after a Post has been up for a while.

Display Order of Comments

Traditionally, blogs have shown the oldest comments first. Part of the reason is that comments can often flow in the form of a discussion—you need to know what's been said earlier to follow what a later commenter is reacting to.

However, some people prefer to show the most recent comments first. One theory is that visitors who keep returning want to first see what's new in the comments area, without having to scroll (sometimes a long way) to the bottom.

WordPress makes it possible to choose between the two. The default is still oldest comments first, but under Settings ⇨ Discussion in the Other Comment Settings area, you see a drop-down menu enabling you to first select Older or Newer Comments.

Threaded Comments

No matter what order comments display in, comments often don't flow in an orderly manner. If someone is commenting on a point made 15 comments earlier, it can get difficult to keep track of the conversation. That's why WordPress has threaded or nested comments enabled by default. This creates a Reply link with each comment in addition to the general comment box at the bottom of the Post. If visitors use the Reply link, the comment shows up inside the comment they're replying to.

You can turn off this feature under Settings ⇨ Discussion Settings. Look for Enable Threaded (Nested) Comments. You can also allow the nesting to go up to 10 comments deep. (The default is 5.)

> **NOTE** *Be aware, though, that not all themes properly display threaded comments. Even if yours doesn't, plugins are available to help you manage them, or you can have your style sheet modified to do so.*

KNOWING YOU HAVE COMMENTS

Assuming you retained the default settings that require comments to be approved (at least the first time someone comments) and for the administrator to be e-mailed about it, you'll know there are comments waiting because you'll get an e-mail.

But you'll also know there are comments waiting from several indicators on Admin screens, as shown in Figure 23-2.

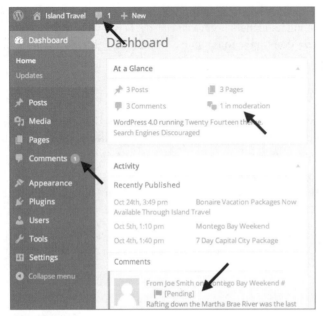

FIGURE 23-2

You'll also see any new comments for individual Posts or Pages when you open their Edit screen. The Comments meta box is shown in Figure 23-3.

FIGURE 23-3

The Comments meta box automatically appears on Post or Page Edit screens after the first comment is made, but you can still manually control its appearance from Screen Options.

APPROVING, EDITING, OR DELETING COMMENTS

The most common way of managing Comments is through the link on the main Admin menu, taking you to the Comments screen, as shown in Figure 23-4.

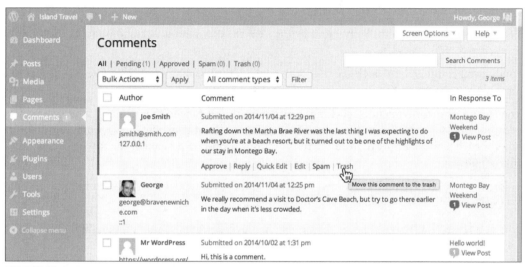

FIGURE 23-4

For each comment, you see the author's name and a URL if the author entered one. Then you see the comment itself, along with the date and time it was submitted. Underneath the comment, if you mouse over the row, you see a menu with the following options:

➤ **Approve**—You can approve the comment (or unapprove it, depending on context).

➤ **Spam**—This marks the comment as spam, so the information can be used by antispam plugins to learn what to block.

➤ **Trash**—This removes the comment to the Trash area. From there, you can restore it later or permanently delete it.

➤ **Edit**—Use this to edit the parameters of the comment, including the body, so you can remove bad language and so on.

➤ **Quick Edit**—This enables you to perform virtually all Edit tasks without going to a new screen.

➤ **Reply**—This enables you to reply directly to the comment in the way described earlier when talking about threaded comments. If your theme is set up to do so, your reply is shown with the comment it's in response to.

On the far right of the comments listing, you see the title of the Post that the comment was responding to with a link to its Edit screen. The tiny speech bubble icon shows how many comments that Post or Page has, and the View Post link takes you to the item on the front end of your site.

At the top of the screen is the standard filtering menu, where you see comments based on whether they're Pending (awaiting approval), Approved, Spam, or sitting in the Trash.

You can filter the comments by Comments or Pings. Lesson 25, "Connecting by E-mail," explain pings or pingbacks in more detail, but basically these are links to your Post, as opposed to someone making a comment through your site.

You can also sort results by Author and by the item the comment is in response to by clicking their respective column titles.

Finally, you can search through the text of the comments by using the Search Comments box at the top right of the screen. You can take any of these same actions.

You can approve a comment by clicking Approve on the text menu that displays when you mouse over a comment on the Comments screen. If you have a lot of comments to approve, just check the box for each, choose Approve from the Bulk Actions drop-down menu at the top or bottom, and click Apply.

Before or after you approve a comment, you can edit the contents by clicking Edit on the text menu. You see a screen such as the one in Figure 23-5.

FIGURE 23-5

From this screen, you can edit all the parameters, including the date and time it was submitted (see the Status box).

Notice that the comment Content Editor is available only in Text mode. Visitors do not get any formatting buttons when entering comments, but plugins are available that offer all sorts of options in that regard.

As always, remember to click Update when you finish editing.

To move a comment or comments to the Trash, you again have the choice to do it individually or in bulk when you're on the Comments screen. When you edit an individual comment, you can trash it from the link in the Status box.

> **NOTE** *If you set WordPress to e-mail you whenever a comment is held for moderation, the e-mail contains direct links for approving or deleting the link, or marking it as spam.*

DEALING WITH SPAM COMMENTS

Although spam comments are dealt with from the same menus as approving or deleting, they are covered in a separate section. WordPress comes with a number of methods for dealing with spam comments but there are also Plugins that can help. Some are mentioned at the end of the lesson.

The first line of defense with spam comments is to make sure you require all comments to be moderated (not counting those visitors you've approved once already—if you keep that setting in place). That way, you don't have just anything appearing on your site without knowing about it.

On the Settings ⇨ Discussion screen, you'll find several settings under Comment Moderation that can help deal with spam comments. The first checks how many links are contained in a comment and holds it for moderation if the threshold is exceeded. The default setting is 2, the idea being that spam comments often contain multiple links. This option functions no matter what other moderation settings you have.

> **WARNING** *Never set this number to 0 or make the field blank. That would send every single comment to moderation, no matter what other settings you have in place.*

The next option enables you to specify words, names, URLs, e-mail addresses, or even IP addresses against which WordPress will check each comment—be sure to have only one item per line. If anything on this list appears in a comment, it will automatically be held for moderation—again, no matter what your other comments settings are.

The final moderation option enables you to create a blacklist. You specify words, names, and so on, but in this case, if a comment contains anything on the list, it's automatically marked as spam, not simply put into moderation. You can still approve a comment if it wrongly is caught by this blacklist.

> **NOTE** *I keep using the term "mark as spam," which means that not only will comments marked as spam not appear on your site, but also they'll stay in your database and can be used by antispam plugins to compare with future comments and help determine if they're spam, too.*

FARMING OUT COMMENTS

If you don't want to use WordPress's Comments system, there are a number of alternatives.

Disqus is a popular comment application that has good integration with WordPress. It has many more features than the WordPress commenting system, including voting comments up or down, seeing who else voted, built-in social media sharing, antispam, replies notification, and much more. Another advantage here is that users can log in to Disqus using Facebook or other social logins, and they stay logged in when visiting any of the more than 1 million sites using Disqus. In that sense it becomes its own social network.

Other popular third-party commenting applications that make integration easy with WordPress include LiveFyre and IntenseDebate.

Another alternative is to use Facebook Comments, which enables people to comment right on your site using their Facebook account. Google+ offers a similar commenting interface that embeds in your site. The drawback here, of course, is that you have to use part of Facebook or Google+ to comment. In the case of Facebook, that's still a large audience, but you may not want to limit yourself.

> **WARNING** *One of the drawbacks of a third-party commenting application is that it may be slow to load or occasionally not load at all.*

PLUGINS

Comment spam is a huge issue, so here are some plugins for that, along with ones that modify the WordPress comment system to make it more powerful or easier to manage.

ANTISPAM

You could write an entire book about protecting your WordPress site from spam, not just comment spam, but also form spam and registration spam. A few of the more popular of these plugins are mentioned, but if you type in **antispam** in the WordPress Plugin Directory, you'll have plenty of reading.

➤ **Akismet**—This popular and powerful antispam service from Automattic, the company that runs WordPress, has a plugin that comes with WordPress. You need an account with WordPress.com to activate it, and it's free only for non-commercial use.

➤ **SI CAPTCHA Anti-Spam**—Using a captcha method, this very popular plugin works for comments, forms, and registration forms.

➤ **Captcha**—Another popular antispam plugin that uses simple captcha techniques to block spam from comments, forms, and registration pages.

➤ **Anti-spam**—Anticomment spam protection without any captcha or other kinds of requirements.

➤ **Anti-spam by CleanTalk**—Stops spam comments, spam registrations, form spam, and spam trackbacks without any captcha, questions, or other actions required by users.

➤ **Email Address Encoder**—Automatically protects e-mail addresses in content, widgets, and other areas without the need for any settings, shortcodes, or JavaScript.

COMMENTS FUNCTIONALITY

➤ **Disable Comments**—Enables administrators to disable comments completely according to post type: Posts, Pages, Attachments, and Custom Post Types. And by completely disabling, you couldn't allow comments on a particular Page if you disabled them for Pages.

➤ **Greg's Comment Length Limiter**—Enables you to put a limit on the length of comments and displays a "characters left" notice for visitors as they type.

➤ **Subscribe to Comments Reloaded**—Enables visitors to sign up to be notified if there are other comments or replies on the Post or Page they commented on.

➤ **WP-Ajaxify-Comments**—Instead of reloading the page when a user submits a comment, this plugin uses Ajax to submit the data without reloading. This is particularly handy if there are errors and the user doesn't have to use a Back button to return to the comment.

➤ **Comment Images**—Makes it possible for visitors to upload images in their comments. Could be useful, but you'd need to keep track of what's uploaded.

ALTERNATIVE COMMENT SYSTEMS

➤ **Facebook Comments**—An example of a plugin that makes it easy to integrate Facebook Comments into your WordPress site.

➤ **Disqus Comment System**—An example of a plugin that integrates a third-party comment program with WordPress.

TRY IT

In this lesson, you practice approving a comment.

Lesson Requirements

Have someone comment on one of your posts, or you can do it yourself as long as you log out of WordPress before doing so. (If you're still logged in, you'll be commenting as an administrator and automatically be approved.)

Step-by-Step

To approve a comment, follow these comments:

1. Log in to WordPress. On the Dashboard, you should see the new comment in the Comments box, and on the left side menu, there should be an icon beside Comments with the number 1 in it. (Or if you had existing pending comments, the number should have increased by 1).

2. You can approve the comment from the Dashboard if you mouseover the comment and use the Approve link on the menu that appears.

3. If you want to read the entire comment first, click Edit, and when you're satisfied, mark it as Approved in the Status box. Finally, click Update Comment.

4. From the Dashboard, you can also click Pending in the Right Now box, and you'll see a list of comments requiring approval.

> **REFERENCE** *Please select the video for Lesson 23 online at* `www.wrox.com/go` `/wp24vids`*. You will also be able to download resources for this lesson from the website.*

24

Bringing in Content from Other Sites

You know how to enter content into Posts and Pages, but there are some kinds of content you want to display from other places. This involves showing content that actually resides on another site, not quoting from another site.

For example, real estate agents usually have their listings with a third-party service, such as MLS. It wouldn't make sense to re-create all or some of those listings on the agent's website; that's a lot of wasted time and energy. But if the listings from the service could be integrated to seamlessly look like part of the site, visitors wouldn't need to leave the site, and the agent would have to maintain only one set of listings.

When talking about bringing in content from other sites, this does not mean

➤ Stealing content from others (using it without their permission)

➤ Duplicating content that's on other sites (with permission)

Both of these actions have bad consequences, so just don't do it. The first is wrong, morally and legally.

The second can cause, at worst, blacklisting of your page/site by search engines, and at the least, if you duplicate content from your own sites, a potential dilution of your search engine ranking can occur (when some people link to one page or site and some to another).

This kind of content can be divided into three primary groups:

➤ Social media feeds (covered in Lesson 22, "Connecting to Social Media")

➤ Content you pay for or have permission to use that comes from a third party (such as real estate listings)

➤ RSS feeds (a kind of headline listing)

This lesson covers how to integrate the last two into WordPress as well as a bit about the types of content available and how to find them. At the end you can find some plugins that can help with the process.

ADDING CONTENT FROM THIRD-PARTY SITES

Like the earlier example of realtors and their listings, many services now offer the ability to integrate their programs or data into your website:

➤ Shopping cart systems

➤ Ticketing programs

➤ Event agenda programs

➤ Appointment booking systems

➤ Reservation systems

➤ Association and other membership management programs

➤ Form builder programs

➤ Survey programs

➤ Information services, such as weather and stock market information

The list grows every day as the technology for securely integrating these kinds of services becomes more sophisticated and easier to use.

As you saw with social media sites, these third-party services try to make it as simple as possible to integrate with your website. Figure 24-1 shows the variety of widgets (not to be confused with WordPress Widgets) that Eventbrite offers, simply by pasting in some code on your site:

FIGURE 24-1

Because of the popularity of WordPress, many of these companies even provide plugins that make the integration process even easier. Even without a plugin, though, integration can be as simple as pasting in a URL.

When talking about video and audio in Lesson 9, "Advanced Post Functions," that's one form of integrating third-party content into your site. Pasting the URL of the video or audio is enough to trigger a player in WordPress, but even if you have to paste in some HTML, it's fairly straightforward.

An *iframe—inline frame—*is an HTML tag that creates a kind of window in the middle of a regular web page and inserts content, usually from a different site. Often on websites these days, you don't even know there's content being pulled in from another site.

You can use iframes in WordPress, *but you must use Text mode on the Content Editor.* Pasting the code in Visual Mode will break it.

To avoid this problem altogether, it's easiest to use a plugin that enables you to use shortcodes instead of the actual iFrame HTML. (A couple of those are mentioned at the end of the lesson.) But iframes aren't the only way of using third-party content by pasting in code.

When you see a weather forecast on a website, that's often handled using JavaScript. In any case, it's simply a matter of copying the code from the third-party site and pasting it into a text Widget or in the body of a Post or Page (taking the precautions noted earlier).

RSS FEEDS

RSS stands for really simple syndication. A website automatically generates a special webpage or pages that can be understood by an RSS reader; the resulting HTML is published by another website. The beauty of RSS is that it makes the distribution process extremely simple. Literally, paste the URL of that other site into a special program on your site, and you have a feed coming in.

Finding RSS Feeds

Suppose you own a gardening center. On your website, you could display the RSS feed from your favorite gardening show on TV or a popular gardening magazine website. Or there could be an RSS feed from a university that sends out information about seasonal plant diseases for your region. If you have multiple websites of your own, an RSS feeds is a great way for one site to display the latest news from the other. And check if any associations or industry groups you belong to have feeds of current news in your field.

But how do know what feeds are available? Well, most websites generate an RSS feed; you just have to know where to look and what to grab. You can find RSS feeds in two simple ways, as shown in Figure 24-2.

The first way is by checking websites that have content you think would be useful to your visitors on an ongoing basis and looking for an RSS feed symbol. The top half of Figure 24-2 shows how some sites include their RSS feed with social media icons. (The RSS feed symbol is highlighted.) Wherever you find the link, you can right-click and copy the URL.

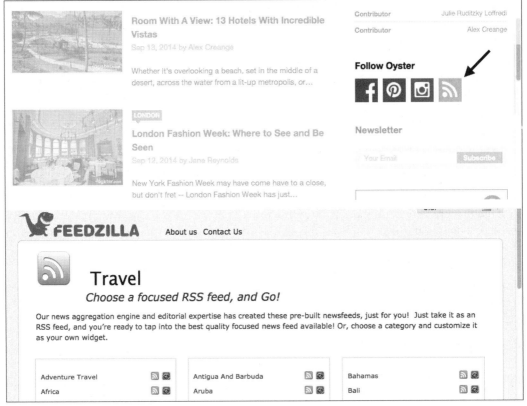

FIGURE 24-2

The second way is by checking directories of RSS feeds. In the bottom half of Figure 24-2, you can see an example of a feeds directory called www.feedzilla.com. Again, you simply right-click the link of whichever feed you want and copy the URL.

Most browsers also have the capability to detect RSS feeds and notify you in some way. If it's not built in they'll have an extension or add-on that provides that functionality.

Displaying RSS Feeds

Displaying RSS feeds from other sites is straightforward in WordPress. Go to Appearance ⇨ Widgets and look for a widget called RSS. Drag it over to the Sidebar area on the right, and it opens up to display the box shown in Figure 24-3 A.

The first thing you're asked for is the URL for the RSS feed. This is the information you copy from the website providing the feed.

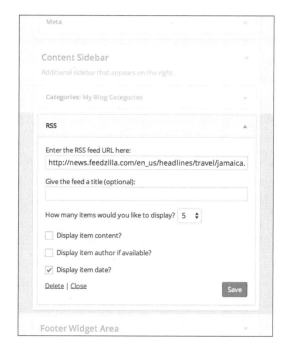

FIGURE 24-3

You then take your copied address and paste it into the WordPress widget where it says Enter the RSS Feed URL Here.

Enter a title that will display above the feed in your sidebar. Next, you have a choice of how many items to display from the feed (the default is 10), along with which parts of the feed you would like to display: Content, Author, and Date.

Click Save and close the Widget. When you refresh your live site, you'll see the RSS feed in your sidebar, like my Jamaican Travel feed in Figure 24-3 B.

If you need an RSS feed displayed in a Post or a Page, rather than in a Widget area, there are plugins that will enable you to do that with shortcode, as mentioned at the end of the lesson.

Make sure you check out any new feed, maybe even put it on a page that's not linked to your site as a trial run, and ensure it has the relevant, useful information you were expecting. Sometimes, you'll want to adjust the settings to show only the title and the date or only the title and content.

PLUGINS

The third-party application plugins you might need are too numerous and too specific to mention, but RSS feed plugins work for any feed, as do iFrame plugins.

THIRD-PARTY APPLICATION INTEGRATION

Start by checking the website for the application and look for a WordPress plugin. If there's no official plugin, someone may have written one, so check the WordPress Plugin Directory by entering the application's name. If you're still not finding anything, you could search by the application type (surveys or appointments or whatever).

➤ **Indeed Job Importer**—Show jobs from your Indeed job listings account in WordPress. Example of a plugin that enables you to easily integrate content from a third-party site.

➤ **SlideShare for WordPress by Yoast**—Easily embed Slideshare presentations. This is a good example of the many plugins that make embedding from public sharing sites simple.

IFRAMES USING SHORTCODES

➤ **Advanced iFrame**—Makes it simple to embed content from other websites in iframes using simple shortcodes.

BRINGING IN RSS FEEDS

➤ **Super RSS Reader**—An alternative to the built-in RSS Widget from WordPress. This enables you to have images in your feeds, automatic scrolling, tabbed content, and more.

➤ **RSSImport**—Enables you to display an RSS feed in the content area of your Posts or Pages using shortcodes.

➤ **WP RSS Multi Importer**—A powerful tool for displaying RSS feeds on your site, including the ability to place them in Posts and Pages using shortcodes.

➤ **FeedWordPress**—Takes material from an RSS feed and creates a Post for each feed item, allowing you to create an archive. Great for curating news from your field of business, for example.

OTHER PLUGINS

➤ **Broken Link Checker**—If you use a lot of YouTube and other third-party videos on your site, part of what this plugin does is check whether a video is still active. However, this plugin can use a lot of resources, so it's best to deactivate it when not in use and then activate it, say once a month, and run it.

TRY IT

In this lesson, you practice putting an RSS feed in your sidebar.

Lesson Requirements

Have the URL of a content feed that you would like to put in your sidebar. One simple way is to go to a friend's blog and get the URL for his feed.

Step-by-Step

To add an RSS feed to the sidebar, follow these steps:

1. Have the URL of the RSS feed available on your clipboard or in a text file somewhere.

2. Go to Appearance ⇨ Widgets.

3. Locate the RSS feed Widget in the Available box on the left side.

4. Click the RSS Feed Widget, and choose a Widget Area; then click Add Widget.

5. When the Widget opens up, paste the URL into the field marked Enter the RSS Feed URL Here.

6. Give the feed a title if you like.

7. Check Display Item Content if you want more than just the title of each item.

8. Do the same for Author if you want that to display.

9. Do the same for Date.

10. Click Save.

11. Refresh your website and view the feed live.

12. If you see nothing or you have an error, double-check the URL of the feed once more and try again.

> **REFERENCE** *Please select the video for Lesson 24 online at* www.wrox.com/go /wp24vids. *You will also be able to download resources for this lesson from the website.*

25

Connecting by E-mail

Although social media has become an important way to connect with your site visitors, e-mail remains an equally important tool. This lesson shows you some easy ways to:

➤ Have visitors contact you by e-mail

➤ Collect visitor e-mails

➤ E-mail visitors automatically when you update your site

Some of this involves setting up third-party services, but they're either free or low cost.

CONTACTING YOU BY E-MAIL

When you want visitors to reach you by e-mail, the two most common ways on websites are:

➤ Putting your e-mail address somewhere in the text

➤ Providing a contact form

WordPress makes both of these methods quite easy.

E-mail Addresses

Let me say at the outset: *Do not put e-mail addresses anywhere on your site*. That's because spammers regularly sweep your site looking for e-mail addresses to "harvest" and put on their lists.

If you choose to ignore this warning, at least do the following: Install a WordPress plugin that will attempt to hide your e-mail address from the evil spammers. Several of them are mentioned at the end of this lesson, but here's a bit about how they work.

Some plugins automatically detect that you've put an e-mail address into a Post, Page, or Widget and use various techniques to make it unreadable to the programs the spammer send around the Internet. Other plugins have you use a shortcode to enter e-mail addresses.

So if you're going to put an e-mail address in your text, what's the best way to do it?

You can enter an e-mail as text, but it's a better idea to use the Link button of the Content Editor and create a mailto link so that people can click the address and it automatically opens their e-mail program to send you an e-mail.

Highlight the text you want the address linked to, click the Insert/Edit Link button, and enter the link, as shown in Figure 25-1.

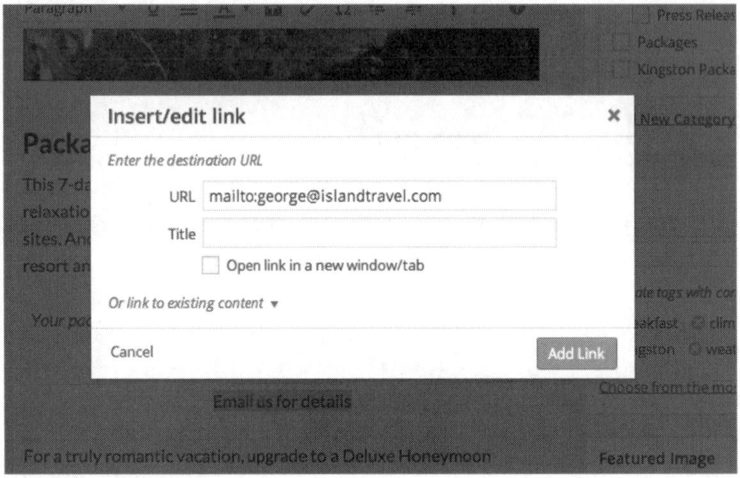

FIGURE 25-1

The key is emailto:you@youremail.com because without that, the triggering of the e-mail program won't work.

Read the documentation of your e-mail hiding plugin because it may take care of the mailto function for you. And make sure the plugin allows e-mails to trigger a mail program.

However, let me end this section where I started: *Ignore everything I just said and don't put e-mail addresses in your text*. Read the next section instead.

Contact Forms

A contact form is a better alternative than leaving your e-mail address out in public, not simply for a bit more security, but also because it's useful for guiding people to give you the information you need. It could be something as simple as asking what department the e-mail is for, or you might ask how long users have owned your product and so on. Plus by making certain fields required, you're ensured of getting the details you need. Figure 25-2 A shows a simple appointment form for Island Travel.

Figure 25-2 B shows how the form was built using Contact Form 7 and a series of tags. The plugin has a simple tag builder system shown in Figure 25-2 C; you simply fill in the field information and it generates a tag. There are many other contact form plugins for WordPress; a few more are listed at the end of the lesson.

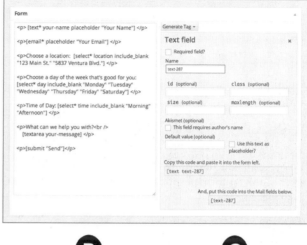

FIGURE 25-2

It's best to use a plugin to create forms. Although you may know enough HTML to build your own contact form, the big issue is how to hook it up so that it sends you an e-mail. WordPress already has a send mail function built in, so it's easiest to use a form plugin that takes care of hooking into that function.

Most readers will be using a shared hosting account for their WordPress site, and sometimes you can run into problems with your form properly sending mail. Some form plugins make it possible to send e-mails through another server, such as Gmail/Google Apps. There are also plugins which add that functionality to a form; see the end of this lesson for one such plugin.

Dealing with Form Spam

E-mail addresses out in the open are not the only target of spammers; contact forms are also on their hit list. I've had a few clients who've never had a form spammed, but for many it starts happening a few days after the form goes live. Whether you choose to do it from the start or when the problem starts happening, there are ways to combat it.

Some contact form plugins have a built-in option for thwarting the spambots (automated programs used by spammers), or you can use a separate plugin to do that.

The most common method, of course, is the dreaded captcha test; visitors have to figure out some hard-to-read letters and numbers, and then fill in a field proving that they're human beings and not spambots. Not all systems use obscure characters, and some ask a simple math question, as shown in Figure 25-3, whereas others use techniques such as dragging a particular image to a certain position.

The easier the captcha is for people to use (while still thwarting the spambots), the more likely it is visitors will complete the form, so finding an easy-to-use captcha is important.

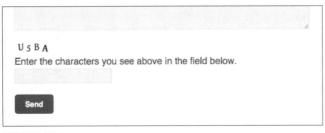

FIGURE 25-3

Fooling spambots into revealing themselves without real users filling out a captcha field is, of course, even better. Look for form plugins that create invisible fields, which visitors cannot see, but spambots will. If the field is filled in, you know that the e-mail is from a spammer. With a bit of CSS knowledge, you can even create your own invisible field. Give the field a special class, and then set the display to "none."

> **NOTE** *An invisible field is different from a hidden field. A hidden field is a special type of form field that users also don't see, but spambots can identify as hidden, so they may avoid filling it out. A field which has been made invisible through CSS is less likely to be identified by a spambot.*

COLLECTING VISITOR E-MAILS

You see them all the time on websites: small forms where you can sign up to join a mailing list or subscribe to a newsletter. This collecting of e-mails can be invaluable. It's a way for you to reach out to your visitors at any time and not worry about whether they're on a particular social network.

Although you could collect e-mails through the kind of contact form mentioned earlier, that's not recommended. It means having to collect the e-mails in, say, a spreadsheet or a program such as Outlook and then trying to manage mailouts from there.

You're much better off using a dedicated mailing list manager service, such as MailChimp or Aweber. Although they do cost money, these services not only manage the sending of the e-mails (with nice-looking layouts), they also offer real-time statistics on whether people are opening the e-mails and clicking any links within them.

Perhaps more important, though, these mailing list managers handle the sign-up process in a special way using *double opt-in*. This automated process takes the addresses visitors first enter and sends an e-mail with a special link. By clicking that link, visitors agree to be on your mailing list and receive another confirmation e-mail stating that they're on the list. This is important to prevent accusations of spamming or being added to a list without consent.

The managers also track whether e-mails are bouncing and handle the process of cleaning up the list from time to time. Even if you had only 100 people on your list, handling these functions yourself would be time-consuming.

> **NOTE** *MailChimp offers free mailing list services for up to 2,000 subscribers, which is one of the reasons I recommend it to small business owners. The free plan does not, however, include autoresponders (automated follow-up e-mails).*

Integrating Mailing Lists with Your Site

Services such as MailChimp and Aweber make it easy to integrate a sign-up form with your website. As with social media sites, they provide simple code for you to paste into a Page or a Widget, as shown in Figure 25-4 A.

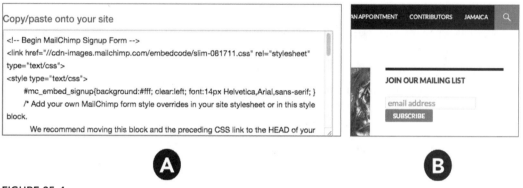

FIGURE 25-4

You can see the result in the sidebar of Island Travel in Figure 25-4 B.

Normally, when people click Send, they're taken to a notification page telling them to watch for a confirmation e-mail. You can use the provider's default notification page, but it's better if you create a page on your website and use that.

Mailing list managers also make it possible now for people to stay on the page where they submitted the form and simply be shown a success message stating that a confirmation e-mail is on the way. People can sometimes be confused by being taken to another page, even if it's on your site, so this feature can be handy.

When visitors click the confirmation link in the e-mail, you definitely want to make sure they're taken back to your site rather than to the default message screen of your mailing list provider. That page is where you'll provide their reward for signing up, such as a free PDF.

Why Not Use a Plugin?

There are plugins for WordPress that offer mailing list functionality. That's attractive in a couple ways: You don't have to log in to a separate service to manager your list, plus your mailing list isn't separate from your list of WordPress users.

However, the potential problems with relying on your hosting account to do even small mailings on a regular basis, coupled with the powerful features of a third-party mailing manager and relatively low cost, makes the plugin route not that attractive. And if you want your list to mirror your WordPress users, there are plugins for some mailing list managers that can coordinate the two.

For those who are still interested, a couple mailing list manager plugins are mentioned at the end of the lesson.

E-MAILING SITE UPDATES

A great way to keep visitors up to date about your website is to automatically e-mail them when you put up new content. Although that may sound like a lot of work to set up, there's a simple way to do it using the mailing list managers just mentioned.

The example of MailChimp is used here, but other mailing list managers use a similar process called RSS to E-mail. The idea is to use the RSS feed that WordPress automatically generates to send out an e-mail to all or part of your mailing list telling them about the newest Posts on your site.

In MailChimp, a one-time mailing is called a campaign, and there are several types. Here you want the RSS-Driven Campaign, as shown in Figure 25-5.

FIGURE 25-5

Then you tell MailChimp what the address of the RSS feed is; it could be all your Posts or only ones from a certain Category. There are other types of feeds that WordPress automatically generates. As Figure 25-6 shows, if you're not certain of the address, just put in your domain name, and MailChimp tries to figure it out:

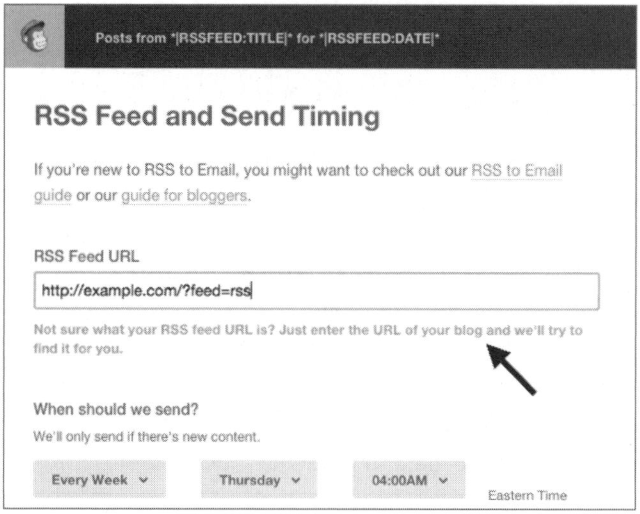

FIGURE 25-6

Then you specify the frequency with which you want the e-mails sent. The beauty of the system is that, say you had them going out weekly on a Thursday, if there were no new Posts since the last mailing, then nothing would be sent, so your subscribers wouldn't get an e-mail repeating old entries.

There are alternatives to using a mailing list manager, such as the subscription service offered by WordPress's parent company Automattic, by way of its Jetpack plugin. Or there's Feedburner from Google. But one of the drawbacks in both these cases is that you can't e-mail your list yourself; it works only when there are new Posts. In addition, most websites should have a mailing list manager for e-mails other than notifying about new content, so why operate two different systems?

Although using RSS to generate e-mails is your best method of keeping visitors up to date automatically, the RSS feeds themselves can still be used by those with RSS readers (programs that notify users of new items for feeds subscribed to).

WordPress is generating those feeds automatically, and reader programs notify visitors if a site has a feed. Still, it's a good idea to include RSS on your social media follow icons.

If you want visitors to follow a particular Category of your Posts rather than all of them, you could create a link to just that Category. Next you can find an example of plugins that enable users of RSS readers to choose from available feeds on your site.

Of course, the problem with regular RSS feeds is that you don't know who has subscribed, so you are unable to send out special e-mails to them.

PLUGINS

There are hundreds of plugins at WordPress.org dealing with e-mails and form creation. Here you'll find some of the most useful.

ANTI-E-MAIL HARVESTING

➤ **WP Mailto Links—Manage E-mail Links:** Protects e-mail addresses from spam harvesters. Works automatically on e-mail addresses entered as text, or you can use shortcodes to enter the addresses for protection.

➤ **Email Address Encoder—**Automatically protects any e-mail address from spammers. No shortcodes are necessary or available.

➤ **Email Encoder Bundle—Protect Email Address:** Automatically protects e-mail addresses from spam robots but also works on phone numbers and addresses.

FORM BUILDERS

➤ **Contact Form 7—**A simple but flexible and powerful form creation plugin with many additional plugins to give it even more power.

➤ **Fast Secure Contact Form—**Build contact forms or any type of form. A powerful plugin with many settings and built-in spam control.

➤ **Contact Form—**For creating a contact form only. Easily drop into any Post, Page, or Widget and you're ready to go immediately. Few settings; the idea is to remain as simple as possible.

➤ **Visual Form Builder—**Build contact forms or any other type of form using a simple interface allowing you to drag and drop fields into any order. Includes antispam functionality.

➤ **Formidable Forms—**Drag and drop form builder.

➤ **Ninja Forms—**Another drag and drop form builder.

➤ **WP Mail SMTP—**If you're experiencing problems with your form sending e-mails, this plugin enables your form to send through a server other than your own.

CAPTCHA TESTS

A number of antispam plugins are listed in Lesson 23, "Managing Comments," which can also work for forms, for example:

➤ **Really Simple CAPTCHA—**A captcha module for forms, which was originally made for Contact Form 7 but can be used with other plugins.

MAILING LIST MANAGERS

Many third-party mailing list managers, such as MailChimp, Aweber, Constant Contact, and more have WordPress plugins, either official or made by others.

You can, of course, just paste in code from these services, but plugins can make it even simpler or add some functionality.

➤ **MailPoet Newsletters**—A full mailing list manager that works from within WordPress. It's possible to assign the task of sending out e-mails through a third party if your server is causing problems sending hundreds of e-mails.

➤ **Newsletter**—A mailing list manager that runs in WordPress.

NEW POST SUBSCRIPTION MANAGER

Subscribe2—Enables visitors to subscribe and be notified whenever new Posts are added, all from within WordPress.

RSS FEED SELECTOR

Category Specific RSS feed Subscription—Offers visitors a drop-down RSS subscription list for your Categories and not just your blog feed as a whole. You can also create feeds for your Tags.

TRY IT

There isn't anything specific to try for this lesson, but what you can do is begin researching a mailing list manager service that fits your needs and budget. Apart from an easy to use interface, look for the ability to segment your mailing list into useful groups. Can you easily do a mailing to everyone who didn't click on the link in your last e-mail? Can you easily send an e-mail only to people who have signed up through your Facebook page? Find out what mailing list managers your friends and colleagues are using, and ask what they see as the pros and cons.

> **REFERENCE** *Please select the video for Lesson 25 online at* www.wrox.com/go/wp24vids. *You will also be able to download resources for this lesson from the website.*

26

Managing Multiple Site Users

One of the ways you can make your site social is to give special access to certain visitors: pages that only they can see or documents only they can download. These visitors could be your clients or members of your local association, or they could be anyone who wants to sign up. Whatever the case, you grant them this special access by making them Users in WordPress.

A *User* is someone who can log in to your WordPress site, and every User has one of five possible *Roles*, which determines what they're allowed to do when they're logged in. What actions they're allowed to take are referred to as *Capabilities*.

Now, it's possible you'll be the only User your site will ever have, but in most cases there are going to be at least some additional Users and this lesson is about how to manage them.

USER ROLES AND THEIR CAPABILITIES

As mentioned, five User Roles are built in to WordPress and, in order of decreasing capabilities, they are

- ➤ Administrator
- ➤ Editor
- ➤ Author
- ➤ Contributor
- ➤ Subscriber

In the case of Island Travel, with its two offices, I could have a single Administrator to take care of technical aspects of the site, and a single Editor who oversees all site content. Each travel agent could be an Author managing their own posts, with a few non-agency people who act as Contributors. Customers and potential customers could be Subscribers, who can view website content the public can't see but have no control on the back end or administrative side of WordPress.

With these examples in mind, let's go through each of the five User Roles in a bit more detail:

➤ **Administrator**—Has full access to every function in WordPress, including editing theme files, changing themes, and adding plugins, user details, and so on. You'll want to limit how many Administrators you have, in part for security (if someone gets ahold of one of those passwords, your site is wide open) and in part to minimize the need for coordination.

➤ **Editor**—The Editor role allows the maximum amount of control over all the content of the website, without changing settings that control the site itself, such as themes or plugins. Editors can add, edit, or delete any content-related items in WordPress, including Categories, Posts, and Pages. They have full access to the Media Library and can add and delete users (though not edit user information). One limitation on Editors which is not so obvious is that they can't access Widgets or Menus because they're blocked from the entire Appearance section of the main Admin menu.

➤ **Author**—Authors within WordPress are meant to be like columnists in a newspaper or magazine. They have full control over their own Posts (not Pages)—adding, editing, publishing, and deleting—but no one else's. This includes the ability to upload files to use in their content. Authors cannot, however, add or delete Posts or Categories. They also can't use unfiltered HTML—code such as JavaScript or certain HTML tags or attributes pasted from a program such as Dreamweaver.

➤ **Contributor**—Contributors can create, edit, or delete their own Posts, but they cannot publish them, only save drafts or submit for review. They also cannot upload files, even to their own Posts. And after a Post is published by an Editor or Administrator, a Contributor cannot edit or delete that Post. Contributors appear on the Post Author drop-down menu and typically are included in lists of Authors that might be generated by themes or plugins.

➤ **Subscriber**—Think of a Subscriber as a registered visitor—someone who can see content or take actions on a site that unregistered visitors can't. Basically, the only permission subscribers have in the admin section is the ability to change their Profile (name, e-mail, interests, avatar, and so on).

For complete details on and an up-to-date list of each Role's Capabilities, check out the WordPress site at `http://codex.wordpress.org/Roles_and_Capabilities`.

As stated earlier, these are the Roles built in to WordPress, but one of the powerful features of WordPress is the ability to not only add new Roles with their own unique sets of Capabilities, but to also change which Roles have which Capabilities. For example, you may want to give Editors the ability to create and edit Widgets, while still keeping them out of Themes. At the end of the lesson some plugins are mentioned that make use of these functions.

> **WARNING** *If you hire someone to work on your site with Administrator powers, be sure to delete that User when they finish. Or if you give her your login information, make sure you change the password when she finishes.*

ADDING A USER

You can add a User to a WordPress site in two ways:

➤ A visitor filling out a registration form

➤ An Administrator adding a User through an admin screen

The registration form will mostly be used to sign up large numbers of visitors as Subscribers, while adding a user yourself through the Admin screen is usually limited to adding a few higher Roles, such as Editors and Authors.

User Registration Forms

By default, the registration form is disabled. You can activate it on the Settings ⇨ General screen by checking the Membership box, as shown in Figure 26-1.

FIGURE 26-1

However, the best advice is to leave the automatic sign-up disabled. If you deal with a lot of membership sign-ups, you'll probably want to use a plugin anyway, and these plugins handle the sign-up process in a different manner. The word *membership* for that setting is a bit confusing because what you're setting is the ability for people to register themselves as new users on the system. There is no User role called *member* and you may or may not think of the users who sign up as members. The wording on the drop-down menu just below is clearer: New User Default Role. In other words, you're setting the Role that users will be assigned if they can register themselves, but it's also the default Role in the drop-down menu when manually creating new users. By default, that role is Subscriber.

> **WARNING** *Don't change the Default User Role unless you've thought things through. Even allowing just anyone to become a Contributor opens up your system to people posting content (even if they can't publish). And you certainly wouldn't want to allow just anyone to be an Author, Editor, or Administrator.*

The Add User Function

To manually add a new User to the system, click Users ⇨ Add New on the main Admin menu and you'll be greeted with the Add New User screen, as shown in Figure 26-2.

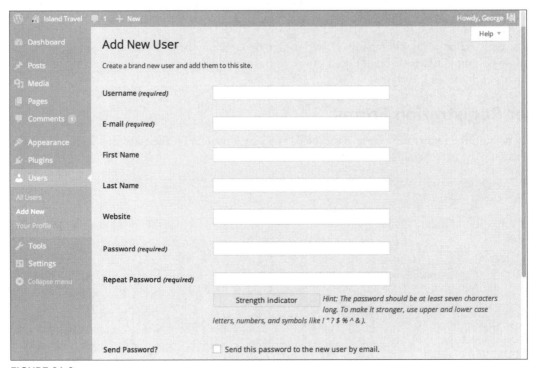

FIGURE 26-2

Only three items are required to create a new User:

➤   Username

➤   E-mail address

➤   Password

Users can fill in the other details as they choose after they log in for the first time.

Always double-check which role you're assigning to the User. (The default is Subscriber.) If you'd like the log in details sent to the User by e-mail, be sure to check the Send Password box. After users have their login information, they can change or fill in any of the fields on the Profile screen you saw in Lesson 5, "Basic Admin Settings" (except the username).

> **NOTE** *Usernames and e-mail addresses must be unique. WordPress warns you if either already exists in the system.*

CHANGING A USER'S ABILITIES

Need to promote a Contributor to Author status? Tired of another Administrator always switching themes and you want to bump them down to Subscriber?

An Administrator can change any User's Role from the Users screen, as shown in Figure 26-3 A.

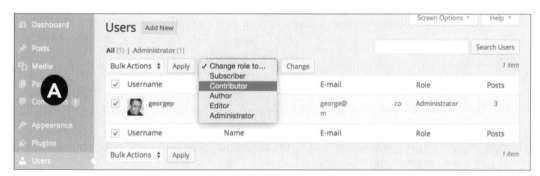

FIGURE 26-3

Check the box next to their name, choose a new role from the Change Role To drop-down menu, and click Change. If several Users need to be changed to the same Role, you can do them all at once by checking the box next to each, and then using the drop-down.

If you have additional information to change, you can do it all from the User's Profile screen, as shown in Figure 26-3 B. Just below the username is the drop-down menu for their Role. Select the new Role and click Update Profile.

If you have a lot of users on the site, you can change the number of users displayed using the Screen Options menu at the top right. In addition, you can filter one particular Role at a time using the links at the top left of the Users screen.

USERS AND SECURITY

Following are three key points concerning users and security:

> **Choose the lowest possible Role**—Don't make someone an Editor when they just need to be an Author. The higher the Role, the more power you're entrusting to the User. And if you turn on the self-registration feature, don't allow users to sign up as anything more than Subscriber.

➤ **Emphasize the importance of tough passwords**—You may give new users a diabolical password, but they can go in and change that later. Impress on them the need to not use natural language words, and to use uppercase and lowercase, numbers, and so on. WordPress has this reminder and a strength indicator that gives users an extra nudge; even better are plugins that force the use of strong passwords. A couple are mentioned at the end of the lesson.

➤ **Monitor your users**—The unexpected appearance of a User you've never heard of with a Role such as Administrator or Editor could be the sign of a hacker. You can quickly check for possible intruders by filtering the list of Users by Administrator or any other Role.

PLUGINS

Many plugins help you set up a Membership site, and those are discussed in Lesson 36, "More Plugin Suggestions" Following are plugins that modify or expand the User management functions of WordPress.

MANAGING USER ROLES AND CAPABILITIES

➤ **Members**—A powerful plugin for modifying existing Roles and their Capabilities, adding new Roles, restricting access by Role, and even making your entire site Private (can be seen only if someone logs in). Not a membership plugin in the typical sense of paid memberships.

➤ **User Role Editor**—You can change the Capabilities of various Roles in WordPress—for example, allowing Editors to use Widgets. You can also add new Roles and give them whatever capabilities you'd like.

MANAGING USER ACCESS

➤ **Advanced Access Manager**—Manage the Capabilities of User Roles as well as User access to various types of content.

➤ **Press Permit Core**—Gives you fine-grained control over what Roles can see what material on the website. Block access by type of content (Posts or Pages), by Category, and by individual content items. This plugin replaces the popular Role Scoper plugin.

➤ **Author Category**—If you want to limit the Categories that users can choose for their Posts, this plugin creates a section in each user profile where an administrator can make the restriction. Could even restrict them to a single category.

OTHER USER MANAGEMENT PLUGINS

➤ **amr users**—Organize lists of users, display a directory of users, and manage users in bulk, based on a variety of user parameters. You can also create public lists of users.

> ➤ **Force Strong Passwords**—Does not let Users enter weak passwords.

> ➤ **Simple Local Avatars**—Creates an upload function on User Profile pages so that they can upload their own photo to be used by themes that display an author image.

> ➤ **New User Approve**—Changes the registration process so that new Users must first be approved by an Administrator.

> ➤ **User Spam Remover**—If you're overrun with spam User accounts, this plugin makes it easy to get rid of them. In fact, it does it automatically, but keeps a backup in case you want to restore a deleted user.

> ➤ **Email Users**—E-mail all Users at once or in groups. Users can even e-mail one another.

> ➤ **Peter's Login Redirect**—Enables control over where Users are taken after logging in or logging out.

TRY IT

In this lesson, you practice adding a new User.

Lesson Requirements

You need an e-mail address you can access that is different from the one you're using for your WordPress administrator role.

Step-by-Step

To add a new User, follow these steps:

1. Go to Users ⇨ Add New.

2. Enter a username.

3. Enter an e-mail address that you can access. (It must be different from the e-mail you use in your current profile.)

4. Enter a password. (Follow the suggestions given by WordPress.)

5. As you enter the password the first time, the Strength meter will tell you how good it is. Make sure you get the green Strong signal.

6. Enter the password a second time.

7. Make sure the Send Password box is checked.

8. Select a role for this User (other than Administrator).

9. Click Add User.

10. Log out of WordPress as an Administrator.

11. Check your e-mail for your User information.

12. Try logging in with your username and password. As long as the new User's role was not Administrator, you shouldn't see Settings on the main admin menu, and depending on the User level, you may not see other parts of the menu either.

13. Be sure to delete the User after this exercise.

> **REFERENCE** *Please select the video for Lesson 26 online at* www.wrox.com/go /wp24vids. *You will also be able to download resources for this lesson from the website.*

SECTION VII
Choosing and Customizing Themes

27

Overview of WordPress Themes

One of the biggest advantages of a content management system is the ability to easily change the look of your site without having to redo all your pages, and WordPress makes it easy with its use of themes. With thousands of themes (free and paid) to choose from, the question is this: How do you choose?

The key to choosing a theme is not to be taken in by looks. That sounds strange to say when one of the principal tasks of a theme is to control the look of your site. But when you understand what themes do and how they can differ widely, you'll understand that "looks aren't everything."

WHAT IS A WORDPRESS THEME?

A *theme* is a set of files, graphics, and scripts that, most obviously, controls the look of your site: layout, colors, typography, and so on. However, behind the scenes, these theme files perform an equally, if not more, important job.

Think of WordPress as a set of functions waiting to be used—functions that pull information from a database, manipulate it, organize it, and display it. It's your theme that makes use of those functions to output the content that's stored in the database, and at that point applies the design elements.

WordPress themes have two distinct roles:

➤ Functionality

➤ Design

Figure 27-1 A shows the default Twenty Fourteen theme for Island Travel with a lot of files to run the site, of which only one is solely devoted to looks—the CSS style sheet.

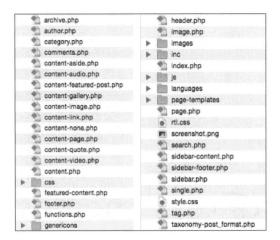

FIGURE 27-1

Figure 27-1 B shows some of the coding in a theme file that uses WordPress functions to get content and settings from the database.

Plugins also use WordPress's functions—to add Facebook-like buttons, show random content in a sidebar, and so on—but the basic functionality of a site is controlled by the theme.

In the last few years an explosion has occurred in the ways themes use and extend WordPress functions. In particular, themes have increasingly modified the back end or administrative screens so that your WordPress and my WordPress can be quite different. Just as some people use more or different plugins than others, the theme used by one person can provide far different administrative options and site functionality than the theme used by someone else. For example, Figure 27-2 shows four very different options screens from two different themes.

Increasingly these days, when people ask me questions about using WordPress, the questions turn out to be about how their particular theme works. Unlike the elements of WordPress that we all share, these sophisticated add-ons put us in different places for how we use the software. That's not a bad thing; it's just a noticeable change from the world of WordPress only a few years ago.

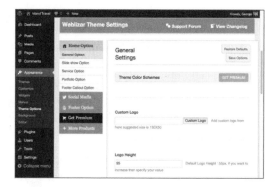
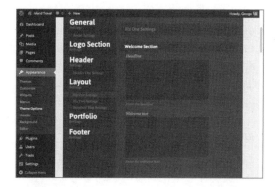
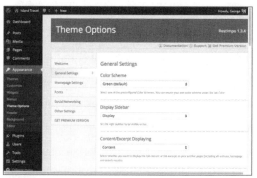

FIGURE 27-2

CHOOSING A WORDPRESS THEME

My rule of thumb for picking a theme is:

Quality, functionality, and flexibility first, design second.

The reason? It's much easier (read, lower-cost) to make a site look exactly the way you want than it is to make the quality of coding better or create new functionality (especially easy-to-use functionality).

Having said that, one of the must-have features for themes today is responsive design, which means, it displays well on any size of device screen. An alternative is to use a theme-switcher plugin that displays a different theme (and even different content) to mobile devices, but a quality responsive design is as effective and a simpler option.

DIY Design?

One of the features that a lot of people are impressed with in a theme is the ability to quickly switch layouts and change colors, fonts, and all kinds of design elements through easy-to-use interfaces.

Don't get me wrong, I think a lot of these do-it-yourself design interfaces are not only cool, but also extremely well-thought-out and brilliantly engineered. But think about design for a moment: How often do you need to change colors and layouts? And if you do it often, should you? Does it help you get and retain visitors or does it confuse them?

The point is that these useful tools are great when you're first setting up a site and they enable you to change your mind a lot, but after you settle on something, how often do you need them again? And, not to be too blunt about it, maybe you should be hiring a designer to set up some of these things, anyway—they have an eye for it.

I know, I'm back to the "functionality is a bit more important than design" rant, but that's because it's those functions that you're going to use day in and day out. A theme that makes it easy to create and manage your own custom widget areas is more valuable than one that focuses on cool color wheels for picking the shade of your H2 headers. If the theme can do both, more power to it.

There's also a part of me that worries about complexity in the back end. It takes a lot of programming to produce these amazing interfaces, and that's just one more point at which something can go wrong. I would rather see simpler (but clear and usable) interfaces that produce good functionality on the site than be wowed by cool effects and massive back ends. OK, rant over.

> **NOTE** *I'm not talking here about visual page builder functionality, which is discussed in Lesson 36, "More Plugin Suggestions." These page builders are about laying out content on individual pages, not setting design elements for the whole site.*

Do Your Homework

The key, then, is not to grab the first theme you like the look of or that has a lot of fancy design functions. You need to check the theme's and the theme-maker's reputation:

➤ Does the theme appear on a number of Top 10 WordPress themes lists?

➤ Is it made by an author or a company who receives good reviews for other work?

➤ How many people are downloading it (if it's available at WordPress.org) and what are they saying about it in the forums?

➤ Put the question to the forums—what are other people experiencing with this theme?

This sounds like a lot, but this theme is going to run your website (along with WordPress) hopefully for several years to come. It should be the backbone on which to hang all future design changes. You want to get this right.

You also need to ask questions based on your needs:

➤ Is it well built; does it offer the functionality you need (not simply for controlling the design); and is it flexible?

➤ What do you need your site to do, and will this theme help make that possible and easier?

➤ Is it worth paying a consultant for one-half hour to pick out a good theme with you?

Following are a few more actions you can take to ensure you have a great theme.

Checking a Theme for Best Practices

What are best practices? It's another way of saying "follows standards," and just like there are standards for using HTML or CSS, WordPress has a certain way of doing things.

Using best practices is about making your experience, and ultimately that of your visitors, better. Part of it involves consistency: Using up-to-date WordPress coding means your theme isn't going to cause conflicts and break, and using built-in WordPress tools rather than creating new ways to do something means you don't have to spend time learning a new function.

Some checks for WordPress best practices are easy:

➤ Does it use the menu system?

➤ Does it use the header and background interfaces?

➤ Does it use the customize interface?

Others are not so easy to quickly spot. For example, I recently had a call from a client who couldn't figure out how to change the header image on a particular page. It turned out that the theme they switched to used a special Custom Field for unique page headers instead of the built-in Featured Image function of WordPress. That's just sloppy theme building.

Some sloppiness occurs at the coding level, so how is the average user to know when that happens?

When WordPress is deciding what themes to put in its directory, it has a plugin to help assess the quality of the theme's coding and other factors. You can download and use this plugin. It's called Theme Check, and even with themes approved for the WordPress directory, it can tell you some things to watch for, as shown in Figure 27-3.

RECOMMENDED: No reference to **add_editor_style()** was found in the theme. It is recommended that the theme implement editor styling, so as to make the editor content match the resulting post output in the theme, for a better user experience.

INFO: Possible hard-coded links were found in the file **footer.php**.

```
Line 20: <?php printf( __( 'Theme: %2$s by %1$s', 'moesia' ), 'aThemes', '<a
href='http://athemes.com/theme/moesia'>Moesia</a>' ); ?>
```

FIGURE 27-3

The theme checker is pointing out that this theme does not style the Content Editor to look exactly the way your content will look on the live site. It's also alerting you to possible issues with a link that's coded into the theme. It turns out the link is harmless because it goes to the theme maker's site, but it could just as easily have gone to some phishing site or other nasty place.

> **NOTE** *A type of best practice to look for is the design of an administrative interface, and this applies to plugins as well as themes. Does the interface look like other parts of the WordPress admin screens? If it doesn't, it is harder to locate elements on a screen. Consistency in design is important on the back end as well as the front end.*

Important Theme Features

Following are some key features to look for in a theme, in addition to using built-in WordPress features and back-end design standards, passing Theme Check, having clear documentation, and so on:

➤ A lot of Widget areas, especially ones that you can place anywhere on the page. (Not the Widgets themselves, but the areas in which you can place Widgets.)

➤ Many front page control options—easy to update and control slide shows, user-selectable content areas (allowing you to put either a Post or Page, or custom Post-type content, into these areas).

➤ Several areas (or even the ability to easily create areas) in which you can have menus that use WordPress's built-in menu system.

And what's interesting is that when you find themes with these kinds of features, they're usually good-looking themes, too. So design and functionality *can* live harmoniously....

Does This Feature Belong in a Plugin?

This is an important question to ask when looking at the features of a theme. And it's easily answered in the following way:

> *If you need this feature even when you switch themes, it belongs in a plugin.*

The classic example is Search Engine Optimization (SEO). There was a big push several years ago to include SEO functions within themes. At first it seemed so much simpler to have these functions available as soon as you installed the theme, but when people switched themes and suddenly lost all their SEO tweaks, well, a lesson was learned.

Following are some other examples of functionality that belong in a plugin and not in your theme:

➤ Social media follow and share buttons

➤ Contact or other forms

➤ Events calendars

➤ Portfolio items

➤ Special photo gallery functions or sliders

Now you might say that some of these functions also involve styling and won't there be a clash with your theme? Well-written plugins will either automatically match your styling (because they use best practices for coding and naming) or allow you to easily change the styling to match your theme.

Of course, if an otherwise good theme happens to have some of this functionality, you can simply ignore it and use a plugin.

Theme-Recommended Plugins

A recent trend with WordPress themes is to recommend or even auto-install plugins. Figure 27-4 shows a theme suggesting several plugins and even offers to install them for you:

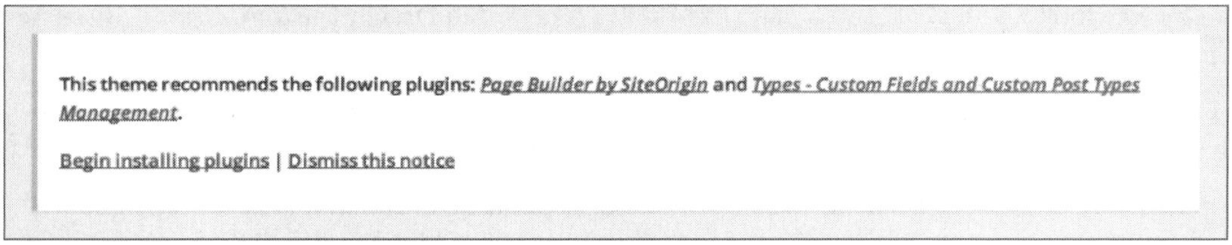

This theme recommends the following plugins: *Page Builder by SiteOrigin* and *Types - Custom Fields and Custom Post Types Management*.

Begin installing plugins | Dismiss this notice

FIGURE 27-4

This can be a helpful feature given the large number of available plugins and the remote possibility they could clash with your theme. What the theme maker is saying here is that these are good plugins that work with this theme. However, recommended plugins might be ones theme makers are pushing for themselves or their affiliates, so you still need to check and see if those are good plugins.

Auto-installed plugins are another matter. Aside from installing something without my permission, I've seen some situations in which the theme will break if one of those plugins is removed. At worst, only some function of the theme should be affected, not the entire theme. The other thing to watch for with auto-installed plugins is that sometimes the updating process is not automatic for those plugins, and you have to do it manually with the potential to mess things up. These are just some of the reasons I'm not a fan of auto-installed plugins.

It can be user-friendly to have helpful plugins installed automatically, and not everyone wants to take the time to check if the plugins are good ones. Nevertheless, being offered the choice of having plugins installed for you is preferred.

> **NOTE** *Lesson 36, "More Plugin Suggestions," mentions some plugins and some services that can help with installing multiple plugins at a time, independent of any theme.*

CHANGING THEMES

Although changing themes is as simple as clicking a button, it's important to understand the implications. First, you will probably lose certain functionality by changing themes. I warned earlier about using theme functions that actually belong in a plugin, because switching themes loses that functionality, but here I'm talking about functions that do properly belong in a theme.

For example, consider one theme that may enable you to have a different header on each Page, while the one you switch to may not. Or consider one that makes it easy to switch off the date that displays with each Post, whereas the next theme may not.

One of the ways around this constant change in functionality is to use a theme framework.

Theme Frameworks

WordPress makes it possible to have Child Themes that work off the files of their Parent theme, adding only those files they want to change, most notably the style sheet. They're used primarily to alter the look and feel of the Parent. (Lesson 29, "Advanced Design Customization," discusses Child Themes.)

Many theme makers use this Parent-Child relationship to create Theme Frameworks. The themes they offer are the children of a single Parent theme, each offering a different design from the next.

Another way to think of a Theme Framework is the separating of functionality and design: The Parent in the Framework handles the functionality, and each Child handles the particular design. Some theme makers don't explicitly separate Parent and Child, but within each theme they have a set of common files that essentially act like a Parent.

The advantage to you is that the back end of every theme running on the framework looks and operates the same way with only minor additions. So switching themes truly is a matter of just switching design.

Copy and Redesign

The other option that a lot of people aren't aware of is that any theme can be made to look any way you want. In other words, if you like the way your current theme works or it has some customizations you've spent money on, you don't need to throw it away just to have a new look.

Simply make a copy of your theme, give it a new name and new credentials, and then alter the design. Of course, that's going to take knowledge of CSS and WordPress, but for anyone who knows what they're doing, it's a straightforward process. Lesson 29 discusses this more in the "Advanced Customization" section.

> **WARNING** *Over the years I've seen many site owners be told by some developer that they have to toss out the WordPress theme they spent time and money customizing, and start again, merely to get a new look. That's just false.*

PLUGINS

These are plugins directly related to themes in general. In the WordPress Plugin Directory you will find some plugins designed for use with a specific theme or theme framework; simply search by the theme's name.

THEME TESTING

➤ **Theme Check**—Makes sure a theme meets WordPress standards and displays errors and recommended changes. Used by WordPress to help with vetting themes for its directory.

➤ **Theme Authenticity Checker (TAC)**—Scans a theme's files to look for malicious code.

➤ **Theme Test Drive**—Enables Administrators to try out a new theme while the public sees the current theme.

MANAGING THEMES

➤ Disable Updates Manager—If you don't want particular themes or plugins to be updated, either automatically or manually, this plugin enables you to block that process. If you've made the mistake of altering your theme files, this prevents updates from wiping them out.

➤ Delete Multiple Themes—If you accumulate a lot of themes in your Theme Library or a WordPress auto-installer has put in a lot of themes, deleting them one at a time can be a nuisance. This plugin enables you to delete them en masse.

MOBILE THEME SWITCHERS

If you're not using a theme with a responsive design, you can still give mobile users a good experience by using a plugin that switches to a mobile theme automatically.

➤ **WPtouch Mobile Plugin**—Detects whether a visitor is on a mobile devices and serves up your existing website in a mobile theme or whatever pages you want to be shown through a separate menu.

➤ **WP Mobile Detector Mobile Plugin**—Switches your site's theme depending on the mobile device it detects.

➤ **Any Mobile Theme Switcher**—Detects what mobile device a visitor is using and displays a theme of your choosing, while showing your regular WordPress theme to desktop visitors.

TRY IT

There is nothing specific to try in this lesson except getting to know what themes are available. Start in the themes directory at WordPress.org, including the list of commercial vendors on the left menu. (It has grown by leaps and bounds over the past couple years.)

All themes at the WordPress directory offer a live demonstration, but it's even better if you have a WordPress installation where you can try out the themes. Some commercial theme authors allow you to try out a theme on their site or have a free theme you can download to give you an idea of their work.

If you have a working site, some plugins allow administrators to try out a new theme without the rest of the world seeing it (not to be confused with allowing visitors to switch themes).

> **REFERENCE** *Please select the video for Lesson 27 online at* www.wrox.com/go /wp24vids. *You will also be able to download resources for this lesson from the website.*

28

Theme Installation and Basic Customization

Up to this point in the book you have been working with the default WordPress theme. Now it's time to install and activate the theme for the Island Travel site.

No matter which theme you choose, you need to customize the design, if only to insert your own logo or change some colors to better match your logo or branding. So this lesson also shows you some basic ways themes enable you to alter the look of your website without knowing CSS or HTML.

INSTALLING AND ACTIVATING A THEME

You need to understand that installing a theme is not the same as activating it. You can have many themes installed in your WordPress Theme Library, but you can activate only one of them at a time. The active theme is the one your visitors see.

You can install new themes and add to your WordPress Theme Library in two ways:

➤ Using the built-in theme selector for the WordPress.org Theme Directory

➤ Uploading the zip file for a theme, usually one you've purchased

To get to the Add Themes screen, however, there is no Add Themes link on the main Admin menu; you must go to Appearance ⇨ Themes and click the Add New link at the top, as shown in Figure 28-1.

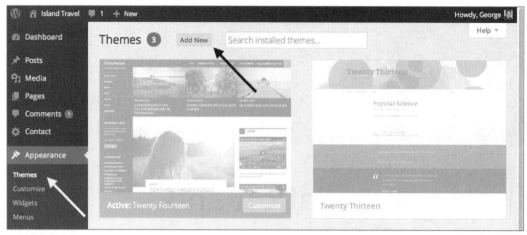

FIGURE 28-1

Searching the WordPress Theme Directory

What you first see when you get there is a series of screen shots of themes from the WordPress Themes Directory, as shown in Figure 28-2.

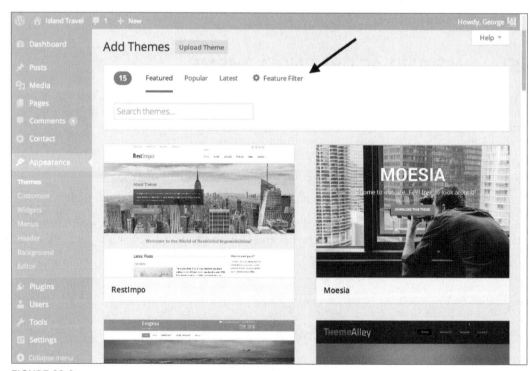

FIGURE 28-2

The default setting is to show the current Featured themes from the directory, but at the top of the screen I've highlighted a menu that also includes the most Popular and the Latest themes, which are self-explanatory. You can also search the directory.

But there's also a link called Feature Filter that enables you to do a search according to all kinds of parameters, such as colors, layout, WordPress functions, and more. A portion of the filter system is visible in Figure 28-3.

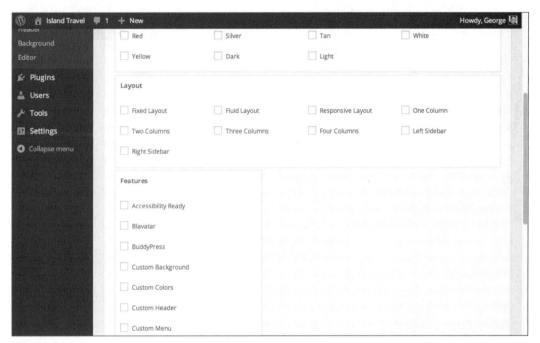

FIGURE 28-3

However you look for themes in the WordPress Theme Directory, the great thing is that you can preview them from this screen simply by mousing over a screen shot and clicking Details & Preview or just Preview.

Depending on the browser width of your device and whether the theme has a responsive design, the resulting version of the theme varies. Part of this is the result of the details sidebar, as shown in Figure 28-4 A. You can collapse that using the lower-left corner button (expanded below Figure 28-4 A), which gives you more room and a different view of the theme, as shown in Figure 28-4 B.

One of the great features of this theme browser is that you can scroll between themes without having to close the window and return to the theme listings. Simply use the left and right arrows at the top of the details sidebar (as highlighted in Figure 28-4 C).

When you find a theme you're interested in, simply click the Install button, either from within the theme browser or on the theme listings screen.

Remember, installing a theme simply makes it a part of your theme library; it won't be visible to the public because it isn't the active theme.

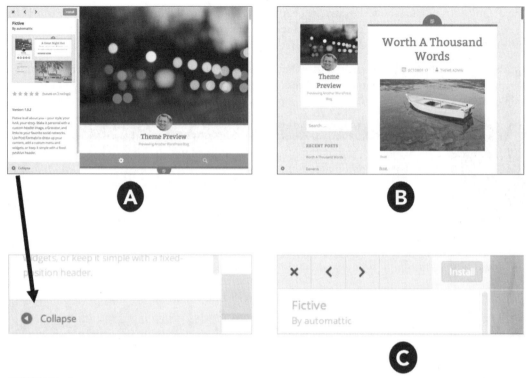

FIGURE 28-4

Uploading a Theme

The other method of installing a theme is to upload its zip file. When you purchase a theme from a commercial vendor, for example, you'll be given instructions for downloading the zip file.

You can also go to the WordPress.org Theme Directory and download a theme's zip file from there, but there's not much point because you can install the theme using the previous method.

There are two key points to keep in mind when downloading commercial theme files:

➤ **The zip file you receive may not be the zip file you're going to upload to WordPress.** Some vendors provide a zip file that contains instructions or graphics files along with the actual theme zip file. They should make this clear, but if WordPress rejects your zip file, that may be why; you just need to unzip the main file and use the zip file inside it.

➤ **If your theme depends on a Parent theme, you should receive two zip files.** You'll need to upload the Parent zip file to WordPress first and then the Child theme zip file. Again, the vendor should make it clear that there are two files required, but WordPress will tell you if you're missing a Parent theme.

To upload a theme's zip file, you need to click the Upload Theme button at the top of the Add Themes screen, as highlighted in Figure 28-5 A.

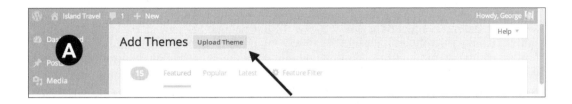

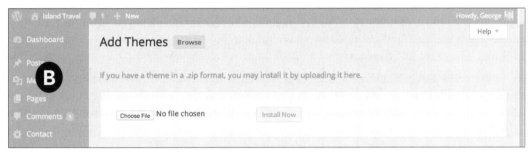

FIGURE 28-5

And the resulting version of the Add Themes screen is a basic file uploading screen, as shown in Figure 28-5 B, where you select the file from your device and then click the Install Now button.

Activating a Theme

After a theme is installed, it's available to be activated and made the theme that the public will see on your site.

When you're on the Themes page, sometimes referred to as the Theme Library, the currently active theme is always displayed at the top left and clearly labeled, as shown in Figure 28-6.

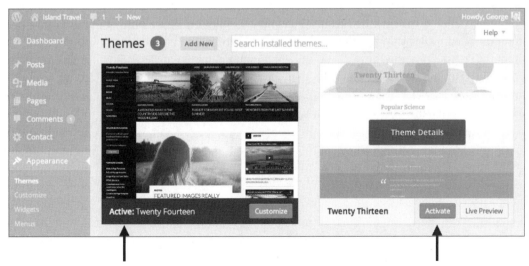

FIGURE 28-6

And when you mouseover any other theme that you have installed, a blue Activate button becomes visible, as you can see on the right side of Figure 28-6. Clicking the Activate button makes that theme live on your site.

But before you make any theme active, there are some tasks you need to perform.

When you switch themes, a number of key pieces of information are changed. In particular, the Menus and the Widgets you've chosen are tied to your current theme's settings. When you make that theme inactive (by activating another), its settings are deactivated as well.

Another way to think of this is that the new theme you're about to activate does not have any settings yet; it has no Menu settings and no Widget settings. (Although WordPress will try to put the Widgets from the last theme into what it thinks are equivalent Widget Areas in the new theme.)

You could, of course, just activate a new theme and then quickly add Menus and arrange the Widgets, but WordPress makes the whole process easier through its preview and customization function, which is just one of several native features of WordPress enabling you to customize your site's design.

BUILT-IN WORDPRESS DESIGN FUNCTIONS

WordPress offers theme makers a number of built-in functions to make it easy for users to change the look of their site. The idea is to have a uniform interface for these functions, no matter what theme is used.

However, theme developers do not have to use these default functions, so they may or may not be active in the theme you use. In that case, themes tend to have their own Theme Options area, either under Appearance or with its own section on the main admin menu. (You saw some examples of these in Lesson 27.) Here I'm concerned only with the functions built-in to WordPress.

The Customize Interface

From Appearance ➪ Customize or from the Preview button on a theme's listing in the Theme Library, a window displays, like the one in Figure 28-7 from the Twenty Fourteen theme.

On the right it shows a real-time version of the front end of your site; in this case, the width of the screen is forcing a tablet-width view of the Island Travel site. On the left you have elements of the site that can be changed. You see the changes as they'll appear on the live site, but until you click the Save button, the changes are not actually applied.

What's available to edit on the left side of the Customize screen is entirely dependent on your theme. Figure 28-8 shows Customize panels from three different themes.

Many of the options on the Twenty Fourteen theme are standard WordPress options that most themes include and are covered here.

FIGURE 28-7

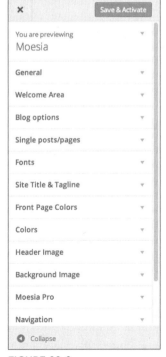
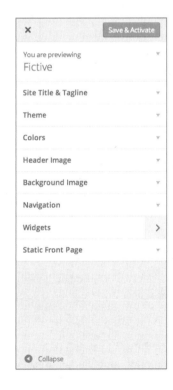
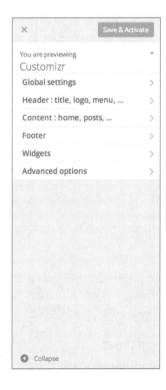

FIGURE 28-8

Navigation

As mentioned, WordPress does not carry over menu location assignment settings when you switch themes. That's because each theme has its own locations, and there's no way to tell which corresponds to which.

As you can see in Figure 28-9, you can set up the navigation from the Customize or Preview section. You can also change navigation on a live site from here.

You can, of course, still choose menu locations from Appearance ⇨ Menus. You can work with Widgets from this screen as well, but for now move on to some settings that deal with the look of the site.

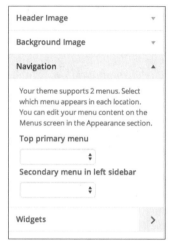

FIGURE 28-9

Header

If your theme has a header image function, you can work with it from here, as shown in Figure 28-10.

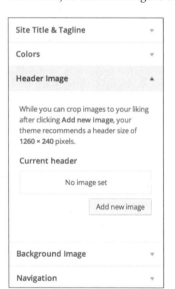

FIGURE 28-10

From here you can upload images or select from the Media Library. Or if there are existing header images, you would see their thumbnail here and be able to select one, or you can get rid of the header image altogether.

Background

If your theme has a background image function, there's a Customize interface for that, too, as shown in Figure 28-11.

FIGURE 28-11

As with header images, you can upload, select from the Media Library, or select from existing backgrounds. Or you can delete the background image completely.

Colors

You can find color elements for the header and background in the Color section, as shown in Figure 28-12.

FIGURE 28-12

If the Site Title is going to be displayed along with the header image, you can select its color here. And if there is no background image, the color you choose here is the one that will be visible.

Because the Customize screen works in real time to show you the effect of your changes, it's easier to see it in action in the video that accompanies this lesson.

For both the header and background images, many WordPress themes activate the individual admin screens for them, which appear as submenu items under Appearance.

Custom Header

The header image functions shown on the Customize screen are all available in one place on the Custom Header screen, as shown in Figure 28-13.

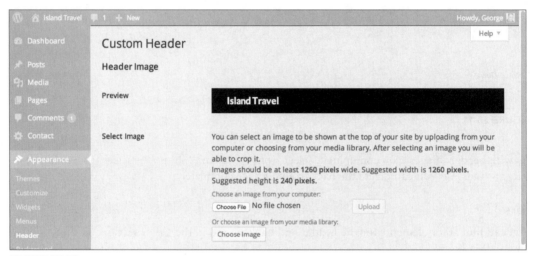

FIGURE 28-13

Some important wording is highlighted concerning the image size, which varies considerably between themes.

Some themes, such as the Twenty Fourteen theme, make the header image the full width of the site, whereas others make the header image a logo that's placed on a colored header background. In that case the dimensions will be much smaller than you see in Figure 28-13.

Whether a full-width banner or a logo, there's another important element to header dimensions: if the image needs to match the dimensions exactly.

Some themes force you to upload an image of a specific width and height, and crop any image larger than that. There's a built-in crop function in WordPress, so you can do it right on the screen.

Other themes give you suggested dimensions and the ability to crop an image to those dimensions, as shown in Figure 28-14. But if you choose to skip the cropping (the button on the right), the theme publishes your image at its full size.

The final choice you may be given with header images is whether to display an HTML version of the Site Title along with the image. In some themes, if you leave the title in place, it will be superimposed over the header image; others place it below or above the image. For the Twenty-Fourteen theme, the title goes below the image, as shown in Figure 28-15.

FIGURE 28-14

FIGURE 28-15

If I choose not to show the title, and the theme shows a full width header image rather than a logo-sized image, one option is to make the header image with the logo built in, as shown in Figure 28-16.

FIGURE 28-16

In any case, you'll need to experiment with your theme to know how it will use header images, and the beauty of the Customize or Preview function is that you can do that before committing to the theme.

> **NOTE** *Well-coded themes will make sure search engines can still read your site title, even if you've chosen not to display it as text to visitors (visitors see the logo image). You can confirm this by viewing the source code of a page and looking for the site title as an* <h1> *near the top of the page.*

Custom Background

As with headers, some themes will use WordPress's Custom Background screen as an alternative to working with the Customize screen.

It's similar to the Custom Header screen but without image size recommendations or restrictions. That's because background images work in a particular way in HTML; they tile, which means they'll be repeated in a certain pattern that is specified by CSS. After you upload an image, you can see the tiling options, as shown in Figure 28-17.

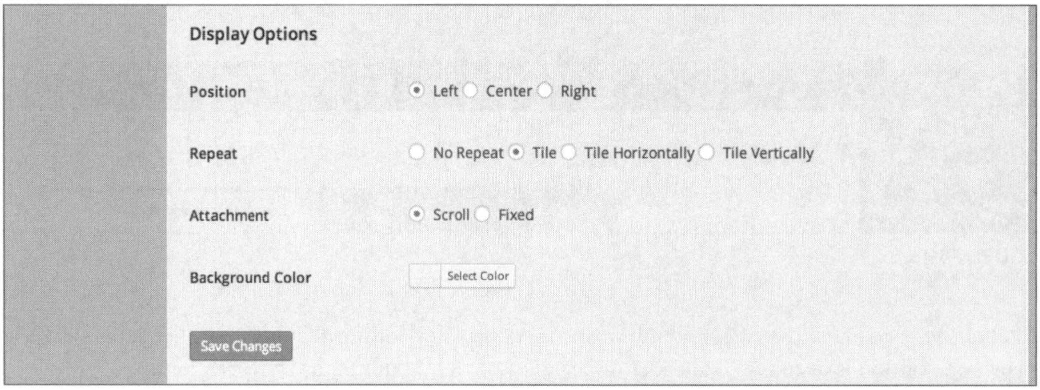

Display Options

Position   ● Left ○ Center ○ Right

Repeat   ○ No Repeat ● Tile ○ Tile Horizontally ○ Tile Vertically

Attachment   ● Scroll ○ Fixed

Background Color   [Select Color]

[Save Changes]

FIGURE 28-17

The background color option enables you to choose the color to be shown if there's no image or if the image does not cover the entire background.

> **NOTE** *As of WordPress 4.1, separate Custom Background and Custom Header screens have been eliminated and everything is done through the Customize interface.*

THEME OPTIONS

As you saw in Lesson 27, themes sometimes create their own ways of customizing the look and layout of your site, and these are referred to as Theme Options screens.

Typically you'll find these screens under Appearance ⇨ Theme Options, although the name can vary, sometimes including the theme name followed by Theme Options or even a completely different submenu name under Appearance. The other common way of listing theme options is through a separate section of the main Admin menu, usually named for the theme.

In either case, you're presented with a screen or set of screens or a single tabbed screen containing all the settings possible with that theme. And those settings vary widely, from just a few to several screens.

These settings, like the ones you've seen in Customize, make it easy for site owners to change the look and structure of their site without having to know any CSS or PHP.

When I was talking about choosing a theme, I mentioned the importance of checking what options a theme offers, either through the Customize screen or a Theme Options section. It could be the difference between two themes that each look great.

PLUGINS

Here are some plugins that can help with modifying or expanding control over design elements.

The Customize function is still fairly new and no doubt there will be many plugins developed to modify and expand it, but a couple of the following do just that.

➤ **Background Manager**—Extends the WordPress background function to allow more control over background images in particular. Enables full-screen background images and different backgrounds based on the page.

➤ **Custom Background Extended**—Extends the built-in WordPress background function to allow individual backgrounds on any Page or Post.

➤ **WP Display Header**—Gives you easy control over what site header image is shown on any given Page. Can make the image random on specific Pages as well.

➤ **Site Layout Customizer**—Change the layout of your front Page or other Pages using the WordPress customize function. May not work with all themes.

➤ **Styles**—Modifies the WordPress customize function so that you can make style changes no matter which theme you use. Enables you to style many color elements as well as fonts.

➤ **Fourteen Colors**—Modifies the default Twenty Fourteen theme's customize function so that you can adjust colors easily.

➤ **Easy Google Fonts**—Enables you to add Google fonts to your site, for all themes you use. Integrates with the WordPress customize function so that you can preview your fonts in real time.

➤ **WP Google Fonts**—Easy interface for adding Google fonts to your site and choosing which elements will use which fonts.

TRY IT

In this lesson, you install a new theme and change the background color in the Customize screen.

Lesson Requirements

A WordPress installation is required.

Step-by-Step

Install a new theme and change the background color by following these steps:

1. Go to Appearance ⇨ Themes and click Add New at the top, or if you see a large + symbol in your Theme Library, click that.

2. Pick one of the themes you see in the Theme Browser, and click Install for a theme that's not already installed.

3. When the install process is complete, click the Live Preview link.

4. On the left menu, look for a section called Colors, and click it so that it drops down to reveal the options available.

5. Look for Background Color, and click Select Color. On the right side of the screen, you should see some part of the background color change.

6. If you don't see any change or you never found Background Color as a choice, click the X at the top left and leave the Customize screen. Click the Return to Theme Installer, and try another theme, using the same preceding steps.

7. When you finish changing the background color, you can either click Save & Activate to see what the theme looks like on your site (only if it's a test site and not a live site). Or you can click the X and leave the window.

8. Make sure you delete the theme afterward if you don't want it.

> **REFERENCE** *Please select the video for Lesson 28 online at* www.wrox.com/go /wp24vids. *You will also be able to download resources for this lesson from the website.*

29

Advanced Design Customization

Depending on the theme you use, the sophistication of built-in design customization can vary greatly. Even a powerful design interface has its limits. The ultimate control over design lies with more advanced techniques, and that's what this lesson is all about. This lesson deals with *cascading style sheets* (CSS). Although they're not difficult to use, they do require precision, which is a nice way of saying that you can easily mess things up simply by leaving out a bracket or misspelling a word.

If you find that intimidating, then calling on the services of a professional for those kinds of changes makes a lot of sense. But what you'll learn in this lesson is that the changes are not that difficult for a professional, so shouldn't cost too much.

The basic idea behind advanced theme customization is that you're going to override the theme's styling, and there are two ways of doing that:

➤ Adding custom CSS at some point after the theme CSS has loaded

➤ Making a Child theme that uses the original theme as its Parent

Both enable you to add your own CSS, but the Child theme method opens up the possibility of modifying or adding theme files as well.

USING CUSTOM CSS

Many themes, even ones with sophisticated design interfaces, have a method of adding your own custom CSS. Whether it's a box in the Customize menu (Figure 29-1 A), a Custom CSS plugin screen (Figure 29-1 B), or a theme's custom CSS option box (Figure 29-1 C), you can write CSS that overrides the theme's styling.

You need to understand that whether you do it yourself or hire someone to make these styling changes, tools like this are useful because they don't change anything in the theme itself. So even if you do make a mistake or change your mind, you can easily get back to the original theme instantly.

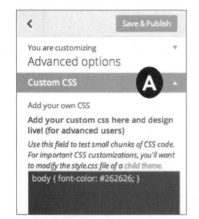

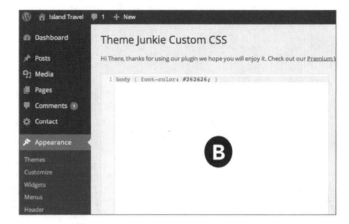

FIGURE 29-1

What if your theme does not provide one of these ways of overriding CSS? Fortunately, several plugins can add that functionality; several are mentioned at the end of the lesson. Ensure that the plugin properly loads the CSS so that it overrides the theme and not vice versa.

> **WARNING** *Some people say that you can add CSS to the end of the current theme's style sheet, and they readily admit that an update of the theme can erase those changes. They also advise you to keep a copy of your changes, and then add them back in after the update.*
>
> *Bad idea.*
>
> *Aside from the possibility of losing your backup of some or all those changes, there's the possibility of messing up the CSS file while you're working on it, especially if you're trying to make the changes live through the Theme Editor built in to WordPress.*
>
> *In addition, the methods in this lesson are so straightforward, there's no reason take a chance with any theme files.*

USING A CHILD THEME

If you need to do more than adjust a few style sheet rules, you probably need to create a Child theme.

What Is a Child Theme?

The concept grew out of the realization that often the changes people wanted to make to a theme require modification of the actual template files and not just adding a custom style sheet of some sort. For example, people want the menu placed in a different spot or need some extra widget areas.

So the WordPress developers devised a simple answer: a parent-child theme hierarchy, which says, if the necessary files don't exist in the child theme, look in the designated parent theme. For example, if you want to modify the `header.php` file in the parent theme, simply copy it, make changes, and drop the new version (still named the same way, of course) into the corresponding location in the child theme folder. Because the child theme is active, WordPress first checks its folder. In this case, it would find `header.php` and not look in the Parent folder. If the file isn't present in the child theme folder, WordPress looks for `header.php` in the parent theme folder.

> **NOTE** *One file that WordPress does not use in this either/or manner is* `functions.php`. *If there's one in the parent and one in the child folder, the two are combined.*

But why not simply make a copy of the original theme, rename it, and then start making your own changes? That's certainly an option, but there are several reasons why you should use the Child theme route:

➤ Many child themes are primarily concerned with changing the look of the parent, so they consist of just a style.css file and maybe some graphics files or a `functions.php` file. It's much easier to deal with these few files than a full-fledged theme.

➤ You'll miss out on upgrades to the original theme.

➤ It makes it easy to know what you've changed because you're dealing only with the files that are different from the parent.

➤ You always have the original set of files to fall back on—they're already installed in WordPress.

➤ The parent theme remains intact and your modifications are clearly separate. (Make sure you give credit in your child theme—parents always like that.)

In addition, when you see how easy it is to make a child theme, you'll just say, "Why not?" Let's start.

> **WARNING** *For this next section, you need to use a plain text editor program, so put away any word processing program you have. If you don't use a plain text editor, you'll end up with all sorts of nasty hidden code that word processors use behind the scenes, and that will likely cause things not to work properly on your server.*
>
> *For Windows, there's a plain text editor called Notepad in the Accessories folder of Programs, or there are many free editors to download, such as Notepad++.*
>
> *Mac users have TextEdit, which comes with OSX, but it does not work in plain text mode by default, so check your preferences before using it; set them to Plain Text, and turn off all spell checking and auto anything. (Better still, search the Web for* **plain text editor mac** *and download another program such as TextWrangler).*

Creating a Child Theme

Only one file is required to create a child theme: `style.css`. That's it.

As long as it's formatted correctly (which is easy) and placed in a uniquely named folder in the `/wp-content/themes` directory, WordPress will see it as a theme and display it in the Theme Library. I'll go over that again shortly, but I want you to start building the `style.css` file.

I've created an example of the most basic file you need in Figure 29-2.

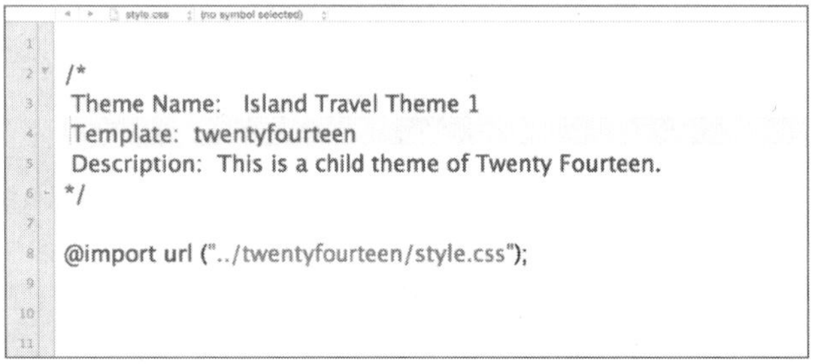

```
/*
Theme Name:  Island Travel Theme 1
Template: twentyfourteen
Description: This is a child theme of Twenty Fourteen.
*/

@import url ("../twentyfourteen/style.css");
```

FIGURE 29-2

The first line must have the `/*` because that tells the system that it's a comment and not part of the rules for the style sheet.

On the next line, type **Theme Name:** followed by the name of your theme. The actual name can be whatever you want. Make it something clear because this is the name that will appear in your Manage Themes directory, and it should make it easy to know which one you're choosing. I'm going to use **Island Travel Theme 1**.

The only other required line must begin with **Template:** followed by the name of the folder where the parent theme resides. That's why the name is in lowercase—it's not the Theme Name like the one you just created. This is the folder name in the Themes directory of `wp-content`. This is how WordPress will know where to look for files that aren't in your child theme.

> **NOTE** *Just to be clear, this example is for the Twenty Fourteen theme. You would use the folder name of whatever theme you use as a parent; that's the name you put after "Template."*

There's other information you can put in the comment area of your Child theme. In this case I've put a Description line, which will be used in my Theme Library listing and help remind me who the Parent is for this theme.

Now you need the closing comment symbols `*/`. (Notice that it's reversed this time—asterisk first, then the forward slash.) This means the comments are over and it's time for the CSS rules.

But there's one more thing you need to do: Tell your browser to load the Parent stylesheet or you'll have no styling at all:

```
@import url("../twentyfourteen/style.css");
```

Use the `@import` rule to do that, and the URL you specify needs to be relative to your child theme. The `...` tells your browser to look outside the child theme for a folder called `twentyfourteen` and go in and grab `style.css`.

> **WARNING** *There can't be any CSS rules above `@import` and before the closing comment characters `*/`. If there are, the import function won't work. So, start any of your custom CSS after the line with the import rule.*

That's all you absolutely have to have in your child theme's `style.css` file.

> **NOTE** *There are plugins that can help automate the process of creating a child theme of varying complexities. Some are mentioned at the end of the lesson.*
>
> *Keep in mind, though, that you still need a plain text editor to work with the files made by a child theme creator plugin.*

With the basics of your style sheet done, save the file from your text editor by creating a new folder with a short but unique name, so there's no chance of another theme having the same folder name. This is the folder that's going to be put into `/wp-content/themes`, so it has to be lowercase with no spaces. (A dash is okay between words or numbers.) I'm going to use the name `island-travel-theme-1`. That's not going to be only unique, but it also allows me to keep it straight should I add other Island Travel Child themes in the future.

If you're comfortable using an FTP program to transfer files to your server, you can simply upload this folder in to `/wp-content/themes`.

If you prefer to use the upload method of installing themes explained in Lesson 28, "Theme Installation and Basic Customization," you need to first compress or zip up the folder.

Make sure the Parent theme is in your Theme Library. If it's not, the upload process will give you an error. Or if you FTP the folder, there will be an error when you go to the Theme Library.

> **NOTE** *To compress or zip a folder on a Windows machine, you would actually select all the files inside the folder (in this case, just one) and then right-click, at which point, you choose Send to Compressed Folder. You then need to rename the folder with the lowercase theme name you decided on earlier.*
>
> *On a Mac, simply highlight the child theme folder, right-click, and choose Compress Folder. You end up with* `island-travel-theme-1.zip` *(or whatever you named the folder) followed by the* `.zip` *extension).*

MORE WAYS TO CUSTOMIZE

When you work directly with CSS, either through a custom CSS file or a Child theme's style sheet, the possibilities for change are virtually unlimited. Add in the capability of a Child theme to include new templates or change existing ones, and you have complete control over the look of your site. But there's another option available in some themes: *hooks*.

For example, say you wanted a navigation bar to appear above the header area instead of below it, and your theme does not have a Customize option to do that. There are two ways to accomplish this in any theme:

➤ Changing some CSS rules

➤ Copying the `header.php` file to your Child theme and physically moving the code that creates the navigation bar

But some themes are coded in such a way that you can add your own code at certain points in the layout without touching the theme files. These points are called hooks. Not only can you add your own code, you can remove the theme's code.

With the example of moving a navigation bar in mind, the third option becomes removing the theme's coding for the navigation from one hook and placing it into another.

You work with hooks in the `functions.php` file of a Child Theme, using PHP and HTML, so this certainly isn't an option for everyone, but if you're hiring a developer you'll have a sense of how they are able to manipulate your theme.

Here's another example: making the date of a Post disappear.

➤ You could write some CSS rules to hide the date: `.entry-date { display: none; }`

➤ You could copy the file where the date is inserted and save it in your Child theme, and then comment out the date coding or remove it altogether.

➤ Or there may be a hook in your theme for the area just below the Post title that enables you to remove the date from the display, using a PHP function in the `functions.php` file of your Child theme.

And just so you know: WordPress has hundreds of hooks and many plugins have them as well, so the extent to which you can customize without touching core files is almost limitless.

In addition, any theme can be manipulated to look as different as you want, to the extent that you can keep using the same Parent theme forever and simply update the look of your site by creating new Child themes.

> **WARNING** *This is a good time to repeat something: Do not get fooled by unscrupulous developers who tell you that they have to ditch all your existing customizations to give the site a new look.*
>
> *There may, of course, be good reasons to ditch everything: if the customizations were poorly done in the first place and are making your site slow, for example, or are not compatible with the latest WordPress coding standards. The point is, you need good reasons to throw out all the time and money that was originally spent, and now you know the questions to ask.*

PLUGINS

Following are some plugins that can make advanced design customization easier.

CUSTOM CSS INTERFACES

➤ **Simple Custom CSS**—Adds a CSS editor Admin screen with syntax highlighting. Works with any theme, but it won't necessarily override all CSS because of where its style sheet is placed in the head area of the HTML page.

➤ **Theme Junkie Custom CSS**—Adds an Administrative screen where you can add CSS using an editor with syntax highlighting. The plugin also puts the CSS box into the WordPress customizer so that you can preview the CSS changes. The custom css is added in such a way that it can override not only a theme's style, but also any plugin styling.

➤ **Lazyest Stylesheet**—Adds a CSS editor with syntax highlighting and overrides any theme or plugin styling.

CHILD THEMES

➤ **Child Theme Configurator**—Provides an interface for selecting Parent theme style elements you want to change, enabling you to first preview the changes. Then when you're ready, it creates the child theme files for you.

➤ **Child Theme Creator by Orbisius**—Automatically creates a child theme from any nonchild theme and includes a theme editor.

➤ **Child Themify**—Automatically creates a child theme from any other nonchild theme.

TRY IT

There is nothing specific to try in this lesson, unless you would like to follow the instructions for creating a Child theme style sheet in a plain text editor. You may be interested, however, in pursuing a study of CSS to customize your theme.

One of the best tools for learning CSS is your browser. Virtually any modern browser has a function called "inspect element." By right-clicking on any element on a web page, you're shown the HTML and the list of CSS rules governing that element. Even better, the inspect element interface allows you to change the CSS to see what those changes look like. The change only happens in your browser at that moment; you don't actually change the website files.

While this browser function is invaluable, you'll want to understand how CSS works. Here are some great online CSS tutorial sites:

➤ http://www.codecademy.com/en/tracks/web

➤ http://learn.shayhowe.com/html-css/getting-to-know-css/

➤ http://www.w3schools.com/css/

➤ http://www.cssbasics.com/introduction-to-css/

➤ http://learnlayout.com/

> **REFERENCE** *Please select the video for Lesson 29 online at* www.wrox.com/go/wp24vids. *You will also be able to download resources for this lesson from the website.*

SECTION VIII
Becoming Search Engine Friendly

30

Optimizing Your Content

The most common way for people to find what they want online is through search engines, but although searches return thousands, even millions, of pages of results, few people go past even the second or third page. It's no surprise, then, that so much attention is paid to achieving high search-engine rankings.

Search engine optimization (SEO) is a complex and constantly changing topic, well beyond the scope of this book, but in this and the following lesson, you see some things you can do in WordPress to better your chances of good rankings.

The healthiest way to think about SEO is to first think about your visitors' needs. Remember, the goal of search engines is to deliver the most useful, reliable, best-quality web pages that meet the search parameters. If you work hard to make your site useful to visitors, you have a better chance of ranking well. Having said that, you also have to take into account the ways search engines read and interpret that content.

WRITING SEARCH-FRIENDLY TITLES

This section covers the importance of relevant titles for Posts and Pages. There are other kinds of titles used in HTML coding for images and links, which are discussed in their respective sections later in this lesson.

Having good titles for Posts is crucial because of the number of ways WordPress uses them, all of which relate to search-engine ranking:

➤ In many themes, the `<title>` tag of the post's HTML page is created simply by combining the title of the Post with the title of your website (set under Settings ⇨ General).

➤ When the title of a Post is linked to its full-text version, WordPress themes typically create a title attribute for the link tag, which says something like, Permanent Link to [the title itself goes here].

➤ As the H1 element in the content section of the HTML, a Post's title sits high in the semantic (meaning) hierarchy of the web page.

➤ Also, if you have custom permalinks turned on, and depending on the setting, the title is likely used to create the ending portion of the web page's URL: `yourdomain.com/aruba-beach-famous-for-sunsets` by replacing spaces with hyphens and making everything lowercase.

These are all elements that search engines use in various ways when calculating the relevance of a web page—it's up to you to make sure the title itself is relevant.

By relevant, I don't just mean relevant to the content of the Post. A title also needs to match the wording visitors are likely to use when searching. You need to think of not only what information your audience wants, but also the wording that best conveys that information. Very likely, those same words are ones they'll use when searching.

Take the title of one of the Posts I've been working with on the Island Travel site: 7 Day Capital City Package. Looking at this from both a visitor and a search engine standpoint, it's not a good title. Notice it doesn't mention the word Kingston, when that's the name of the city the Post is about and likely a keyword people would enter in a search.

It would also be good to say a bit more about the package. Is it an escorted tour? Is it focused on nightlife? Is it a family package? Is the hotel on the ocean? Not only will this be more informative, it will also help distinguish the package from other Kingston vacations undoubtedly offered by Island Travel.

Though the details of what makes a relevant or useful title will always depend on the particular Post, a few guidelines can be helpful from a search standpoint:

➤ **Be succinct.** If you look at the titles of results in search engines, you'll notice that they're truncated if they're too long. (Approximately 60 characters is the typical stopping point.) It would be nice for your entire title to show in the search results, but at the least, have the most important words first.

➤ **Use key search terms.** Look at some search results and you'll see that search terms are highlighted everywhere, including in the search results title, which is taken from your Title tag. If your Title tag has that search term, you'll benefit from the highlighting.

➤ **Be upfront.** Put the key search terms as near the beginning of the title as you can. Search engines interpret what comes first as more important.

➤ **Don't try to be fancy.** If you can work a good turn of phrase into a title while keeping it clear and succinct, more power to you, but don't worry about being clever (unless that's important to your visitors).

Keep in mind that while the title of a Post may be used in custom permalinks and the Title tag, you can still control the wording of both.

For custom permalinks, if you have them turned on, that's done on the Post edit screen, as shown in Figure 30-1.

FIGURE 30-1

For title tags, it will depend on your SEO plugin, but usually there will be a box on the Post edit screen. The plugin will typically add more to the title tag, such as your Site Title, but the wording for the Post title portion can be edited. If you have trouble boiling down the content into a succinct title, it may be that you're covering too much information in a single Post. Would the material be better handled as several Posts?

Looking at it from a search engine's point of view, if too much of the content is not directly related to the title, it seems to the search engine that relevance is lost and the ranking could go down. Your visitors may see the relevance, but search-engine algorithms aren't as sophisticated.

However, you need to balance breaking up content with not having so many extra web pages so that visitors have to do a lot of clicking to get all the content.

Also, search-engine experts disagree about the maximum length of a single web page of content, so you should focus more on the needs of your visitors and the context. An academic paper is different from a product description—they each have a different criterion for length.

> **WARNING** *When you consider a WordPress theme, check the source code to see if it's creating SEO-friendly HTML, for example, not making web page titles H3 or not leaving off the title attribute on title links, and so on. This is separate from any SEO functions a theme may offer. Those functions belong in a plugin, which is discussed in Lesson 31, "Optimizing Behind the Scenes."*

WRITING SEARCH-FRIENDLY CONTENT

The content you offer on your web page is the key to visitor satisfaction and therefore to search-engine ranking. If you have high-quality, relevant content, visitors will be happy and so will the search engines. But as previously mentioned, search engines aren't as sophisticated as visitors, so you need to structure your content in certain ways to ensure that they get the relevance.

For search engines, the primary factor for the relevance of content is keywords. They scan web page content to see how well it relates to the words entered by the searcher.

The details of how search engines scan content for relevance vary between search engines and over time as well—their algorithms are constantly being tweaked to achieve better results. However, here are some basic tips concerning keywords, which, even if they somehow stopped being helpful with rankings, are still helpful to visitors:

➤ **Be consistent.** If your title says the Post is about all-inclusive resorts, don't use only the term "full-service resorts" in your content. Your visitor might understand that they're the same, but you can't take the chance that search engines will understand. It is true they've become increasingly sophisticated at recognizing synonyms. For example, if you enter "all-inclusive resorts," you will get results with the terms "all-inclusive packages" or "all-inclusive vacations" highlighted. Even so, it's better to make sure your keyword is dominant among any synonyms.

➤ **Use keywords early.** If the term "all-inclusive resorts" is in your title and yet doesn't appear until your second or third paragraph, your visitors and the search engines may be excused for wondering if they're reading the right page. Visitors may well continue on, but search engines are less forgiving.

➤ **Don't repeat a term too much.** Visitors know from the title that the Post is about all-inclusive resorts; it is annoying to see the term in every single sentence. The search-engine equivalent is to assume that the repetition is meant to trick it into seeing the web page as relevant. And apart from lowering your ranking, such behavior, taken to an extreme, could get your web page (or even your site) marked as spam.

As the last point suggests, relevant content is not simply about having a lot of keywords. Search-engine algorithms have become increasingly sophisticated over the years, and keyword density, as it's called, is only one of several factors for which content is analyzed.

Assuming all the content in a long Post is focused and relevant, it's still helpful to visually and semantically group that content. To do this in a search engine–friendly way, you need to use HTML heading tags, which is easily done using WordPress's Text Editor in Visual mode (the Format drop-down on the second row of the button bars). Headings within content should take the next heading after the title. In other words, if your Post title is an H1, all first-level headings should be H2, headings grouped under an H2 should be H3, and so on.

Write your headings with the same criteria you would for writing titles: succinct, and keywords at the front, without repetition.

> **WARNING** *Never copy text from another site without quoting it and linking back to the site. Not only is it wrong, but it's also usually illegal to take content from elsewhere and claim it as your own. (You'd be amazed at the number of people to whom this comes as a surprise.) Always check the fair use and copyright laws for your country.*
>
> *Keep in mind, too, that search engines are becoming more sophisticated at spotting duplicate content and this can affect the ranking of pages. If your site is nothing but duplicate content, it could even be blacklisted.*
>
> *Aside from entering a large chunk of your unique content into a search engine (enclosed within quotation marks), there are also services that site owners can use for ongoing checks for plagiarism, such as Copyscape or Plagspotter.*

CREATING SEARCH-FRIENDLY LINKS

Search engines also determine the relevance of your site to someone's search by looking at links from two perspectives: inbound and outbound.

Inbound links are ones on other sites that point to your site, and although these are important to search-engine rankings, getting other sites to link to you is far beyond the scope of this discussion. Be concerned here with links in your Posts that point to other sites.

Search engines look at two aspects of outbound links in particular:

➤ Relevance to the content of the Post

➤ The popularity of the site to which you're linking

When you create links to other sites, always think of your visitors' needs and you're more likely to meet the standards of relevance.

If the link promises to send you to a site with more information about great resorts in Jamaica and that site turns out to be a sales pitch for a time-share the writer is affiliated with, you will not be a happy visitor. What you read is what you want to get. (If the link said you were going to find a great deal on a time-share, it would have been a relevant link.)

> **NOTE** *In the pop-up link editor window of WordPress, there's a Title field. It's good practice to enter a short description of what you're linking to, even if it's just the name of the site or the Page. It's useful for your visitors and it's thought to have some role in search-engine ranking.*

Even when they're relevant, you can help improve the value of your outbound links—both to visitors and to search engines—by doing a bit of research. If there are two good sites and one ranks higher in search results than the other, go with the higher-ranked site. Either site would be useful to your visitor, but the higher-ranked one may be given more weight by search engines. Of course, you would put both sites in a links list, but I'm talking here about making choices within the content of a post—you don't want to crowd the body with too many links or it gets a bit overwhelming.

And don't forget about linking to related material on your own site. This internal linking helps visitors and search engines find you material and the Link to Existing Content feature of the Insert/ Edit Link window makes it easy to do. Lesson 36 also talks about plugins that can automate the process of finding related content on your own site and linking to it.

MAKING IMAGES SEARCH-FRIENDLY

Although search engines are getting more sophisticated at analyzing the content of images, they still rely on two attributes of the HTML image tag to tell them details about the image, as shown in this sample code:

```
<img src="http://yourdomain.com/images/image.jpg" title="My New Car"
alt="Photo of my new Toyota Prius sitting in the driveway">
```

It's important that all your images have this descriptive text and in Lesson 13, "Working with Images in the Content Editor," you can see the screens in WordPress where you can enter information for these attributes. Now, look at these attributes with search engines in mind:

➤ **Title**—Titles should be simple, leaving the details to the ALT attribute and giving the two or three keywords that describe the content of the image. Don't load up the title with keywords that aren't relevant to the immediate content. If the image is of a beach in Aruba, use Beach in Aruba, not Caribbean Travel Deals on Beaches in Aruba. Your Post may be about travel deals in the Caribbean, but that's not what the image is about. Stick to the facts. Also, keep in mind that WordPress automatically uses your image's filename for the Title attribute. Sometimes, people think you're stuck with that, but you can change it to a proper title. WordPress just tries to make sure there's something for the Title attribute.

➤ **Alternative Text**—This is the name that WordPress gives to the content that's put in the ALT attribute. The architects of HTML wanted an alternative for visually impaired visitors, and this attribute was intended as a written description that could be read aloud by special browsers. Search engines realized they could make use of the attribute to understand the images on a web page, so the ALT attribute has taken on a fairly important SEO role. Although you can have a lot of detail in here, again, you need to stick to the facts. Avoid using nonrelevant material, and don't try to stuff the alternative text with keywords. For example, don't say, "Picture of a beach in Aruba. Beaches in Aruba tend to be less crowded especially this one located in Northern Aruba." Not only is it annoying to visitors, but you could get penalized by the search engines. However, do make sure you say, "Aruba," if that's a keyword for your post.

> **WARNING** *Even though you're going to write your own image title attribute instead of using the filename that WordPress automatically places there, it's still important to have descriptive filenames rather than the ones generated by your camera. Having aruba-beach.jpg is much better than img67474.jpg.*
>
> *Make sure you use hyphens to separate words in the filename and not underscores because search engines ignore the underscore and lose the separation of the words.*

PLUGINS

Here are some plugins directly related to SEO within content. In Lesson 31, "Optimizing Behind the Scenes," you'll read about SEO plugins for the entire site.

OPTIMIZING CONTENT

➤ **SEO by SQUIRRLY**—A limited, free version of a paid plugin that analyzes your content as you write, telling you when it's well optimized for search engines. The free version is good for two or three Posts per month.

➤ **SEO Smart Links**—Enter a word or phrase, along with the URL you want it linked to (on your site or another site) and the plugin finds the word or phrase in your content and automatically creates links.

➤ **Duplicate Title Checker**—If you write a lot of Posts, it may be hard to remember if you've used a title before. This plugin warns you if there's a Post with the same title.

IMAGE TITLE AND ALT TAGS

➤ **SEO Friendly Images**—Automatically adds `alt` and `title` attributes to all your images based on settings you can modify.

➤ **Format Media Titles**—When you upload images to WordPress, the system automatically makes the filename the title attribute of the image, but if the filename isn't well formatted, search engines and the public won't read them easily. This works well, however, only if you've already given descriptive filenames to your images before uploading.

TRY IT

In this lesson, you optimize one of your important Posts or Pages.

Lesson Requirements

A Post or Page with three or four paragraphs of text, some links, and an image.

Step-by-Step

To optimize content, use the term Post for simplicity's sake:

1. Open your Post in the Edit Post screen.

2. Read through the Post and, in another program or on a piece of paper, write a short sentence describing what the Post is about. Set aside this summary for the moment.

3. List two or three of the most important words or phrases in the Post.

4. Ask yourself if these keywords are ones that people would use to search for the topic covered by your Post.

5. Do some research by entering those keywords into a search engine and see what comes back—are these sites related to yours? Ask friends, coworkers, or customers to do a search related to your site and note what keywords they use. Check online keyword tools such as Google's (`http://adwords.google.com/select/KeywordToolExternal`) to get a sense of how people are using your keywords and what possible alternatives might be.

6. Revise your list of keywords as necessary.

7. Check the title of your Post—does it use the most important of your keyword(s) and does it convey what that short sentence from step 2 conveyed?

8. Take the summary of your Post that you wrote in step 2 and compare it with your opening paragraph. Does that paragraph clearly convey your summary? If not, rewrite it. (Later when you have an SEO plugin installed, the summary will be used for the *meta description.*)

9. Check that your opening paragraph uses your keywords. If not, rewrite it.

10. Check the rest of the Post to make sure your keywords appear several times in the text in a natural way. Rewrite as necessary.

11. Check your links to make sure they're going to useful sites and make sure the wording of the link indicates where the visitor will be taken.

12. Check that any images in the Post have clear and accurate titles and alternative text attributes, and, where appropriate, they use the keywords chosen earlier.

13. Remember to update your Post.

> **REFERENCE** *Please select the video for Lesson 30 online at* www.wrox.com/go /wp24vids. *You will also be able to download resources for this lesson from the website.*

31

Optimizing Behind the Scenes

The previous lesson talked about optimizing your content in ways that help increase your rankings in the search engines. Now, it's time to look at behind the scenes settings that affect how search engines rank your site, as well as how to monitor your site statistics to see how well your SEO and marketing efforts are paying off.

OPTIMIZING ADMIN SETTINGS

A number of settings in WordPress have an effect on the way search engines see your site.

Search Engine Visibility

When you first installed WordPress, you had the option of making your site visible to search engines, which was a good idea to keep it hidden until you were finished building it. Now, it's time to unblock your site, which you do under Settings ➭ Reading, as shown in Figure 31-1 A.

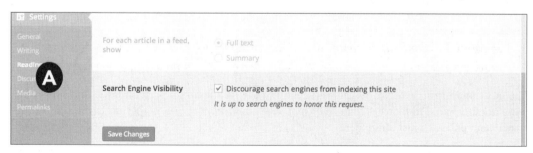

FIGURE 31-1

If you forget to uncheck this box, search engines will not index your new site. Most good SEO plugins warn you if you forget, as shown in Figure 31-1 B.

Site Title

Another admin setting that's important is your Site Title under Settings ⇨ General. Even if you use a graphic in your header instead of the default text title that many WordPress themes use, this Site Title setting remains important because, as mentioned in Lesson 30, "Optimizing Your Content," it's used by most WordPress themes when creating the HTML Title tag, which, in turn, displays at the top of your browser window. Make sure the site title is the one people likely would use if they're looking for you or your business.

Customizing Permalinks

Every web page on a WordPress site has a *permanent link*, or *permalink*. This is a unique URL that never changes unless you actually delete the element in WordPress that creates that web page, such as a Post, Page, Category, and so on.

Permalinks are valuable because it means the web page always works when that URL is used to link to it.

However, the permalinks generated automatically by WordPress are not easy for people to remember because they look like this:

```
http://www.mydomain.com/?p=45
```

Even if you delete this Post or Page, no other Post or Page can have that number. The question mark indicates that what follows is a query string, which is used to query the database and find all the parts necessary to create the web page.

From an indexing standpoint, this permalink is fine for a search engine. Your Page is not going to be left out of the indexing process because it has a query string in its URL.

From a ranking standpoint, however, having a keyword in the URL does help search engines confirm what the Page is about. As Google puts it in its Search Engine Optimization Starter Guide:

> *If your URL contains relevant words, this provides users and search engines with more information about the page than an ID or oddly named parameter would.*

The most important factor in all this is the ease of use for visitors. I prefer a URL that says something about where I'm being taken—such as `http://www.mydomain.com/destinations/aruba`— rather than one with just a number.

That's what custom or pretty permalinks in WordPress are all about: creating more user-friendly and search-friendly URLs. And you choose the structure of pretty permalinks under Settings ⇨ Permalinks, as shown in Figure 31-2.

What is the best setting for Custom Permalinks? There's some disagreement about this, but the one most recommended is the Post Name setting, which essentially leaves out any date or category names in the resulting URL. Figure 31-3 shows the Permalinks Settings when this is chosen.

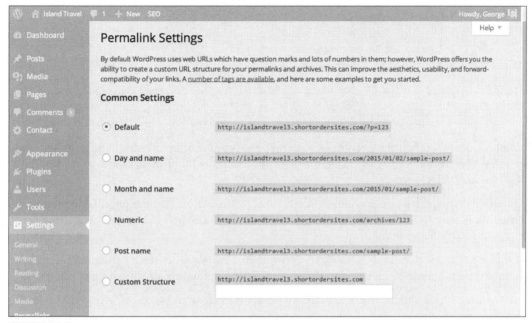

FIGURE 31-2

FIGURE 31-3

However, different types of sites may require different permalink settings or even customization of the settings through the use of specialized plugins. E-commerce sites in particular, with a large number of categories and subcategories, require a lot of attention to permalinks. And search engines may have specific rules for specific types of content. For instance, Google requires news-related sites to have a unique ID in the URL of news stories.

Editing Individual Permalinks

The trouble with WordPress's custom permalinks is that they're anything but permanent. A user can change a custom permalink at any time, as shown in Figure 31-4.

FIGURE 31-4

Not only does this defeat the purpose of a permalink—any existing links to the page will no longer work—but also any search ranking for that link will be lost (unless steps are taken; see the "Redirecting URLs" section).

Remember that search engines rank pages, and the URL is like an ID for a page. Changing a custom permalink is actually like creating a new page in the eyes of a search engine; you're starting from scratch to establish a ranking.

Set it and forget it—that needs to be your motto when creating the custom permalink for a Post. That means you should be careful about the wording of a permalink because it must last forever.

First, remember this about titles: Keep custom permalinks clear and succinct. Avoid URLs such as the following:

```
http://www.yourdomain.com/aruba-testimonials/our-favorite-spot-in-aruba-for-
dining-and-dancing-all-night-long.
```

Even if you want that as the title of the Post, at least tidy up and shorten the custom permalink by editing it, for example:

```
http://www.yourdomain.com/aruba-testimonials/our-favorite-spot-aruba-dining-
dancing-all-night.
```

Many SEO plugins can help with this process by removing *stop words* such as: *in, a, and, for,* and so on. Stop words are ignored by search engines, and shorter urls are easier for visitors to visually scan.

> **NOTE** *Changing a permalink before your site goes live to make it easier to read or more search-friendly is fine because search engines haven't indexed it and no one has linked to it.*

Redirecting URLs

If you make changes to your site that affect a URL, anyone who follows a link to that URL is going to get a 404 Page Not Found error, including the links in a search engine's listing. Not only is that bad for visitor experience, but also search engines give you negative marks for broken links.

These kinds of changes include deleting, changing slugs (the lowercase version of titles used for URLs), or moving from one Category to another. All these affect the URL of the web page, so you need to do something about it. Similarly, suppose you converted your website into a WordPress site. Very likely the URL for each web page would be different and you wouldn't want your visitors getting error messages if they used the original URL.

Redirection is a kind of change of address; it tells the world to go somewhere other than the original location of the URL. That could be to the homepage of the website or to the same or related content in another location. There are several types of redirection, such as permanent or temporary, and you would need to research which is best for your particular situation.

For search engines, proper redirection is vital because it not only stops any negative points for pages not found on your site, but it also transfers the ranking for the old Page to the new Page.

On Apache servers, which run the vast majority of sites, you can redirect through a special file on your server called the `htaccess` file or even through your hosting Control Panel, but there are plugins for WordPress that can make the process easy, as mentioned at the end of the lesson.

META TAGS

A meta tag is a type of HTML tag that's hidden in the head area of a webpage. They're used for various purposes, one of which is for search engines to understand what a Page is about.

It used to be that everyone was worried about the keywords' meta tags. If you didn't have the right words in those tags, search engines wouldn't index you properly. However, the meta tags for keywords have little if any role in search-engine ranking these days.

The description meta tag, however, is extremely important.

Not only do search engines look for the search words in the description meta tag, but also they compare what's said in the description to see if it aligns with the content of the Page. In addition, the description meta tag—if it meets these criteria—is often used as all or part of the two lines shown below the Page title in most search engine results, as shown in Figure 31-5.

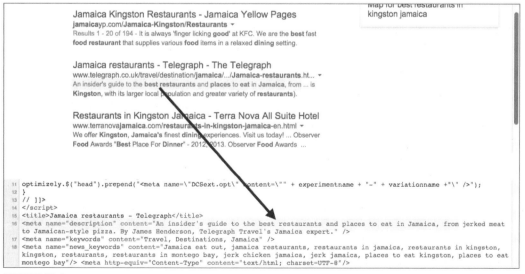

FIGURE 31-5

Clearly, it's important for your site's Pages to have good description meta tags. Some themes include the tag on Post or Page screens, but as previously mentioned, do not use any SEO functions created by your theme. The proper way to handle meta descriptions is with an SEO plugin, as mentioned later in the lesson.

Technically a web page's title tag is not a meta tag, but because it's hidden in the head area and used by search engines, it belongs with the current discussion.

The important difference with meta tags is that most WordPress themes create a title tag using, at least in part, the Site Title from Settings ⇨ General. So in that sense, you have some direct control of the title tag in virtually any WordPress installation.

You can see how a theme uses your Site Title by looking in the browser tab of one of your web pages. If you don't see it there, don't worry because you can take control of what displays in the title tag by using an SEO plugin.

PLUGINS FOR SEO

Because WordPress does not offer an interface for creating meta descriptions or controlling title tags, you need a plugin for that.

There are plugins that control only meta tags, as mentioned at the end of the lesson. But because there are many other elements to SEO, you should use a plugin that offers a wide range of tools.

One of the most powerful and popular of the complete SEO plugins is WordPress SEO by Yoast. And one of its key features is a meta box that appears on all Edit screens, as shown in Figure 31-6.

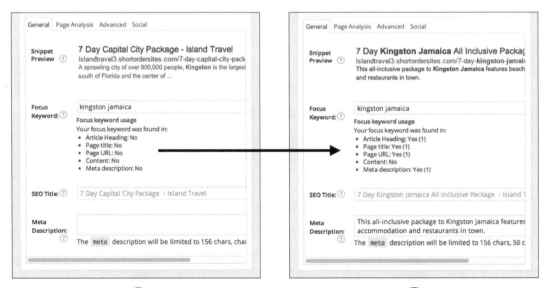

FIGURE 31-6

In Figure 31-6 A you can see how, when I've told the plugin that my keyword for this page is *kingston Jamaica*, it told me I'm missing that keyword in important places.

By making changes to my Post title, the custom permalink, and entering a meta description, Figure 31-6 B shows the plugin giving me better marks.

One limitation to the plugin is that it looks for the keyword as a single phrase, while search engines look at instances of each word individually. If your keyword phrase flows naturally in a sentence, then this won't be an issue. If not, you may need to use this focus keyword tool a bit differently.

For example, a better keyword for this page would be "kingston jamaica vacation." Since the plugin only looks for that exact phrase and it would never appear in a sentence, I chose a part of the phrase that would be used in normal writing. I would then use the tool to check for the word "vacation."

The most helpful part of this plugin is the Page Analysis feature, as shown in Figure 31-7:

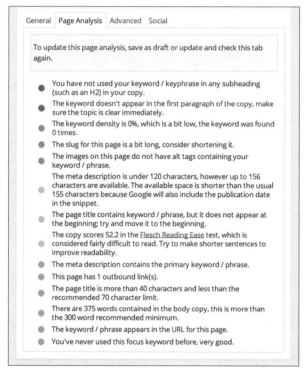

FIGURE 31-7

This powerful tool looks at the content of your Page and rates it from a search engine standpoint, and not just based on the keyword you claim to be optimizing for. There's a lot to this plugin, as there is to any SEO plugin that aims to give you a complete set of tools for optimization. These plugins have settings that, if you handle them incorrectly, can actually hurt your rankings.

For example, with WordPress SEO, the Advanced tab of the meta box enables you to block search engines from indexing the page or follow links on the page, provides a canonical URL that overrides any permalink settings, or even permanently redirects users to another Page. Clearly you need to know what you're doing with these settings, which is why many SEO plugins provide a way of hiding these advanced functions from other users with editing abilities.

MONITORING SITE STATISTICS

There is no built-in statistics system for WordPress, but you have a number of choices for finding out detailed information on who's visiting your site and what they do there.

One method is to use the statistics provided by your hosting company. It will have at least one package—such as Webalizer or AWstats—that can give you a lot of details about your site visitors. Sometimes, you can access these stats through a URL, or you may need to go through your web hosting panel (such as cPanel). Check the host's knowledge base for instructions on accessing stats.

The disadvantage is that these statistics are more difficult to read and less comprehensive. Server statistics can also be misleading in certain ways. For example, the same person coming back four times in a day could look like four people visiting the site. Other statistics methods use javascript to track the activity of visitors, allowing them to distinguish one visitor from another as well as gather far more information than your server does.

However, if someone has their javascript turned off they won't get tracked by this method, so it's useful to have both types of statistics.

Some statistics plugins keep track of visitors using the database of your WordPress installation. Although some of them are good, it can add a load to your server, and they're also one more thing to maintain on your site.

There are also plugins that tie into third-party site statistics services, such as Google Analytics or StatCounter, that run on their own servers so that you don't have any kind of load or maintenance worries. WordPress.com offers its own server, which can be used by self-hosted versions of WordPress using a plugin such as JetPack.

Google Analytics offers the most comprehensive set of visitor-tracking tools. All you need is a Google Account, and you can get Analytics. You can also run multiple site statistics from one account. There's a unique code that needs to be placed on each site, and although many themes offer a place to paste your Google Analytics (GA) code, you shouldn't go that route.

Site statistics should not be dependent on your theme, just as SEO functions should be kept separate. Fortunately, there are many plugins that not only take care of placing your GA code correctly, but some even display GA reports in your WordPress Dashboard. Some of the plugins are listed next.

PLUGINS

Here are some useful SEO tools to check out.

COMPLETE SEO TOOLS

➤   **WordPress SEO by Yoast**—A complete SEO tool with an excellent page analysis tool that helps you write content in a more SEO-friendly way.

➤ **SEO Ultimate**—Like other complete SEO plugins, this gives you control over title tags, noindex, meta tags, Open Graph, slugs, canonical, autolinks, 404 errors, rich snippets, and much more.

➤ **All in One SEO Pack**—As the name suggests, this plugin offers a wide range of SEO tools, including a meta box on Post and Page screens for writing meta descriptions, title tags, and so on.

SPECIFIC SEO TOOLS

➤ **Add Meta Tags**—Add basic meta tags to all areas of WordPress: Posts, Pages, Categories, Custom Post Types, and more. You can also add Opengraph, Schema.org Microdata, and other types of specialized SEO tagging.

➤ **HeadSpace2 SEO**—Manages the meta tags for all areas of WordPress, and also enables you to load plugins only on specific web pages.

➤ **All in One Webmaster**—Makes it easy for you to submit to various webmaster tools, such as Google, Bing, Facebook, Quantcast, Clicky, and more.

➤ **Google Author Link**—Manage Google author links for single or multi-author websites.

REDIRECTION

➤ **Quick Page/Post Redirect Plugin**—Adds a redirection meta box to Post and Page screens, allowing all types of redirection: temporary, permanent, or meta.

➤ **Simple 301 Redirects**—Creates an admin screen where you can easily set up permanent 301 redirects for any number of URLs.

➤ **Redirection**—A plugin to manage 301 redirections as well as tracking 404 errors and more.

GOOGLE ANALYTICS

➤ **Google Analyticator**—Add Google Analytics coding to your site and display reports in your WordPress Dashboard.

➤ **Google Analytics by Yoast**—Makes installation of Google Analytics coding easy and gives you an interface for customizing the tracking that Google Analytics can do.

➤ **Google Analytics Dashboard for WP**—Enables you to display Google Analytics reports live in your WordPress Dashboard.

OTHER STATISTICS

➤ **Jetpack by WordPress.com**—One of the many plugin functions available through this single plugin is a site statistics system run through WordPress.com so that there's no extra load on your site.

➤ **WP Statistics**—Standalone site statistics that work in WordPress.

TRY IT

There's nothing specific to try with this lesson.

Reading the Google starter guide is an excellent idea because it offers a great overview of a complex subject. You can download it here:

```
http://static.googleusercontent.com/media/www.google.com/en//webmasters/docs/
search-engine-optimization-starter-guide.pdf
```

If you have a live website, **do not touch Permalink Settings without consulting a professional** or carefully researching what to do in your particular situation.

Whatever stage you're at, you should install an SEO plugin and begin working with the basics of meta descriptions and so on.

REFERENCE *Please select the video for Lesson 31 online at* `www.wrox.com/go` `/wp24vids`. *You will also be able to download resources for this lesson from the website.*

SECTION IX
Maintenance and Security

32

Keeping Up to Date

Like any software, WordPress is constantly being improved—more features, more efficient code, increased security, and so on—as are themes and plugins. Not having an up-to-date WordPress installation is a common cause of malfunctions and one of the key reasons sites get hacked. **You must keep everything up to date**. Fortunately, updating is a simple task. In addition to that, you can maintain your WordPress site to keep it running smoothly in other ways.

UPDATING WORDPRESS

Following are two types of updates for WordPress:

➤ Automatic minor updates, for example, 4.0 to 4.0.1

➤ Major version manual updates, for example, 3.9 to 4.0

The minor updates are for security and minor functionality fixes, whereas the major version updates have key new features, along with some security fixes. As the name suggests, the automatic updates occur without any need for action on your part.

WordPress is clear about the availability of major updates or minor updates that for various reasons cannot be automatically applied. A warning message with a link to perform the update displays at the top of every admin screen until the update is completed, as shown in Figure 32-1.

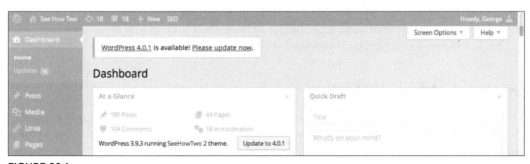

FIGURE 32-1

If you're logged in as any role other than Administrator, the message tells you to notify your administrator of the update. Also, an Update button appears on the Dashboard if there's an update available—displayed next to the name of the version you're running.

For automated updates, the administrative e-mail is sent a notification that the update has taken place.

Automated Updates

At one time, all updates for WordPress had to be done manually, but to make life easier for users and to ensure that minor updates were applied, because they often involve security fixes, it decided to automate non-major updates.

It was also possible to automate these updates between major new releases because they rarely involve changes that could affect plugins or themes. Nevertheless, you always need a regular backup routine in place just in case something negative happens because of any update.

Although WordPress has tried to make its automated updates work on as many server configurations as possible, there may be some situations in which they do not work. In that case, your admin screen can show a message saying an update is available and you need to do it manually.

You can also turn off automatic updates if you prefer to do them manually. Some plugins for that purpose are mentioned at the end of the lesson.

Major Version Updates

When WordPress undergoes significant changes, the update is not automatically applied, but the process is still extremely simple: You press a button.

The trick is to do a full backup of your files and your database prior to pressing the button, and WordPress reminds you of this. Unless your regular backup routine happens to have fallen on the day of the update, you should do a special backup so that you have a snapshot of your site at the moment before the update.

The reason for the caution is that there is a slight chance of something going wrong during a major update. Out of literally thousands of updates to hundreds of site clients over 7 years, I can count on one hand the number of times I've had to revert to a backup.

> **NOTE** *If your server does not work with automated updates, all you have to do is follow the same procedure as a major update: Do a backup and press a button.*

Completely Manual Update

There can be situations in which pressing the Update button does not work, but you'll know this already because you also won't be able to upload media files without having to enter your hosting account information.

If your hosting company won't fix this problem with file ownership and you haven't bothered to find a new hosting company that will, then you have to do a fully manual update of WordPress.

There isn't enough room here to go into the details of a manual update because there are a lot of variables. WordPress.org has a handy three-step manual updating process (`http://codex .wordpress.org/Upgrading_WordPress`), but even with that, it warns you that you may need even more details on its extended upgrade instructions page (`http://codex.wordpress.org/ Upgrading_WordPress_Extended`).

Troubleshooting WordPress Updates

As mentioned, it's rare for there to be problems even during major updates, but if you do encounter them, they fall into three main groups:

➤ WordPress loads but has error messages; weird characters appear at the top of the screen; or certain functions aren't working.

➤ Your screen is white except for an error message.

➤ Your screen is completely blank (white screen of death).

In most of these cases, a plugin is clashing with WordPress. What you should do depends on the state of your screen.

If you can access the WordPress admin screen, the first thing to do is deactivate all your plugins. If you don't have a lot of them, you can try re-activating them one at a time until you find the culprit.

If you have a lot of plugins, first try activating one-half of them. If you're still running fine, activate the other one-half. When you know which half caused the problem, you can start deactivating that half one at a time until the site works properly.

If you can't access the admin screen, but you have an error message, there may be a clue in that message as to which plugin is causing the problem. In that case, you can use an FTP program to go into your plugins directory and change the name of the plugin's folder. That will cause it to deactivate, and when you refresh the WordPress admin screen, it should be up and running.

However, often the error message relates only to a symptom and not the cause of the problem. In other words, the file mentioned in the error message is one that's not working because of a problem somewhere else. Fortunately, if the error message doesn't help or you have a completely blank screen, the process of checking plugins previously described can be done through your FTP program.

Through your FTP program, rename your plugin directory to something such as **plugins-old,** which has the effect of deactivating all the plugins. You should now have access to the backend of WordPress. Next, you create a new directory called plugins. Then, one at a time you drag a plugin's folder from one directory to the other until you find the problem plugin.

Whenever you find a broken plugin, simply leave it deactivated while you research what's happening. Check the plugin's page on the WordPress Plugin Directory to see if others are having the same issue. It may be a matter of waiting for the author to come up with a fix, or it could be there's a conflict with an update in another plugin.

If you purchased the plugin, e-mail the company and explain what happened, what version of WordPress you're running, what version of PHP your server uses, and what other plugins you have.

If it's vital to have that plugin working immediately, you could consider using a different plugin. Or if that's not an option, it may be that the previous version will continue to work. You can get earlier versions from the Developer link on the plugins page in the WordPress directory, or if you have a paid plugin, you should have the earlier version on your hard drive. Try reinstalling and see if that works.

WordPress Cleanup

In addition to keeping WordPress up to date, some maintenance tasks can be useful to perform from time to time, depending on the size and activity of your site. Some of the key tasks are described here, and you can find lists of plugins at the end of the lesson, which can help you with each of them:

➤ **Revision Cleanup:** By default, WordPress keeps all revisions you make to Posts or Pages. Many of these, particularly as time moves on, probably are not worth keeping. There are plugins that can help you clear out old revisions in bulk or change the revision function, so WordPress keeps only the last four or whatever number of revisions you choose.

➤ **Media cleanup:** Between uploading different versions of files or uploading ones you never end up using, your media library (and hence your server) can become unnecessarily bloated. Coupled with the multiple images that WordPress creates for each one you upload (and this could be a dozen or more depending on the theme and plugins you use), you can see how stuffed your server can become. Deleting unneeded media files can be a huge help. There are plugins that can make the process easier by tracking down whether a file is used anywhere.

➤ **Trash cleanup:** By default, WordPress clears out files in the Trash area 30 days after they've been placed there. However, it can be good to go through it after you've done any major house cleaning and delete them right away.

➤ **Database Repair:** Over time, databases can become filled with unnecessary data, or table information can become corrupted. This can slow down your site. But there are plugins that can help without having to know anything about databases.

Your website is like a big closet. Easy to stuff with lots of unneeded items—and just as easy to keep clean with a bit of effort.

UPDATING PLUGINS

When plugins require updating, the most visible notice from any screen in the admin area is a tiny graphic displayed next to the Plugins link on the main admin menu, as shown in Figure 32-2.

FIGURE 32-2

The number in the circle tells you how many plugins need updating. The admin toolbar also has an update indicator showing total Plugins and Themes needing an update.

Figure 32-2 also shows the Plugins page—plugins needing updating have a color-coded highlight and a notice about a new version. You can also view only the plugins that need updating by clicking the Update Available link on the text menu at the top of the Plugins screen.

Following are two ways to do the actual updating of plugins:

➤ From the Plugins page you can click the Update Now link for an individual plugin or use the Bulk Action function to update several at once.

➤ From the Dashboard Updates link on the main admin menu, choose one or more plugins, and click the Update Plugins button.

If you ever experience a problem after updating a plugin, see the section "Troubleshooting WordPress Updates," earlier in this lesson.

Over time, you may accumulate plugins that have been deactivated and are no longer used. It's important to delete these.

Even if plugins are not activated, WordPress has to process them to a certain extent for listing on the Plugins page. It may not be much for each plugin, but if you have 10, 20, or more plugins you're not using, you might as well delete them.

There's also a security issue involved here. As long as a plugin remains installed, its files are sitting on your server. If a security flaw is discovered by hackers, those files could be used by them to cause problems, despite the plugin not being active.

Remember, plugins are easily reinstalled at any time, whether from the WordPress Plugin Directory or a paid plugin, which you'll have a copy of on your hard drive (right?).

> **NOTE** *Sometimes, there will be a plugin that you activate every so often to perform a specific function and then deactivate it again. That's fine, but make sure you update it to try and prevent any security issues, even when it's not active.*

UPDATING THEMES

Like plugins, themes may need updating for various reasons. It could be that they have a special functionality that relied on something in WordPress that has now changed. Or the new version of the theme takes advantage of new features in WordPress. In either case, you need to perform an update.

Theme updates are included in the number that appears beside Dashboard Updates on the main admin menu. That's why after having updated all your plugins, you may still see a number listed.

You can do theme updates from the Updates page, just as with Plugins, or from the theme library where you can see a clear notification on the theme's thumbnail, as shown in Figure 32-3.

FIGURE 32-3

Some premium or commercial themes may have their own methods for updating. Following are some examples:

➤ Log in to the company website, download the new version as a zip file, install it through the WordPress theme upload function, and delete the old version.

➤ Log in to the company website, download the new version, manually upload the folder via FTP, and overwrite the old version.

➤ Load a special plugin that handles the updating.

In any case, you should receive some sort of notification, perhaps through the WordPress Updates area of the menu, with instructions on how to perform the update.

Just as with plugins, it's not good to keep more than a few themes in your theme library at any one time. In particular, there can be security issues with outdated themes.

Some automated WordPress installers include dozens and dozens of themes from the WordPress.org site. There's no good reason for this, when it's so simple to preview and then install a theme at any time. Get rid of all these extra themes.

Or if you're working on a site redesign and you've been loading several possible themes, make sure you delete them after you've made your choice.

PLUGINS

Some of the plugins listed here enable you to disable elements of WordPress's updating system. Make sure you know what you're doing when using those features.

UPDATING

➤ **Background Update Tester**—If your WordPress installation does not enable you to have automated minor updates, you can try running this plugin to help identify what the issue might be.

➤ **Disable Updates Manager**—If you don't want particular themes or plugins to be updated, either automatically or manually, this plugin enables you to block that process.

➤ **Block Plugin Update**—If you have a plugin that you need to keep at its current version for some reason, this enables you to block updates for individual plugins.

➤ **Update Control**—Gives you full control of how automated minor updates will be applied. Also useful for developers who want to control how beta versions of WordPress are updated.

➤ **Disable WordPress Core Updates**—WARNING: This completely disables the WordPress check for updates. You may want this if you maintain a site for someone else and you want to take care of updates without them being troubled or confused by the process.

➤ **ManageWP Worker**—If you have more than one WordPress site, this tool enables you to manage them all from a single admin interface, including updating plugins and so on.

➤ **No Update Nag**—Sometimes, you don't want other users of WordPress bothered by the update notification message, so this can disable it.

CLEANING UP

➤ **Thin Out Revisions**—Enables you to manage the Revisions function in WordPress, including doing a bulk cleanup of old revisions and on-going automated cleanup.

➤ **Better Delete Revision**—Tool for managing the Revisions function, including bulk deletion.

➤ **WP Media Cleaner**—Goes through your media files and looks for ones that are not used anywhere, and then lists them and gives you the opportunity to delete them.

➤ **WP Clean Up**—Cleans up the WordPress database by taking out revisions, auto drafts, and so on.

➤ **WP Clean Up Optimizer**—Optimize WordPress: Offers a wide range of optimization functions to make WordPress run smoothly.

➤ **Optimize Database After Deleting Revisions**—Despite the name, this plugin is for optimizing your WordPress database in general.

➤ **WP-Optimize**—Tool for optimizing the WordPress database.

TRY IT

Because you may not have any plugins that need updating, you see how to get one that needs updating. This gives you practice deleting a plugin, downloading one manually, uploading and installing it manually, and, finally, updating it.

Lesson Requirements

This exercise has no special requirements.

Step-by-Step

For this exercise, you find a plugin, upload a new one, update it, and then delete it.

1. Go to `http://www.wordpress.org/plugins/`.

2. Search for **fighting the lyrics.**

3. You should get only one result. Click Fighting The Lyrics to bring you to its main page.

4. Click the Developers link.

5. Under Other Versions, click 1.05.

6. Save the file to your desktop.

7. Return to your WordPress admin screen.

8. Click Plugins ⇨ Add New.

9. On the text menu at the top, click Upload.

10. Click Browse and then select your Fighting the Lyrics zip file from the desktop.

11. Click Install Now.

12. When you see that it's been installed successfully, click the text link Return to Plugins page.

13. You see the orange-colored background on the Fighting the Lyrics listing that tells you there's an automatic upgrade.

14. Click Update Now.

15. When you see the message Plugin Updated Successfully, click the text link Return to Plugins page.

16. Find the Fighting the Lyrics listing. You'll see the Delete link.

17. Click Delete.

18. On the Delete Plugin screen, click Yes and Delete These Files, which removes the plugin completely.

> **REFERENCE** *Please select the video for Lesson 32 online at* `www.wrox.com/go/` `wp24vids`. *You will also be able to download resources for this lesson from the website.*

33

Keeping Backups

Back up or die. It should already be your mantra for your home devices; now do the same for your website. Without a backup of your data, you face disaster if something happens; it rarely does, but the key word is "rarely." Because it's even remotely possible for your server to crash or a hacker to mess up your files, you must keep backups.

And for backing up WordPress, there is only one course of action: *Automate your backups.*

I've tried many different ways over the years to educate clients and readers about how to back up WordPress, how often to do it, and how to get into a routine of doing backups. Almost without exception, it doesn't happen. We get busy, we forget, we get intimidated by the process; whatever the cause, people do not take the time to back up their sites.

The good news is that it has become so easy to do automated backups with free and paid plugins, or third-party services, that there's no point in even trying to develop a manual backup routine. Whatever method you use, make it an automated one that's easy to restore.

THE ELEMENTS OF BACKING UP

After being blunt about the "why" of doing backups, I'll now briefly consider the what, where, when, and who, followed by some details on the how.

What to Back Up

Following are two elements to a WordPress backup:

➤ Site files (WordPress, themes, plugins, and your media files)

➤ Site database (settings and all your text content)

You need to understand that these are completely separate on the server and require different methods of backing up. Check that a plugin is doing both, or understand which plugin is doing what, so that you're covering the other backup by some other means.

Where to Keep Backups

The golden rule of backing up, whether for your home devices or website, is to store the backup somewhere else. Even better is to have two backups, each in a different location. I remember years ago storing a backup hard drive for my computer at my parent's place. Luckily I never had to wake them in the middle of the night to access my data. These days there are better options.

When you're looking into backup options for your WordPress site, you need to make sure the backup is not being stored on your server. The whole point of the backup is to restore it if something happens to your server.

One solution is to get a hosting account with a different host and store your backups on that account. An advantage of this method is that if your current site crashes and you decide it's time to switch hosts, your files are already at the new location, speeding up the switchover.

The cloud is a popular choice for backups these days, because it's somewhere other than your server and services like Amazon S3, Google Drive, Dropox and many others are usually very cost effective. If you have a large site, storing even just a few backup versions can add up, so you want a low-cost storage solution.

Another location for backup storage, depending on the size of your site, is an e-mail account such as Gmail with plenty of storage. If you're backing up your database separately from your site files, this can be an ideal method for storing the database file, which is typically quite small when zipped up.

And, of course, storing a copy of your website on an external hard drive is another simple and cost-effective solution. Notice I didn't say "stored on your computer's hard drive," because you won't want to be worrying about computer crashes just when you need to restore a backup.

The ideal scenario: one backup in the cloud and another on an external hard drive. Whatever the plan, make sure you choose a plugin or service that can handle it.

When to Do Backups

How often should you do a backup? As often as necessary.

I don't say that to be funny or cryptic. It simply means that the frequency of backups will vary for different sites or for the same site over time.

For example, say you spend 3 weeks getting ready to launch your site. You should set your backup for every day or even twice a day depending on how much you're doing each day. A weekly backup would miss a lot of material. After the site is launched and you're adding a new Post once a week, say, then a weekly backup would be reasonable.

Who Should Do Backups?

Everyone. Whether you run a personal blog, a site for your soccer team, or an online store, you need backups. Your content is valuable and you need to protect it. Besides, backup solutions cost nothing or very little, and when they're automated they don't require your time.

Following are some excuses I've heard for not backing up, all of which are just wrong:

➤ I have a very reliable host.

➤ I update my content only a couple of times a year (!).

➤ I have all my original Word docs and images on my hard drive.

These people are delusional: Accidents happen to any host. Even if your content isn't changing, WordPress and plugins are, and the point of a backup is so that you don't have to reconstruct your crashed site from scratch.

How to Do Backups

The two choices previously mentioned were: plugins or third-party services. Now we'll consider the latter, and end with plugins in general. Then a list of some plugins is provided.

Third-Party Backup Services

Although you may store your backups with a third party, such as Amazon S3 or Dropbox, this section discusses third parties that actually handle the backup software as well as the storage.

Your hosting company is actually a backup service you should consider first because it already takes care of your website files. However, you need to keep the following in mind: *Do not rely on your hosting company's default backup system.*

Most hosting companies regularly make backups of their servers, but those are rarely kept longer than the next backup, and these are typically images of the entire server. For them to extract your particular site's data is not worth their time. And if you read the fine print of most hosting companies, they do not guarantee a backup of your files.

Currently, more and more hosting companies advertise individual site backups as part of certain hosting plans. So it's definitely worth looking into what your hosting package includes.

Most hosting companies do offer a backup service for an additional fee, but here's an important question to ask: Where do they store the backups? If it's on your hosting account or even on the same server where your account is located, that's a problem. If the entire server goes down, not only is your site inaccessible, but also are your backups.

In addition to your hosting company, you can also check with other hosting companies to see if they have accounts for backing up sites. That way your backups are stored on a completely different server system, and if you need to switch hosting companies, you're already set up with one.

Another type of third-party backup service is one such as VaultPress, which is run by the folks who make WordPress. Many other backup services are available, such as blogVault, Codeguard, BackBlaze, and DropMySite; search for **website backup services**.

Free and Paid Plugins

With the advent of the cloud and inexpensive hard-drive storage, along with the development of sophisticated automated plugins, you don't need a third-party service to get great backup protection.

Some plugins back up only the WordPress database. You do not want these plugins. If there were plugins that just automated the backing up of site files, then I might say, get both plugins, but there aren't any files-only backup plugins that I know of. Even if there are, I know from experience that average site owners are not going to manually do FTP backups of site files every time they get an e-mail saying their database has been automatically backed up.

Don't set yourself up to fail: Just get a plugin that backs up both your files and your database.

What about plugins for moving websites? Although these do create complete copies of your database and files, their primary purpose is to take a snapshot of a site and re-create it immediately on a subdomain or elsewhere. If the plugin has the capability to schedule automated copying, it might work for backups.

Some plugins do full automated backups but do not have the capability to tie into cloud or other storage services, such as Amazon S3 or Google Drive. For some people, this could work, but in my experience, the average website owner would benefit from the simplicity of a paid storage service.

For example, consider home data storage. For years there have been ways to link all your home devices to a central data storage location, whether on one of those devices or a stand-alone network drive. Yet how widespread has this practice actually become? Not very. But along comes cloud storage with a simple set up, and you hear grandmothers talking about backing up photos of the grandkids.

You should use an automated backup plugin that has the capability to tie into several different storage solutions.

Remember, if a plugin is saving only a full backup to your own hosting account, you're responsible for downloading that backup so that it's stored somewhere else (preferably two other places).

Restoring Backups

It's one thing to have complete backups stored in safe locations, but if you can't easily restore a backup, the value is lost to some extent. Yes, you can pay someone to do a restoration or maybe your hosting company can help, but for many people, the goal should be to have the same plugin do the restoration.

To sum up, following is the ideal backup plugin solution:

➤ Full backup of files and database

➤ Scheduled, automatic backups

➤ Storage to at least one location different from your server

➤ Simple restoration of backups

Although there are a couple free plugins that meet these requirements, you're more likely going to need a paid plugin, including paid versions of some free plugins mentioned next.

> **WARNING** *Under Tools ⇨ Export, you can find a feature of WordPress that appears to do what a database backup does, but it's quite different. This feature extracts only the content from your database and preserves a few elements of the structure in a language called XML.*

PLUGINS

Although my goal in this book has been to mention only free plugins, the small number of free complete backup solutions leads me to list a couple of popular paid ones.

PAID COMPLETE BACKUP SOLUTIONS

➤ **Backup Buddy**—Full backups and easy restoration, with 1 GB of storage on their servers, or you can store files anywhere you choose. Includes easy migration of your WordPress site to a different hosting company.

➤ **Snapshot**—Full backups and restoration, including the capability to make notes about each backup.

FREE COMPLETE BACKUP SOLUTIONS.

➤ **UpdraftPlus Backup and Restoration**—Supports backing up of both files and database to a variety of services such as Amazon S3, Google Drive, an FTP account, and much more. This does site restore as well. Files and databases can have separate backup schedules.

FULL BACKUPS

These plugins do full backups but may limit where you can store or whether you can easily restore. Many have paid versions that extend their functionality.

➤ **BackUpWordPress**—Automated backups of your files and database. However, the free version backs up only to your hosting account. No restore function.

➤ **BackWPup Free**—WordPress Backup Plugin backs up files and databases, with the capability to store backups at any FTP location as well as some cloud services such as Amazon S3 and Dropbox. Does not have a restore function built in.

DATABASE-ONLY BACKUPS

Although these should not be used by the average site owner as a backup solution, here are a couple examples for those who need this limited functionality.

➤ **WP Migrate DB**—Enables you to copy only your database and change all the URLs and file paths so that you can use them in another location. Saves having to do two separate steps of copying the database and then running an update of all paths.

➤ **WP-DB-Backup**—Basic database-only backup that you can schedule. Stores backups on your server, or you can have them e-mailed.

continues

continued

MIGRATION TOOLS

These plugins are meant for moving or copying your site from one place to another. These are not backup solutions as I've defined.

➤ **Duplicator**—Takes care of the entire process of copying your site and restoring it in a new location.

➤ **WP Clone by WP Academy**—Utility for copying and moving your WordPress site to a subdomain, a new server, or a new domain.

TRY IT

There's nothing specific to try in this lesson, but a couple actions are recommended. Read through the details of your hosting account and find out exactly what you may have in the way of backups. At the same time, check what options it has for backup services.

Look into the costs of cloud storage. You can find good pricing, and remember that you can use it for other purposes in addition to your backups, such as storing video or audio files to use on your website.

REFERENCE *Please select the video for Lesson 33 online at* www.wrox.com/go/ wp24vids. *You will also be able to download resources for this lesson from the website.*

34

Keeping Your Site Secure

Every piece of software on the Internet is threatened by hackers. Because of its tremendous popularity, WordPress is a regular target. The good news is that protecting yourself is not nearly as daunting as it might seem.

Two of the most important elements of WordPress security have previously been covered: staying up to date with all aspects of your site's software, and having a backup if something happens.

This lesson shows you six additional steps you can take to increase the security of your WordPress installation. Although these are not exhaustive, if you do all or most of these steps, you're much better off (sadly) than a great many users. Some other issues you need to be aware of in the constant effort to ward off hackers are also covered.

SIX STEPS TO GREATER WORDPRESS SECURITY

None of the following steps are difficult to do; the hard part is remembering to do them or getting in the habit of doing them.

Strong Passwords

Every security expert will tell you that weak passwords are the leading cause of software breaches. As you saw when first setting up WordPress, you need to pay attention to the password strength indicator and use only passwords that trigger a reading of Strong.

Following are the six criteria for a strong password:

- ➤ At least eight characters in length
- ➤ Some lowercase letters
- ➤ Some uppercase letters
- ➤ Some numbers
- ➤ Some characters such as #&!
- ➤ No actual words

And just so it's driven home visually, following are some examples:

➤ **Bad**—Harp78

➤ **Good**—k7Te%w8Xq

I know, you're thinking to yourself the good password is hard to memorize, but that's part of what makes it good. Use a password manager program to store these hard-to-memorize passwords.

While random is best, it is possible to have a password you can memorize yet is still pretty strong. Take a random phrase, such as "The 4 cats drive a Lexus through Dallas each morning at 9" and use the first letter of each word to create this password: T4cdaLtDema9. This is the minimum length for creating a password this way; the longer the better.

Randomness is crucial; don't use a phrase from books, movies, songs, and so on. The more visually memorable the random phrase is to you, the easier it will be to remember.

And do not rely on substitution methods like this: p@ssw0rd, r@nd0miz3, and so on. Hackers easily incorporate these substitutions into the dictionaries they use.

Another approach is to memorize a random set of at least 6 symbols and numbers, such as "7%$9#4." Then take a word of at least 6 letters and add two numbers at the end, such as "debate24." The first number tells you which letter to capitalize and the second tells you the point at which to inject your random symbols and numbers, so the resulting password would be: dEba7%$9#4te. One of the advantages here is that you only memorize one thing, yet you can generate any number of passwords.

> **WARNING** *If you have other users on your site, it won't matter how careful you are with your own password if they go into their profile and use something unsecure. That's why you should use a plugin to force users to choose strong passwords. Some are mentioned at the end of the lesson.*

Two-Factor Authentication

The hot topic in security these days is two-factor authentication, which means requiring two components for logging in. Typically, the components consist of something the user knows (a pin number) and something the user carries with them (a bank card).

Obviously, a physical component is not practical for things such as logging into WordPress, so a second piece of knowledge makes sense, but it needs to be knowledge accessible only by the user at the moment of login. If a temporary second password generated for that transaction could be transmitted to the user, that would be equivalent to possessing a physical object. Enter the mobile phone. A temporary password is simply texted to the phone.

The way it works is you have a plugin on WordPress which, when you sign in with your username and password, immediately triggers a code to be sent to the phone you've already registered. You have to enter this code before you can get into WordPress. At the end of this lesson some plugins that enable this kind of stronger login process are mentioned.

Use Reputable Themes and Plugins

Corrupted or unsecure themes and plugins are one of the leading causes of hackers worming their way into websites. And these themes and plugins tend to come from unreliable sources.

Free themes and plugins should be downloaded from one of only two places:

➤ WordPress.org

➤ A well-known commercial theme or plugin maker's site

Go anywhere else and you could be leaving yourself open to problems. Ask yourself this: If it's free, why isn't it in the WordPress.org directories? Anyone can submit his work, which is then given a thorough check, not just for viruses and malware, but also for coding compliance and other standards.

Some commercial theme or plugin makers put free items on their sites to give you a taste of their work. If they're reliable, that's fine. This is particularly true of themes. If you're not sure of the theme maker's reputation, you can always run the theme through the Theme Check plugin, mentioned in Lesson 27, "Overview of WordPress Themes." There are also plugins that scan all your site files for possible malware, as mentioned at the end of this lesson.

Do Not Use "Admin" for a Username

WordPress no longer automatically gives the first user on the system the username "admin." However, many people continue to enter that as their choice when first installing WordPress. Don't do it.

If you set up a security plugin that monitors access to your site, you would not believe how many people will try to get into your WordPress by entering "admin" as the username. These hackers know that eventually they'll strike a site that's using it, and then they're part way toward getting in.

If you have an account with the username "admin" you need to get rid of it right now!

All you have to do is create a new administrator account with a username unique to yourself. Then log out and log in as the new user. Delete the "admin" account, assigning all its Posts to you.

Change the Database Prefix

When you install WordPress, you're given the option of choosing the prefix for the names of the database tables. The default is wp_ but you can use any prefix you want.

Although I'm not completely convinced that this offers much protection, all installations have the same table names following the prefix—it's an easy step when you're installing WordPress, so you might as well do it.

Vigilance

You can protect yourself in a number of ways by keeping an eye on certain elements of WordPress.

Regularly check your list of users. Filter for administrators and editors. Make sure there are no unknown users suddenly appearing, which could mean that hackers have set themselves up with control over your site and access to your files through the theme and plugin editors.

Delete temporary administrators. If you hire someone to work on your site, create a temporary administrator for the task, and when they're through, erase it.

Delete the accounts or change the passwords of any former administrators, editors, or authors. And there are plugins which will automatically force current users to reset their password after a certain amount of time; see the end of the lesson for some examples.

Make sure no backups of your wp-config file exist. Neglectful developers may make a temporary backup of this crucial file. If they leave it on the server, it won't be protected, and depending on how they saved it, it may be a plain text file. Figure 34-1 shows a backup of a config file exposed on the Internet and how easily it can be opened as a text file, revealing all the database login information:

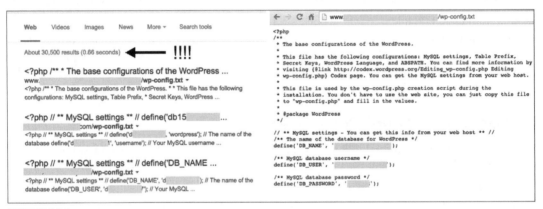

FIGURE 34-1

By the way, I found this file (and thousands more like it) with a simple search using Google. Don't make things this easy for hackers. And just so you know, these kinds of vulnerabilities have been pointed out on the Internet for more than a decade, so there's no excuse for leaving backed-up copies of config files on the server.

You can look for these files on your hosting account using an FTP program or the File Manager of your hosting Control Panel. Look for things such as wp-config.txt or wp-config.php.bak. Any variation other than wp-config.php is vulnerable. Simply delete them, but, of course, *don't delete* wp-config.php.

Limit Login Attempts

Hackers don't actually have to break into WordPress to cause you problems. They could simply flood your login page with attempted logins. When I say flood, I mean hundreds or even thousands of attempts in a short period. On shared hosting, this can often have you shut down as the hosting company works to prevent the server from being overloaded and all other sites suffer.

There are plugins that limit how many times a single user can try to log in before being blocked; a few are mentioned at the end of the lesson.

> **NOTE** *For more ways to help secure WordPress, some of which require a bit of technical knowledge, check this page of the WordPress Codex:* `http://codex .wordpress.org/Hardening_WordPress`.

DEALING WITH SENSITIVE DATA

Some hackers just want to break in for the fun of it or to use WordPress as a tool for larger acts, but others are after data, such as personal or credit card information.

Following are two security elements relating to sensitive data:

➤ Collection

➤ Storage

Common solutions exist for both, in addition to specific steps you should take.

Collecting Sensitive Data

Suppose you have a form on your WordPress site where you need to collect data such as a person's address, insurance policy number, or Social Security number. Unless the page containing the form is protected by secure browsing (an HTTPS in the URL), the data can be stolen as users enter the information.

With an SSL certificate for your site, you can use a WordPress plugin to designate that form page as HTTPS. Actually, you can make your entire site secure that way, including your administrative area.

The other important element in all this is retrieving the sensitive data. The normal action for any form is to have it e-mailed to you; however, regular e-mail is also susceptible to hacking. You can use plugins to have WordPress send your e-mail through a secure mail server. (One is mentioned at the end of the lesson.)

> **NOTE** *Making your entire site HTTPS, whether or not you collect sensitive data, is an important trend in internet security. Google announced in the summer of 2014 that it was giving a minor search ranking boost to sites with HTTPS, and suggested that this boost would increase over time. Check if your hosting company offers an SSL certificate with your account or, if you need to purchase one, they start at about $50 per year.*

Storing Sensitive Data

The short answer to the problem of storing sensitive data in WordPress is: Don't do it!

For data from web forms, plugins exist that write the information to your WordPress database and e-mail it to you. Typically, the reason for doing this is to allow the exporting of gathered data all at one time to be imported into a spreadsheet or an offline database.

If that's the case, you need to retrieve the data every day, or even more frequently if a lot of data exists, and then delete it from WordPress. Do not keep the data stored online.

Better still: find a plugin that offers an automated method for securely transferring the data to a safe location.

Remember: *There are no good reasons for storing sensitive data in WordPress.* It's that simple.

SECURE HOSTING

One aspect of security that sometimes is overlooked is your choice of hosting companies. Although the services offered are almost identical, including the software used to provide those services, important differences can exist in how that software is set up.

Account Firewalls

Most individuals and small businesses have their sites hosted on a shared server. That is, their account is just one of hundreds or possibly even thousands of other accounts on the server. It's an efficient and cost-effective way of providing inexpensive hosting, but it poses an important security problem: keeping those accounts separate.

You could take every security step discussed so far, but if your neighbors on the shared server aren't vigilant and a hacker gets into one of their accounts, that can leave you vulnerable, unless the hosting company has properly insulated accounts from one another. There have been several well-publicized security breaches over the years, in which literally thousands of websites were hacked or brought down because the hackers wormed their way in to others' accounts through the server system after hacking one account.

The most you can do is research this before using hosting companies. Ask what steps they take, check forum postings for signs it has happened before, and Google the company name and **security breach**, and so on.

The ultimate defense you have is a good backup routine. If a server breach occurs, just take your backup and move to a new hosting company. The switch is often faster than waiting for the problem to be fixed.

Visible Directories

Earlier in the lesson you saw a screen shot of someone's file directory where there was a backup of the `wp-config.php` file (refer to Figure 34-1). Well, it wasn't just the readable backup file that was a problem: You should not have been able to view a list of all the files in that directory!

When you browse a domain name, you're actually browsing the home directory on the server. And when you try to browse a directory, the server looks for certain types of files: `default.html`, `index.html`, `index.php`, and so on. If it doesn't find one, the server may, depending on the hosting company's settings, simply display a list of the files in the directory, with a link to each file, as shown in Figure 34-2.

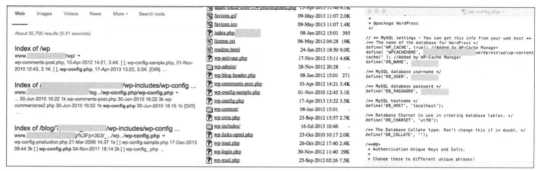

FIGURE 34-2

You can see how a simple search turns up visible directories, and from a directory, you can download a `wp-config.php` file. Notice that I'm not accessing the file through a browser, which would have processed the php file and nothing would happen. What I did was right-click a file and download it to my computer, and that's only possible if the directory is visible.

WordPress protects itself from hosts who leave directories visible by placing blank `index.php` files into all directories that shouldn't be open. You can see this at work by adding the following to the end of your domain name: `/wp-content/themes/`.

If you try to view that URL, you should get a blank white screen; that's the `index.php` file at work. If it weren't there and your host allowed visible directories, you'd see a list of all your theme folders.

If for some reason a WordPress directory is visible, you can solve the problem in the same way, by uploading a plain text file called `index.php`, containing only `<?php //Silence is golden ?>`

Make sure you don't have anything after the closing bracket, not even a space.

You can do the same for any folder you create on the web that does not have an `index.php` file (or other type of default file).

File Permissions

Sometimes, someone in a forum advises others to change the permissions on a folder or file to 777. That means anyone can read the file, edit the file, or delete the file. The advice is usually meant to solve some issue a person has with WordPress or a plugin.

Never change a permission level to 777.

Your problem might temporarily be solved, but you're opening yourself up to much larger ones. No proper fix for a problem should involve changing permissions to that level of openness.

Although different hosting companies have different approaches to file permissions and ownership, at WordPress.org, you can find a good discussion about the recommended types of file permissions you should see in a WordPress installation—and none of them are 777, not even upload directories. Here's the URL:

```
http://codex.wordpress.org/Changing_File_Permissions
```

PLUGINS

For those who want all or most of the security measures discussed in this lesson, here are some comprehensive security plugins, while those who only want individual security features can choose from specific plugins.

COMPREHENSIVE SECURITY

➤ **iThemes Security (formerly Better WP Security)**—General purpose security plugin.

➤ **Wordfence Security**—General purpose security plugin.

➤ **BulletProof Security**—General purpose security plugin.

➤ **Acunetix Secure WordPress**—General purpose security plugin.

STRONG PASSWORDS

➤ **Force Strong Passwords**—Does not enable users to change their password unless it passes the WordPress strength meter's "strong" level.

BRUTE FORCE PROTECTION

➤ **Login Security Solution**—Secures your login by increasing the time period before repeated failed logins get an error message. Also enforces strong passwords when users change their password.

➤ **Login LockDown**—Helps to prevent brute-force attacks by locking out anyone who tries and fails to log in more than a set number of times. You can also adjust how long they're blocked.

➤ **Rename wp-login.php**—Renames your login page to help reduce brute-force attacks.

ADMIN AND LOGIN PAGES PROTECTED

➤ **Lockdown WP Admin**—Hides the admin area and the login page from anyone not logged in.

PASSWORD EXPIRY

➤ **WordPress Password Expiry**—Set the amount of time before a password expires, based on a user's role. They can either reset the password themselves or make it so the administrator has to choose the new password.

➤ **WP Password Policy Manager**—Not only does this provide an expiration date for user passwords and force them to reset, but you can also control what elements must be a in a password (uppercase, numbers, characters, and so on). You can also reset all user passwords automatically with a single click.

SENDING SECURE EMAILS

➤ **WP Mail SMTP**—Handy plugin if you're having problems with the default PHP mail function in WordPress because it enables you to send e-mails through a third-party server, such as Gmail or Yahoo and so on. Also enables you to send e-mails securely.

MALWARE SCANNING

➤ **Anti-Malware and Brute-Force Security by ELI**—Scans your WordPress installation for malware and helps you remove it.

TWO-FACTOR AUTHENTICATION

➤ **Clef**—Two-factor authentication for logging into your site using your smartphone.

➤ **Google Authenticator**—Integrates your site with Google Authenticator for two-factor authentication for logging into your site.

ADDITIONAL SECURITY PLUGINS

➤ **WordPress HTTPS (SSL)**—Enables you to force some or all pages on your site to use HTTPS for secure browsing.

➤ **WP Login Alerts by DigiP**—Alerts you by e-mail when someone tries to log in to your website. It logs the IP address and what username he tried to log in with.

➤ **WordPress Simple Firewall**—Blocks anyone violating the firewall rules you set up. Also has an audit history of site access, protects against brute force attacks, and offers two-factor authentication for logging in.

TRY IT

In this lesson, you practice testing whether your file directories are visible on the Internet.

Lesson Requirements

You need a browser and FTP access to your hosting account files.

Step-by-Step

To test for visible file directories, follow these steps:

1. Enter the domain name of your website into your browser's address bar, and press Enter/Return.

2. After you see your home page, enter the following to the end of your domain name: **/wp-content/themes/**

3. Press Enter/Return. You should see a blank white screen. If you see a list of links for all your themes, your server allows file directories to display and your WordPress installation is missing the `index.php` file that's supposed to be in that directory to produce the white screen and keep people from viewing your files.

4. If you did get the white screen, you can test whether folders would be visible without the `index.php` file. Using your FTP program, navigate to wp-content/themes.

5. Look for the `index.php` file.

6. Using your FTP program, rename the file to something such as **index.php-old**.

7. In your browser, try to view the themes directory again.

8. If you can see your theme folders, you know your host allows visible directories, and you can ask them to turn that off. (They may or may not.) If you get some sort of error or warning about trying to view a directory, you know your host has visibility turned off.

9. In either case, make sure you rename your file back to `index.php`.

> **REFERENCE** *Please select the video for Lesson 34 online at* www.wrox.com/go/wp24vids. *You will also be able to download resources for this lesson from the website.*

SECTION X
Adding Functionality Using Plugins

35

Installing and Activating Plugins

There are a lot of things that WordPress doesn't do, and that's a good thing. The simpler the base, the more secure, the more bug-free, and the more efficient it can be. It's also easier to update a simple structure. But you'll probably want WordPress to do more, and that's where plugins fit in, so to speak.

In this lesson, you learn about finding, installing, and activating plugins. Lesson 36, "More Plugin Suggestions," provides a quick guide to help you sort through the more than 37,000 plugins available—during the week I was working on this lesson, more than 350 plugins were added to the directory!

WHAT IS A PLUGIN?

Plugins are a file or set of files that provide additional functionality to WordPress, from simple tasks such as removing the version number of WordPress to creating a full-fledged shopping cart system.

The name refers to the simplicity of adding these scripts to WordPress—you just "plug" them in with the click of a mouse. You may have to do some configuration, depending on the complexity of the function, but even then the vast majority of plugins are meant to be used by novice and expert WordPress users alike.

One of the best things about plugins is that you can unplug them. That's important because it helps protect your website by keeping the plugins separate from the core WordPress files. If something goes wrong, either because of a conflict with other plugins or when you update WordPress, or you change your mind and don't want it or want a different plugin, all you have to do is unplug or deactivate it.

Plugins are constantly being updated to keep pace with WordPress updates as well as to add new features and security. As talked about in Lesson 32, "Keeping Up To Date," keeping track of those updates is automated for you in WordPress under the Dashboard ➪ Updates area as well as in the Plugins area itself.

Finding Plugins

The best place to go for plugins is Plugins ➪ Add New. That's because WordPress has a built-in search function that directly accesses the WordPress.org plugins directory, as shown in Figure 35-1.

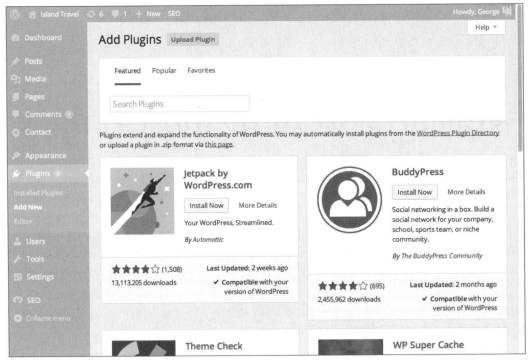

FIGURE 35-1

As mentioned previously, this should be your only source for free plugins. The plugins here have been tested for viruses as well as for meeting basic WordPress coding standards. You can also find a lot of commercial plugin makers by searching the Internet or getting the free version from the WordPress directory.

But how do you choose from the tens of thousands of WordPress plugins?

The video for this lesson walks through the WordPress directory and how to use the information there to make decisions about which plugins to try. But following are a couple tips:

➤ **Run the numbers.** Start with the number of downloads, and then check the ratio of five-star ratings to the number of one-star ratings, with the total number of people who took the time to rate it. A plugin with 500,000 downloads, 50 five-stars to 10 one-stars, and only 85 ratings is less of a candidate than a plugin with 20,000 downloads, 100 five-stars to 2 one-stars, and 170 ratings.

➤ **Read the support forums.** How responsive is the author? Are a lot of the questions raised serious in nature?

➤ **Check out the authors.** Do they have a lot of experience writing other plugins? Are those other plugins well rated?

> **NOTE** *Support free plugins by donating to them. If you use 20 plugins and donate $2.00 to each of them, think of all the functionality you're getting for only $40.00. You couldn't pay someone to write a single plugin for that.*
>
> *If 10,000 people donate $2.00 each to a plugin, the author could better afford to maintain the plugin or develop others. And don't forget to rate plugins at WordPress.org.*

The other important source of information about plugins is the Internet. People enjoy writing top-ten lists about WordPress plugins. However, check out at least four or five lists from important bloggers and see which plugins make it to all or most lists. Sometimes, you'll get actual reviews of plugins, but again, check out a few to spot common points.

Of course, the great thing about free plugins is that you can try them out. If your site is up and running, do this experimenting on a test version of WordPress. You can set up one in a subdirectory of your hosting account using your hosting company's auto-installer.

Installing and Activating Plugins

You need to understand the difference between installing and activating plugins. When you install a plugin, you're actually just putting its folder into the plugins directory of `wp-content`. However, it won't do anything on your site until you activate it.

Installing a plugin is as simple as clicking the Install button when you've found the plugin you want through the search function you saw earlier in the lesson.

If you've downloaded a commercial plugin, you can upload it to WordPress through the Add Plugins screen, as shown in Figure 35-2.

FIGURE 35-2

WordPress tells you when you've successfully installed a plugin, as shown in Figure 35-3 A, and you can verify that by going to Plugins ➪ Plugins, as shown in Figure 35-3 B.

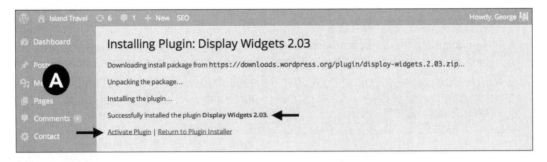

FIGURE 35-3

The color of a plugin's listing depends on its status. White rows are the inactive plugins, blue rows are the activated plugins, and orange-colored rows indicate plugins that need updating, with a link to do the update automatically.

You can also filter what you see on this Plugins screen by using the menu at the top left. You can see All, Active, Recently Active, Inactive, or Upgrade Available. (Options display only if there are plugins that meet their criteria.)

After you install a plugin, activating it is easy: Click the Activate link on the text menu below the name of the plugin. What happens after that depends on what the plugin does and how the author chose to integrate it. Look for one or a combination of these:

➤ A new section on the main Admin menu

➤ A new submenu item on the main Admin menu

➤ A new item on the toolbar

➤ A new Widget

➤ A settings link on the plugin's listing on the plugins Page

After a plugin has been activated, the text menu below the name changes to show Deactivate and Edit (plus any other menu items created by the plugin itself). There is no Delete option anymore because the plugin is activated.

Deactivating and Deleting Plugins

To deactivate a plugin, of course, you just click Deactivate. Although this stops the functions of the plugin, you haven't fully "unplugged" at this point.

After a plugin has been deactivated, you have the choice to delete it completely from WordPress. What that means is the plugin's files are permanently deleted, and WordPress reminds you of this before completing the deletion process, as shown in Figure 35-4.

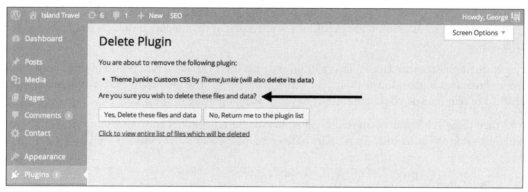

FIGURE 35-4

However, the settings and data for a plugin are another matter. Sometimes, they remain in the WordPress database; sometimes they're deleted; and sometimes there's a plugin setting that lets you decide.

Leaving plugin settings or data in your database is usually fine; it can be quite handy in case you re-install a plugin later. But sometimes a plugin leaves behind a large amount of extra database tables and data, which can reduce the efficiency of WordPress. There are plugins that can help you clean up your database from time to time.

> **NOTE** *If you ever have a problem with your WordPress site, there's a good chance that one of your plugins is causing the issue. Appendix A, "Troubleshooting for WordPress," offers some troubleshooting tips, including how to sort through possible plugin difficulties.*

How Many Plugins Should You Have?

Here's a rule of thumb: *Keep the number of plugins to a minimum.*

That doesn't mean there's a number of plugins that's too many. Some owners may have only 6 plugins, whereas others will have 40. But you shouldn't have more than you need for your purposes or for the efficient loading of your site. The key is to always be keeping an eye on *plugin creep*.

For example, I've seen people with three plugins that essentially do the same thing. They're using one for one purpose and one for another when they could use just a single plugin.

In other cases I see people using plugins that are no longer necessary. For instance, they have a video player plugin when the built-in video player in WordPress would work just as well. Or they have a plugin that orders menu items, when WordPress has an excellent menu system by default.

Plugin resource usage is another factor to consider when assessing if you have too many plugins. For example, you could have 12 plugins that, combined, use fewer resources than a single plugin. In other words those 12 plugins do things that don't put as much of a load on WordPress as the single plugin. A plugin that turns off the toolbar needs far fewer resources than a plugin that creates an entire events calendar.

Plugin quality is another factor. Two plugins may perform the same function, but one is poorly written and requires more resources than the other. That means the inefficient plugin is reducing the amount of plugins you could potentially have by using up more of the load.

And then there's the issue of unused plugins. Lesson 32 talks about the importance of cleaning up plugins that aren't activated. That's part of keeping plugins to a minimum as well.

PLUGINS

Here are some plugins to help you manage your plugins.

➤ **Plugin Organizer**—Enables you to group plugins on the plugins Page, as well as determine the loading order of plugins or choose to not load a plugin under certain conditions.

➤ **WP Manage Plugins**—Provides a set of tools for managing plugins. Disable automatic updates for specific plugins, hide the plugins page from other users, and have an e-mail automatically sent to an administrator when plugins are added, activated, or deactivated.

➤ **P3 (Plugin Performance Profiler)**—Provides a performance report on all your plugins. Helps you spot ones that take up a lot of resources that may slow down your site. Stores reports to allow for comparison over time.

➤ **WP Install Profiles**—If you create multiple WordPress sites, this plugin enables you to create a profile of a set of plugins. You can then download that profile and have all those plugins automatically installed on another WordPress installation.

TRY IT

One of the most popular plugins in the WordPress directory is Contact Form 7. You can use it for simple contact forms or complex forms such as an application form. In this lesson you learn to find it, install it, and activate it.

Lesson Requirements

This lesson has no special requirements.

Step-by-Step

In this section you find, install, and activate Contact Form 7.

1. Go to Plugins ➪ Add New.

2. Do a search for **Contact Form 7**. It should come up as the first result or at least near the top. Look for the author, Takayuki Miyoshi, at the end of the description.

3. Click Install (just below the title on the left).

4. In the resulting pop-up prompt, click OK.

5. In the Installing Plugin screen, if things are successful, you see a link at the bottom to Activate Plugin. Click that.

6. A Plugins screen displays, and you should see Contact Form 7 as a white row, indicating that it's active. Also, on the main Admin menu, you should see the heading "Contact" just above Appearance. If you don't want this plugin, you can delete it later, but in one of the videos for this lesson you see some basics for setting up this powerful plugin, which you can follow along with at home.

> **REFERENCE** *Please select the video for Lesson 35 online at* www.wrox.com/go/ wp24vids. *You will also be able to download resources for this lesson from the website.*

36

More Plugin Suggestions

Throughout this book, I have introduced you to plugins that are useful for the topics of each lesson. Of course, there are many other uses for plugins, so this lesson lists some common topics for which people want plugins.

> **PLUGINS**
>
> The plugins discussed throughout this book are compiled in a handy reference list available online at www.wrox.com/go/wp24vids. The list is arranged by lesson and each one has a direct link to the WordPress Plugin Directory.

PLUGIN CATEGORIES

Following are some of the top plugins for a number of common purposes:

Ad Managers

Although this is not the place to go into the details of running ads on your website, you should know that there are two types of advertising:

➤ Running ads you've sold

➤ Running ads provided by an ad network (such as Google AdSense)

You can, of course, do both on your site, but if you're going to use an ad network, be aware that you need a reasonable amount of traffic to make it worthwhile. Typically, people talk about having at least 5,000 unique visitors per month. Plugins can help you integrate ad networks into your site.

To sell ads, you may not need a large amount of traffic but simply the right targeted traffic for your advertisers. Although you could just stick an ad in your sidebar, a plugin enables you to schedule how long it's shown, where it's shown, and even to whom it's shown, plus, it should provide the important statistics you need to show your advertisers as proof of views and clicks.

You must work hard to get high traffic or find and pitch the right advertiser. There is no easy money.

Having said that, following are some plugins that can help manage both types of ads:

➤   AdRotate

➤   Advertising Manager

➤   Ad Injection

➤   WP125

➤   Ads by datafeedr.com

And for plugins that just run ad network ads, you can use the following:

➤   Easy Plugin for AdSense

➤   Quick Adsense

➤   Google AdSense by BestWebSoft

➤   Chitika

All you need to do is search the name of the network you're going to use, or ask them for details on how to integrate their ads with WordPress. (Many have their own plugins or coding.)

Content

A huge number of plugins can help you put in content and to help you sort through some of them. They're divided into two groups: laying out content and organizing content.

Laying Out Content

The Content Editor of WordPress is a basic sort of text editor that enables you to insert media. However, if you want the layout of your content to appear fancier, you need plugins.

Using shortcodes is the most common way to create complex layouts such as columns, collapsing or accordion content, tabbed content, pull quotes, boxes, and more. You simply wrap the text in the shortcode to achieve the effect. Following are some plugins of that type:

➤   Shortcodes Ultimate

➤   WordPress Shortcodes

➤   Olevmedia Shortcodes

➤   WP Canvas—Shortcodes

➤   Easy Bootstrap Shortcode

➤   Collapse-O-Matic

➤   WP Easy Columns

Tables are an important way of laying out data, and although shortcode plugins can create tables, it's sometimes easier to enter the data into a form and have the table created from there. Following are some plugins specifically for tables:

➤ TablePress

➤ Websimon Tables

➤ ULTIMATE TABLES

➤ MCE Table Buttons

➤ Easy Pricing Tables by Fatcat Apps

➤ Responsive Pricing Table

When you start to get into multiple layout effects and elements on a single page, shortcodes can be difficult to work with. The trend now is toward visual layout builders. Sometimes, they're included in paid themes or commercial plugins, but some free plugins offer this kind of approach to laying out content:

➤ Page Builder by SiteOrigin

➤ Page Builder by WooRockets.com

➤ Plug-N-Edit Drag & Drop HTML Visual Editor with Web Page Builder WYSIWYG

➤ Beaver Builder—WordPress Page Builder

➤ MiniMax—Page Layout Builder

➤ Zedity™ Now Creating your Content is Super Easy!

And finally consider a specific type of page layout plugin: the Coming Soon page. When you first build a site, you want to hide everything but have at least a page explaining what's happening. Rather than just saying "coming soon" or "under construction," these plugins enable you to put up some temporary content—in particular, a form to gather names for your mailing list:

➤ WP Maintenance Mode

➤ Coming Soon/Maintenance mode Ready!

➤ Coming Soon Page & Maintenance Mode by SeedProd

➤ Ultimate Coming Soon Page

➤ Maintenance

➤ underConstruction

Organizing Content

Letting your visitors know about other content on your site is vital. While they're reading what they were originally interested in, you want to show them other material. The plugins in this group help you present that information in various ways.

These plugins enable you to display other content or lists of other content inside a Post or a Page:

- ➤ Top 10—Popular posts plugin for WordPress
- ➤ WordPress slider plugin—Featured Articles Lite
- ➤ Insert Pages
- ➤ Query posts by category...and display posts on page in grid layout without coding—Content Views
- ➤ Page2cat: Category, Pages & Posts Shortcodes
- ➤ Custom Content Shortcode
- ➤ Features by WooThemes
- ➤ Show/Hide Content at Set Time
- ➤ Timed Content
- ➤ Global Content Blocks
- ➤ Insert Html Snippet
- ➤ Insert PHP

These plugins enable you to list content in the sidebar or other Widget areas:

- ➤ AVH Extended Categories Widgets
- ➤ BNS Featured Category
- ➤ IntelliWidget Per Page Featured Posts and Menus
- ➤ Feature A Page Widget
- ➤ Multiple Category Selection Widget
- ➤ Sub Categories Widget
- ➤ T(-) Countdown
- ➤ Related Posts
- ➤ Related Posts via Categories

And these plugins display a list of your Posts related to the current Post:

- ➤ Yet Another Related Posts Plugin (YARPP)
- ➤ WordPress Related Posts
- ➤ Contextual Related Posts
- ➤ upPrev

E-commerce

Selling products or services with WordPress is getting easier and easier with a wide range of plugins available. The trick is to pick one that matches your current needs but leaves room for growth and change in the future.

Following are the four main elements of e-commerce:

➤ Catalog

➤ Shopping cart where you store items

➤ Checkout

➤ Payment processing

You want to leave the final stage—payment processing—to the folks with the secure servers, such as PayPal, Stripe, or your merchant account providers. But the rest can be handled by what I'm calling full-shopping cart plugins.

The most common business model for these plugins is to offer a free base plugin with most of the functionality and then charge for add-ons, such as special shipping modules and so on. Following are three of the most popular plugins today:

➤ WooCommerce—excelling eCommerce

➤ WP eCommerce

➤ Jigoshop

A new trend in full-shopping cart systems is to have a third-party system integrated into your WordPress Pages. Many of the leading shopping cart providers are beginning to offer this kind of integration. One of the leaders that offers a limited free version that you can try is:

➤ Ecwid Shopping Cart

If you're going to use only PayPal and you don't need a full shopping cart because you have only a few products or you're selling only individual services that need a Buy Now button, there are many plugin options, including

➤ WP Easy Paypal Payment Accept

➤ WordPress Simple Paypal Shopping Cart

➤ PayPal Donations

If you're selling only digital products, there are plugins made just for you, including:

➤ Easy Digital Downloads

And if you're selling affiliate products, you can check for plugins that make that integration easier, such as:

➤ Amazon Product in a Post Plugin

➤ Amazon Link

Events

You could create an events category of Posts and use that for listing your events, but an events plugin can offer far more functionality, such as integrated maps, calendar views, and other enhancements for your visitors. Following are some popular events plugins from the WordPress Plugins Directory:

➤ The Events Calendar

➤ My Calendar

➤ Events Manager

➤ WordPress Event Calendar

➤ Event Organiser

Another way to handle events is to use a third-party event or calendar service. One such option is to use Google Calendar and a plugin that integrates it with WordPress, such as Google Calendar Events.

If you'd like to sell tickets to an event, some plugins have the capability to add on that function, but it's even easier to use a third-party service, such as Eventbrite, EventBee, or TicketBud. Shopping cart services such as Shopify can have ticketing functions. Integrating with WordPress can be as simple as dropping in some HTML, or some services provide their own plugin.

Form Builders

Whether it's a simple contact form or a complex application form, some plugins enable you to easily create them. Even when the name of the plugin includes the word "contact," you can create other types of forms. Following are just a few of the free form builder plugins available:

➤ Contact Form 7

➤ Fast Secure Contact Form

➤ Ninja Forms

➤ Visual Form Builder

➤ Formidable Forms

➤ Contact Form Builder

➤ Contact Form

➤ Form Maker

➤ Usernoise modal feedback/contact form

➤ Calculated Fields Form

There are, of course paid form builder plugins (the most popular being Gravity Forms) but there are also third-party form builders that can easily be integrated into WordPress, including Wufoo, Formstack, and MachForm. Google offers a free form-building app, and there is a plugin called Google Forms, which can help integrate it with WordPress.

Maps

Displaying maps in your content has become a must in many situations, and plugins are available to make this as simple as possible. Some plugins for other purposes will include mapping capabilities within them, such as event calendars, but if you need mapping on its own, there's a wide range to choose from for Google Maps:

- ➤ Google Maps Ready!
- ➤ MapPress Easy Google Maps
- ➤ Basic Google Maps Placemarks
- ➤ Comprehensive Google Map Plugin
- ➤ WP Google Maps
- ➤ Google Maps Widget

And don't forget, Google is not the only mapping choice. Here are some plugins that can use OpenStreetMaps and others:

- ➤ Leaflet Maps Marker (Google Maps, OpenStreetMap, Bing Maps)
- ➤ OSM—OpenStreetMap

Some additional features you may be looking for: the ability to add multiple markers to one map, display images or other content when clicking on a map location, or create a visual route on the map.

Membership

Membership sites have become extremely popular over the past few years. They're a great way to keep visitors involved in your site by offering free membership with exclusive content or to generate revenue with paid memberships.

Even if you're not charging for memberships, you need a way to restrict who can view content, and several plugins can make that easy:

- ➤ Members
- ➤ Role Scoper
- ➤ Groups
- ➤ WordPress Access Control

If you want to create a paid membership site, there are many choices of premium or paid plugins, usually in the $50.00 to $100.00 range for a single site license. They include WishList Member, MemberPress, Member Mouse, Restrict Content Pro, Magic Members, and Digital Access Pass.

However, following are some plugins at the WordPress Plugin Directory that enable you to charge for memberships:

- ➤ s2Member Framework (Member Roles, Capabilities, Membership, PayPal Members)
- ➤ Paid Memberships Pro
- ➤ Membership
- ➤ WP-Members

Important features to look for in plugins for paid memberships include the capability to offer free memberships, ease of moving people between membership levels, ease of integration with payment gateways and mailing list managers, ease of specifying which content is open to which members (this should be as fine-grained as allowing part of a Post to be visible to nonmembers and the rest to members only), and the capability to automate the release of content to members over a period of time.

Another type of membership site is the social network, and several plugins are available at WordPress.org offering that functionality:

➤   BuddyPress

➤   Users Ultra

➤   WP Symposium Pro Social Network plugin

➤   WP Mingle

These plugins operate like a mini-Facebook where members can send private messages to one another, join groups, and much more.

Specialty Subjects

Some plugins are aimed at specific industries or organizations, so be sure to search the WordPress Plugin Directory thoroughly with keywords related to your website's topic or field. Following are just a few examples.

Cooking

Following are some plugins to help you organize and display recipes:

➤   Recipe Card

➤   Easy Recipe

➤   WP Ultimate Recipe

➤   GetMeCooking Recipe Template

Jobs

Following are plugins for posting and managing your own job listings:

➤   WP Job Manager

➤   Zartis Job Plugin

And following are others for importing job listings from third-party sites:

➤   Indeed Job Importer

➤   WP Broadbean

Real Estate

Following are plugins that help you manage a real estate site in general, including listings, calculators, maps, and so on:

- ➤ WP-Property—WordPress Powered Real Estate and Property Management
- ➤ FireStorm Professional Real Estate Plugin
- ➤ Simple Real Estate Pack

And following are others designed solely to bring in listings from third-party sources:

- ➤ IDX Broker WordPress Plugin
- ➤ Optima Express IDX Plugin
- ➤ WPL Real Estate

Sports

You can find plugins to help manage your sports team or even a whole league:

- ➤ SportsPress—Manage Leagues & Sports Clubs
- ➤ WP Club Manager
- ➤ LeagueManager
- ➤ Team Rosters
- ➤ Game Schedules
- ➤ Swim Team

Theater and Entertainment

Whether it's managing your theater group's productions listings, your band's schedule, or box office sales, there are plugins to help out:

- ➤ Theater for WordPress
- ➤ TheatreCMS Lite
- ➤ GigPress
- ➤ Gigs Calendar
- ➤ WP Bands Directory
- ➤ StageShow

JETPACK

One of the most popular plugins in the WordPress Plugin Directory is JetPack, which is made by Automattic, the company that runs WordPress. It's in a category of its own because it's a collection of plugins, each of which can be activated or deactivated individually.

At the moment, Jetpack has more than 30 modules, including a contact form, statistics, Widget visibility, social media following and sharing, slider, tiled galleries, related Posts, and much more. To activate Jetpack you need an account at WordPress.com, even though not all the modules need WordPress.com to function.

There are some advantages to using a plugin collection. The first is that you instantly have access to a wide range of functions, all using the same sort of interface. And there shouldn't be any problem with compatibility because all the plugins are written to work together.

However, if you use only one or two items in the collection, one of the disadvantages is that you have a certain amount of extra overhead that you don't need. It's true that the unused plugins aren't taking up any processing power, but the collection itself has to be run. Some people have tried creating versions of Jetpack that aim for less overhead and also don't require joining WordPress.com.

Another disadvantage of Jetpack is that it operates entirely differently from the rest of the WordPress interface. Consistency has always been a hallmark of WordPress and most of its plugins and themes, yet this plugin seems to flaunt all those conventions.

Still, for a lot of people, it's easier to have this plugin choose all their basic plugins for them and not have to sift through tens of thousands of plugins.

PLUGINS FOR OTHER PLUGINS AND THEMES

A lot of plugins in the WordPress Plugins Directory add functionality to other plugins or to themes, including ones from commercial makers. So it's always worth checking if your favorites have any add-ons. Following are some sample numbers:

➤ WooCommerce— More than 1,000 add-ons

➤ Contact Form 7—More than 100 add-ons

➤ Easy Digital Downloads—More than 100 add-ons

➤ BuddyPress—More than 500 add-ons

➤ WP E-Commerce—More than 500 add-ons

➤ NextGen Gallery—More than 200 add-ons

Following are examples of paid themes and plugins that have free add-ons in the WordPress Plugins Directory:

➤ Genesis Theme Framework—Approximately 200 add-ons

➤ Gravity Forms—More than 250 add-ons

TRY IT

To try something in this lesson, search the WordPress.org Plugins Directory to see the variety of functions the plugins can perform.

> **REFERENCE** *Please select the video for Lesson 36 online at* www.wrox.com/go/ wp24vids. *You will also be able to download resources for this lesson from the website.*

SECTION XI
References

- ▶ **APPENDIX:** Troubleshooting WordPress
- ▶ **GLOSSARY**

Troubleshooting WordPress

This book includes the occasional troubleshooting tip. In this appendix, the goal is help you think through the troubleshooting process.

Addressing every particular problem is impossible in a few pages, but following are a few common issues that illustrate some general strategies for solving problems. They also provide some ideas for getting more information online.

SITE VISIBLE BUT WITH AN ERROR MESSAGE

If you can see your site, but an error message displays at the top of the screen, it's likely that you've changed something.

You Just Added a Plugin or Theme

In situations like these, there's an easy initial test:

➤ If you just added a plugin, unplug it.

➤ If you just changed themes, switch back.

If the problem is fixed, check to see if any updates are needed on your site. If there are, do a backup and then do the updates. At that point you can try reactivating the plugin or theme.

If the error message returns, the quick answer is to not use that plugin or theme. If you absolutely need them, your next step would be to go to the plugin or theme's page (at the WordPress .org directory or for the commercial makers, their web page) and see if anyone has mentioned problems with the current version of WordPress. If so, hopefully some solutions are offered.

If you cannot find answers, you need to do some detective work on your own site, as discussed shortly.

You Just Did an Update

What's important here is the nature of the update. If it were one plugin or theme that you updated, you could try the strategy of deactivating it.

If you did a general update of WordPress and several plugins or themes, you need a broad approach to tracking down conflicts.

Finding Conflicts

If you can't find any answers to error messages caused by a free theme, there's not much you can do except not use the theme. If you paid for the theme, you need to deal with the vendor.

For a new plugin (assuming you find no mention of conflicts with the latest version of WordPress) it's time to try deactivating all other plugins. If the errors continue, then the plugin is probably incompatible with the current version of WordPress.

If the errors disappear, you can begin to reactivate the other plugins one at a time. If you have a lot of plugins, you can try reactivating one-half at a time. If no errors occur, activate the other one-half. The goal is to narrow it down to the plugin that's in conflict with your new one. If you find a problem plugin, you have to decide which one must go.

If the error message appears after doing a general update of your WordPress installation, you can apply the same strategy: Deactivate all plugins and reactivate one at a time until the error appears again.

ERROR ESTABLISHING A DATABASE CONNECTION

If you get a blank screen with this ominous message, there's likely one of two common causes:

➤ You're trying to install WordPress and you haven't set up a database yet, or the information you entered for your database is incorrect. (Both problems are easily solved.)

➤ Your hosting company is having problems. (Call them and check, and hopefully they can solve it quickly.)

Another cause for this error is a problem with your database, such as a corrupted table. One way to tell if that's the issue is to try logging in to WordPress. If you still get the same error, it's probably a server issue. However, if there's a database problem, you'll probably get a note saying that you should repair your database.

THE WHITE SCREEN OF DEATH

If you have a blank screen and not even an error message, the first thing is to not panic. Even if you haven't properly backed up your site, it's still not time to panic (maybe later, but not yet).

The first thing you need to do (or hire someone to do) is use an FTP program to get into your WordPress files. What you're about to do is equivalent to the plugin conflict testing I showed you earlier.

Simply rename your plugins folder to something such as **plugins-off**. What you've done, basically, is uninstall all your plugins. Now try to view your site. Likely it's going to be there, although it may look a bit mangled because none of your plugins are working.

The next step is to create a new folder called **plugins**, and then begin dragging each plugin's folder into there, one at a time. Each time you drag a folder, you need to be logged in to WordPress and refresh the plugins page. Then as the plugin appears on the list, activate it.

When you get the white screen of death again, you'll know it was the last plugin that you activated. With your FTP program, move it back into the plugins-off folder, and keep moving the rest of them back into the plugins folder.

If none of this works, and you have a backup, it's time to restore it. If you don't have a backup—not even one from a long time ago—it's time to call your hosting company and hope it has something. If it doesn't, then it's time to panic.

PAGE CANNOT DISPLAY

If your browser is telling you Web Page Cannot Be Found or a similar message, the first thing to check is whether it's just you that cannot find the website, or is the whole world unable to find it. Luckily, sites exist such as http://downforeveryoneorjustme.com/that can tell you. Another approach is to use a site such as http://leafdns.com. If it can see the site, but you can't, it's a problem with your ISP connecting to your server.

If no one can see the website, it's time to call your hosting company and see what's going on.

It's possible that your domain name has expired, but usually when that happens, your registrar puts up a page that may say your domain is for sale. In that case, it's a matter of reregistering your domain name. (Assuming you haven't let it lapse more than 30 days, you'll have to pay a redemption fee and hope that no one else has registered it.)

YOU CANNOT RECOVER YOUR PASSWORD

If you're the only administrator on a site and not only have you lost your password but also the e-mail address for recovering the password is not working, there's no need to panic. It's a matter of getting into your database and manually changing the password using phpMyAdmin. If you're not comfortable doing it yourself, you can hire someone, or your hosting company might do it for you for a fee as well.

FINDING HELP ONLINE

Because problems with WordPress are often specific to your particular circumstances, searching online for someone who has had the same problem is going to be one of your best strategies. Fortunately, there's a huge community of WordPress users that shares its experiences in a variety of ways, and following are some suggestions for finding them.

The WordPress.org Site

The number-one place to start is the Forum section of the WordPress.org website. You can find a wealth of information about real-world applications of WordPress and helpful solutions, as well as ideas on making WordPress do exactly what you need it to do. (I've found a lot of inspiration there for customizations I'd never thought of.) Although you don't need to register to use the forum, it's well worth it so that you can post problems for which you haven't found a solution.

When you think you haven't found an answer to your problem, your first action should be: *Search again*. If you still haven't found the answer: *Search again*! Of course, use different wording for each search; follow suggested threads in the results you do find; and try to approach the search from different angles. *Be a detective*. You'll save yourself (and other people in the forum) a lot of time and trouble, and you won't clog the forum with repeat questions.

Your problem has probably been voiced by someone, even if it hasn't been resolved, and you're better off joining that thread than starting a new one.

On the WordPress.org site, you can also find a helpful set of frequently asked questions (`http://codex.wordpress.org/FAQ`) as well as a whole page of tips on how to find help (`http://codex.wordpress.org/Finding_WordPress_Help`).

Using Search Engines

To search for help online, the best tip is to be as specific as you can in your search terms. Simply typing **website is broken** or **page crashes** is too general, but even if you type **menu not showing properly**, that's still less specific than **the sidebar menu is not showing all my categories**. Another aspect of being specific is to remember to narrow the search to your specific software. If the issue is with WordPress, be sure to include **+wordpress** (you may have to use Advanced Search to force a term to be in the search) along with whatever other terms you're searching for. Or if it's a problem with PHP, use **+php** to make sure you're focused on the right scripting language.

It's also important to put quotes around phrases: *sidebar widget* is a different search from "sidebar widget" because the first will look for each word separately, whereas the second tells the search engine to find them together as a phrase.

If you're getting an error message, enclose the entire message (or if it's long, choose what looks like the most relevant part) in quotation marks, and do your search on that. Including your operating system in the search along with your browser can also get you to your answer faster.

Finally, if the search engine supports it, try narrowing your search results to the past year. WordPress, plugins, and themes change so quickly that often advice from even a year ago can be outdated.

Finding Professional Help

If you can't find an answer online or the answer is difficult to implement, it may be time to hire someone to troubleshoot for you. You can search for phrases such as **wordpress developer**. Most likely, some of the people you know use WordPress for their site—ask for the names of people who have done WordPress customizations for them.

Check sites such as Meetup.com and see if there's a WordPress group in your area where you can meet web designers and developers who work with the platform, or check out one of the many WordCamps (http://central.wordcamp.org/) held throughout the world. You can also post your needs on sites such as CodePoet (http://codepoet.net), which is run by Automattic, or WordPress Jobs (http://jobs.wordpress.net).

GLOSSARY

activate a plugin   The next step after installing a plugin. WordPress displays a list of plugins you've installed, but you need to activate them before they function on your site. You can deactivate a plugin but that still leaves it installed.

Administrator   The highest level of WordPress user. Administrators have full access to all administrative functions, as opposed to, say, Editors, who cannot change the theme of a site nor do anything with plugins.

Admin Bar   The previous name for the Tool Bar at the top of admin screen.

attachment   Any file that has been uploaded to a Post or Page and, as a result, is listed in the gallery for that Post or Page. Though the file can be used anywhere on the site, that uploading process created a unique relationship to the Post or Page and, in that sense, the file has been attached to it.

Auto-Embed   A feature of WordPress that automatically embeds videos from certain video-sharing sites, such as YouTube. Users simply paste the URL of the video on a separate line in the Text Editor and the video is embedded. For security purposes, the list of allowed sharing sites is set by WordPress, though this can be altered by custom coding.

avatar   A small graphic or image used in WordPress comments to represent the person making the comment.

backup   Saving and storing a copy of any information. Backing up WordPress is a two-step process: backing up the database, and backing up the theme and uploaded files.

Blogroll   A list of links. It was originally intended to display favorite blogs or other sites you regularly visit.

bookmarklet   A button on a browser's bookmark bar that enables the user to perform a function quickly and easily. WordPress has a Press It bookmarklet that enables users to instantly blog about something they're viewing in their browser.

capability   A task that a user can perform in the WordPress administrative area. Different users have varying degrees of capabilities, with Administrators having all capabilities.

Category   Categories are used to group broadly related content in the way that a book has a table of contents (as opposed to tags, which are like the index of a book). WordPress has two types of categories: post categories and link categories. WordPress pages cannot use Post or link categories, though it is possible to create custom taxonomies for Pages.

child theme   A WordPress theme that shares files with a parent theme. At the minimum, a child theme must contain a style sheet file.

class   An attribute in HTML that enables a CSS style to be applied to any part of a web page that has that class. Example: `<p class="importantparagraph">`.

CMS   Content management system. A CMS is software that enables users to easily store, organize, and update information, usually for display on the web.

comments   Responses to your content that are submitted using a form and, if approved, are displayed for other visitors to read. You can choose whether to allow the comment form to appear on all, some, or none of your WordPress content.

Content Editor   In WordPress, this refers to the large field on Post or Page editing screens where the content is edited. It has two modes: Visual Mode, which shows a WYSIWYG version of the content, and Text Mode, which displays plain HTML.

cPanel   A popular online tool that enables people to easily manage their web-hosting accounts (adding e-mail accounts, setting up databases, and so on).

CSS   Cascading style sheets. A style sheet language used to control the look, formatting, and layout of a web page written in HTML. The cascading part refers to the ways in which style rules are applied.

Custom Fields   User-generated fields that can be attached to Posts, Pages, or custom Post types. By default, there is a Custom Fields meta box that can be made visible under Screen options, but more user-friendly boxes can be created that offer more choices than just text fields for data entry.

Custom Post Type   Additional types of content, such as Posts or Pages, which can be created by WordPress users.

Dashboard   The homepage of the WordPress administrative interface.

database   Software that stores data of various types and enables relationships to be established between the data. WordPress uses a MySQL database.

deprecated   Functions or template tags in WordPress that are no longer supported and eventually will be obsolete.

domain mapping   In WordPress multisite mode, this is the act of telling WordPress to use a particular domain name for one of the sites on the network.

draft   A Post or Page that has been saved but not yet published; also, the state of a previously published Page that has been unpublished.

Excerpt   A short summary of a Post that is entered separately in the excerpt field or is auto-generated using the first 55 words of the Post.

Featured Image An image that has been specially designated for a particular Post or Page and that may be used by a theme in various ways. For example, the theme Twenty Ten—the default theme for versions 3.0 and 3.1—will automatically replace the header image with a Post or Page's featured image (if the image is a certain size). Featured images can be changed at any time.

feed A data format used to provide users with frequently updated content. WordPress creates many different feeds of your site's content in a variety of feed types, such as RSS.

FTP File Transfer Protocol. An FTP program is used to transfer files back and forth to your server.

Gallery A list of all files associated with a particular Post or Page. Also, a display within the body of a Post or Page showing thumbnails of all image files belonging to a Post or Page.

hosting provider Anyone who runs a server connected to the Internet and provides accounts for people to run their websites and/or e-mail.

HTML Hypertext Markup Language. This is the basic language used to generate pages on the Internet. For example:

```
<p><em>Emphasized text</em> has certain tags around it, while all the text in
this paragraph is surrounded by the opening and closing paragraph tags</p>
```

HTML Mode The name previously used for the mode of the Content Editor that displays the content's HTML; now called Text Mode.

ID An attribute in HTML that allows a CSS style to be applied to a unique area on a web page. In other words, an ID name can be used only once per page. Example: `<p id="best paragraph">`.

install a plugin To use plugins—add-on software that extends the functions of WordPress— you must first install them, which means that the file or files for the plugin have been uploaded to a special plugins folder on the server, using either a file transfer protocol (FTP) program or the automated install process in WordPress.

internal linking Linking to content on your own website.

JavaScript One of the most popular client-side scripting languages for use on web pages. Client-side means that it runs in the visitor's browser, which enables JavaScript to react to clicks, mouse movements, and so on, producing effects such as menus changing color when you place your mouse over them. Not to be confused with the programming language Java.

the loop A section of WordPress template files that automatically runs through all possible pieces of content that meet a certain criteria and displays them according to the coding for that loop. For example, WordPress might loop through all posts in Category 6 and display the date, title, and body of each.

Media Uploader Window The screen that appears over top the main administration screen when you click the Add Media button or other links such as Set Featured Image

meta Typically used when talking about meta tags, which provide information about a web page, particularly to search engines, such as a description or a list of keywords relating to the Page. In WordPress, the term is also used in relation to Posts—Post metadata—for such information as the date, categories, tags, and other details about the Post.

meta box A section of a WordPress administration screen, such as Featured Image or Categories or Publish, which contains functions and can be moved around, and whose visibility can be toggled on or off.

multisite A feature of WordPress that enables a single installation to control more than one website or blog.

MySQL One of the most popular open-source databases. SQL stands for Structured Query Language. MySQL is the database used by WordPress.

network The name for the collection of sites in a WordPress multisite installation. It's also used to distinguish the administrative area of a multisite installation, as opposed to the site administration areas for each of the sites on the network.

Page A WordPress Page is often said to be for "static" content. This is meant to be a contrast with Posts, which typically are organized by date and time. The history of a company would be material for a Page, whereas a press release would be material for a Post. WordPress Pages can be organized into hierarchies of parent and child Pages, but unlike Posts, cannot be categorized or tagged.

permalink This is short for "permanent link." The idea of a permanent link is to provide a way for others on the Internet to always find a Page on your website, even if you change something that could affect that link, such as a Post title.

permissions Attributes of a file or directory (folder) on a web server that determine what action a particular user may take with respect to that file or directory (reading, writing, or executing the content).

PHP This scripting language is one of the most widely used for generating dynamic content on web pages. PHP is a server-side language, which means that it works before reaching the user's browser, as opposed to a language such as JavaScript, which functions in the browser. WordPress is written using PHP. Virtually all hosting providers offer PHP, whether on a Windows, UNIX/Linux, or Mac platform.

phpMyAdmin A popular open-source interface for managing MySQL databases.

pingback One type of notification you receive in WordPress to tell you that someone has linked to content on your site. For this to happen, your site must be pingback-enabled, which is set in the admin section.

Plesk/Parallels A popular online tool that makes it easy for people to manage their web hosting accounts (creating e-mail accounts, setting up databases, and so on).

Plugin A file or set of files that provides additional functionality for WordPress, such as suggesting related content to visitors or displaying maps. To work, plugins must first be installed in WordPress and must be activated.

Post A type of content in WordPress that can be categorized. The order of displaying Posts in a category can be controlled according to several parameters such as date published, title, and so on.

Post Box The name sometimes used for the Content Editor on Post or Page edit screens.

Post format   A set of nine possible designations recognized by WordPress and that, when set up by a theme, can be chosen by users when creating a Post. The idea of Post formats is to recognize certain standard content types that people may want to organize and design differently from other Posts. A Post format makes this easy to do through template scripting and CSS.

Post status   Tells you whether a Post or Page is published, unpublished, in draft mode, or pending review.

Post thumbnail   See Featured Image.

publish   Publishing a Post or a Page tells WordPress to display it on your site. You can always save them as drafts until you're ready to publish. You can also tell WordPress to automatically publish Posts or Pages in the future.

RSS   Really Simple Syndication. This is a type of feed format (see Feed).

scheduling   By default, publishing a Post or Page in WordPress—making it live on your site happens immediately, but you can also schedule it to publish at a future date and time.

screen options   A hidden area at the top right of most WordPress administrative screens that, when displayed, provides the ability to add or remove meta boxes from the screen, change the number of results displayed, and other functions for controlling the look of the screen.

sidebar   The area of a website on the left or right side of the Page where items such as navigation, advertising, and small chunks of content display.

slug   A word or series of words in lowercase lettering containing no spaces. There are slugs for Posts, Pages, categories, tags, and authors, and they're used by WordPress to make URLs more descriptive.

style sheet   A file that contains the CSS used to create the look, formatting, and layout of a web page.

tag   A keyword you assign to Posts that can be shared by other Posts. Posts can have multiple tags. Tags are meant to be specific in the way that entries in the index of a book get detailed (as opposed to categories, which are like a book's table of contents).

taxonomy   A system of classification. Default taxonomies in WordPress include Post categories, link categories, and tags. Users can also create their own custom taxonomies.

teaser   The portion of a Post prior to the point where you've added a More tag to the Post.

template   A file in WordPress themes that provides instructions for assembling HTML Pages. Templates may use other templates in the assembly process.

Text Editor   See Content Editor. The term is also used for programs that edit simple text files.

Text Mode   The mode of the WordPress Content Editor that displays the pure HTML version of the content.

Theme   The set of files that controls the layout, look, and certain aspects of the content on the HTML pages generated by WordPress. A theme consists of at least one style sheet and at least one template file.

Theme Editor   A text editor built into the WordPress administration area (listed under the Appearance menu section as Editor) that enables theme files to be edited.

Tool Bar   A horizontal menu bar that remains stationary as the Page scrolls and is visible to logged-in users of WordPress if they choose. What appears on the bar depends on the user's role and what plugins are used. By default, the bar is visible while logged in and viewing the live website. Separate controls for visibility on the live site and the administration screens are located on a user's profile page.

trackback   One type of notification you receive in WordPress to tell you that someone has linked to content on your site.

update   To replace the current version of WordPress, a plugin, or a theme with a newer one.

Update (button)   When you see this word on a button, it means you must click it to save any changes you've made. It's important to get in the habit of clicking this before you leave a screen, even if you don't remember changing anything.

URL or URI   Uniform Resource Locator or Uniform Resource Identifier. Although a URL is a subtype of URIs, the two terms are sometimes used interchangeably. A URI is any string of characters that identifies a resource on the Internet, and a URL is a URI that includes how to access the resource. In other words, what makes `https://wordpress.org` a URL is the "https://."

user   Someone who is a registered user on a WordPress site. There are five levels of users with varying degrees of capabilities: Administrator, Editor, Author, Contributor, and Subscriber.

Visual Mode   The mode of the WordPress Content Editor that displays content in a WYSIWYG format the way a word processing program would.

Widget   A piece of code that enables you to place chunks of content (for example, a list of categories, recent posts) on your website (typically in the sidebar) using a drag-and-drop interface.

WordPress MU   The original name given to the version of WordPress that enables multiple sites on a single installation.

WordPress Multisite   The name of a version of WordPress that enables multiple sites to be controlled by a single installation. The MU is commonly referred to as multiuser, although it's actually phonetic for the Greek letter μ. WordPress MU was merged with the regular version of self-hosted WordPress as of version 3.0.

WYSIWYG   Stands for What You See Is What You Get. In the WordPress Content Editor, there is a Visual Mode, which displays posts in a partly WYSIWYG format (to see them exactly as they will appear on the web, you need to use Preview), as opposed to Text Mode, which displays the Post with all the code used by the browser to display it.

INDEX

WordPress Video
Gallery, 191
WordPress Video Player,
190
Widgets
amr shortcode any
widget, 246
Custom Sidebars, 246
Display Widgets, 246
Remove Inactive
Widgets, 246
Shortcodes AnyWhere,
246
WordPress Dashboard Twitter,
41
WP Clone, 29
WP User Avatar, 53
Post Box, 408
posts, 408
admin settings, 210–211
comments, allowing/
disallowing, 210
content, importing, 208–210
Custom Post Type, 406
drafts, 406
editing, Bulk Edit, 206–207
Featured Image, 98–100
finding, 201–203
formats, 95–96, 409
listing, 201–202
new
Add New link, 57
Add New Post screen,
57–66
Quick Draft box, 57
pages and, 9
password protection, 91
private, 91
Publish setting, 92
revisions, 91, 93–94
site map, 14–15
status, 409
sticky, 90–91
tags, 97–98
thumbnails, 409

PowerPoint presentations, 196
Profile page, 49–50
Display Name Publicly As,
51
Password Strength Indicator,
51–53
plugins, 53
Toolbar, 50–51
Publish meta box
Revisions link, 93–94
Status setting, 89–90
Visibility setting, 90–92
publishing, 409

Q

Quick Edit, 204–205

R

registration forms, 291
repositioning, boxes, 38–39
revisions, 91
cleanup, 356
plugins
Better Delete Revision,
359
Optimize Database
After Deleting
Revisions, 359
Thin Out Revisions,
359
Revisions meta box, 103–104
RSS feeds, 409
displaying, 274–275
locating, 273–274
plugins, 287
FeedWordPress, 276
RSSImport, 276
Super RSS Reader,
276
WP RSS Multi Importer,
276

S

scaling images, 166–167
scheduling, 409
screen options, 409
Screen Options button, 37–38
searches. See also SEO (search
engine optimization)
content, 336–337
links, 337–338
Media Library, 219–220
permalinks, 342–344
Themes Directory, 310–312
titles, 333–335
troubleshooting help, 402
security
admin username, 369
administrators and, 370
database, 369
hosting and, 372–373
login attempts, 370–371
passwords, 367–368
plugins, 369
Acunetix Secure
WordPress, 374
BulletProof Security,
374
Force Strong Passwords,
374
iThemes Security,
374
Lockdown WP Admin,
374
Login LockDown,
374
Login Security Solution,
374
Rename wp-login.php,
374
Wordfence Security,
374
WordPress Password
Expiry, 374
WP Password Policy
Manager, 374